7·95

The Devils are Among Us

The War for Namibia

Denis Herbstein & John Evenson

C000054793

Zed Books Ltd
London and New Jersey

The Devils are Among Us – The War for Namibia
was first published by Zed Books Ltd, 57 Caledonian Road,
London N1 9BU, UK and 171 First Avenue, Atlantic Highlands,
New Jersey 07716, USA, in 1989.

Copyright © Namibia Communications Centre, 1989.

Cover designed by Andrew Corbett,
Photographs John Liebenberg and John Evenson/NCCT.
Typeset by EMS Photosetters, Rochford, Essex.
Printed and bound in the United Kingdom
at Bookcraft (Bath) Ltd, Midsomer Norton.

British Library Cataloguing in Publication Data

Herbstein, Denis.
    The devils are among us: the war for Namibia.
    1. Namibia.
    I. Title.   II. Evenson, John.
    968.8'03.

    ISBN 0-86232-896-9
    ISBN 0-86232-897-7 pbk

Contents

Acknowledgements

We acknowledge the contribution of Michael and Priscilla Hishikushitja, Andreas Amushila, Justin Ellis, Brian Wood, the Rev. Hidipo Shanyengange, Derek Forbes, John Dugard, who have provided information or commented on written material. At the London offices of the Namibia Communications Centre our work has been greatly facilitated by Hilifa Mbako, Protasius Ndauendapo and Christine Plezia. We also owe a debt to the skilful and often courageous advice offered by two lawyers in Namibia, David Smuts and Hartmut Ruppel. At Zed Books, John Daniel and Anne Rodford have been patient and constructive.

Others have reported their experiences or offered insights from inside the war zone, but we feel it is still premature to mention them by name.
August 1989

Preface

This book has been written in Britain by two journalists whose names on the South African government blacklist have prevented them from working in Namibia. While we might have missed the atmosphere, the human contacts and visual insights vital to a reporter, there are compensating factors in doing an 'outside job'. The story of the war would have been impossible to ascertain under the rigorous conditions of censorship. The facts are more freely retold abroad. However, we make no claims to be presenting the definitive story of the struggle for liberation. That will follow when independence and peace — and access to the archives — are granted to this tragic land.

The Namibia Communications Centre was established in 1984 as an ecumenical news agency to publicise the struggle of the churches and the people of Africa's last colony. The world formally favoured Namibian independence, yet the realization of the goal seemed as distant as ever. Hardly any news came out of the country, and what did was selected and fashioned by the mind of the South African military. The Centre quickly established a territorial network of church-based amateur and professional stringers able to supply news for transmission around the world. The offices in central London became a meeting place for Namibians living in Britain, and a stopping-off point for the churchmen and women, students, politicians, freedom fighters to-ing and fro-ing between southern Africa and the outside world. What we heard from our 'spies' inside the territory, and Namibian visitors to London, forms much of the marerial in this book.

Namibia is unique in the 20th century not for its experience of genocide, for there are the Armenians and Jews and Cambodians; nor for the apartheid shared with blacks in South Africa; nor are they a people starved of a motherland, as are the Kurds or Palestinians; while Eritreans would even dispute the territory's claim to being Africa's last colony. What makes it different is being the last surviving League of Nations mandate administered as a 'sacred trust of civilization'. This

vi

status was unique in international diplomacy for not placing its faith in the good government of subject peoples, but in providing safeguards towards the fulfilment of that aim. It is one of the ironies of the century that the country given the most solid protection under international law should suffer the more for it.

In the scramble for Africa, Europe's undignified carve-up of the 'dark continent', imperial Germany gained Namibia. The German emperor proclaimed a 'protectorate' over its people. In the exercise of this 'protection', his representatives signed treaties with local chiefs which the Germans usually did not honour, but when blacks deviated from the 'contract' they were punished by armed possés, their land seized, yet more onerous treaties imposed. When the Hereros saw that their grazing lands would soon all be stolen, they launched a war of resistance.

A well-trumpeted justification for German protection was to bring peace between Namas and Hereros, who had skirmished over land for a quarter of a century, usually with guns supplied by Afrikaner traders, and on at least one occasion by a German missionary. But joint resistance was not yet possible. In planning the insurrection, the Herero supreme chief, Samuel Maharero, wrote his 'let us die fighting' letter to Hendrik Witbooi of the Namas.

All our obedience and patience with the Germans is of little avail, for each day they shoot someone dead for no reason at all. Hence I appeal to you, my Brother, not to hold aloof from the uprising, but to make your voice heard so that all Africa may take up arms against the Germans. Let us die fighting rather than die as a result of maltreatment, imprisonment or some other calamity. Tell all the *kapteins* [chiefs] down there to rise and do battle. [Drechsler 1980, p. 143.]

Maharero asked Hermanus van Wyk, *kaptein* of the Basters (of Nama and European descent) to deliver the letter to Witbooi. It never arrived. Van Wyk handed it to the Germans. Even so, it is doubtful whether the appeal would have induced Witbooi to change his mind at that stage. Governor Theodor Leutwein later admitted he had been saved from 'disaster' at the beginning of the uprising because Herero and Nama were kept from joining forces for nine months, until October 1904. Divide and rule tactics in which real or imagined differences were played upon by their rulers became a hallmark of the colonial and South African style of government, with serious consequences for Namibia's liberation struggle.

The second lesson which Namibians might have learnt at this early stage was the poisonous power of Western propaganda. In matters of warfare and culture, Germany was perhaps the most advanced civilization the world had seen, though lagging behind the USA, France or Britain in democratic institutions. Yet the German conduct of the war in no way matched that of its 'uncivilized' enemy. Compare the two battle commands. The extermination order of General Lother von Trotha, the German commander-in-chief, issued after the defeat of the Hereros at Hamakari:

> The Herero people will have to leave the country. Otherwise I shall force them to do so by means of guns. Within the German boundaries, every Herero, whether found armed or unarmed, with or without cattle, will be shot. I shall not accept any more women and children. I shall drive them back to their people — otherwise I shall order shots to be fired at them. These are my words to the Herero people. Signed: the Great General of the Mighty Kaiser, von Trotha.

Von Trotha was not quite true to his word. By the end of 1905, some 16,000 of the original Herero population of between 60,000 and 80,000 were still alive, but 14,000 of these were in concentration camps, their land and cattle seized. The Namas suffered almost as badly. By 1911 they were reduced to fewer than 10,000, having lost one-third to a half of their numbers.

In January 1904 Samuel Maharero issued his battle order.'In my capacity as Supreme Chief of the Herero I hereby decree and resolve that none of my people lay their hands upon the English, the Bastaards, the Berg Damara, the Nama and the Boers.' Nor were German women and children, unarmed German men or missionaries to be harmed. The order preceded the Geneva Convention on the conduct of war by four decades. Maherero was true to his word. After the war, a vengeful German public craved just one case of a raped *Deutsche Frau*, or a child murdered by blacks. Governor Leutwein was unable to oblige. Yet the vision of barbarism survived, much as, three-quarters of a century later, the SWAPO nationalists would be portrayed as 'marxists' and 'terrorists'.

In World War One, South African troops occupied German South West Africa in the name of the British king, and were rewarded with the territory under a League of Nations mandate in 1920. General Jan Smuts, one-time Boer leader and co-founder of the League, spoke of the mandatory state looking upon its position as 'a great trust and honour, not as an office of profit or a position of private advantage for its own nationals'. (Du Pisani 1986, p. 1.) Yet that is exactly what it became. The earnest debates before and during the Versailles peace conference, the words of the Trust itself, point to an unprecedented caring for the welfare of subject races and the new Union of South Africa undertook to 'promote to the utmost the material and moral well-being and the social progress of the inhabitants.' It would abide by a group of specific obligations relating to the slave trade, forced labour, trafficking in arms and intoxicating spirits, military training, as well as promises about freedom of conscience and worship, with a special mention for the missionaries (Dugard 1973).

This was not a sweeping statement worthy of a Jefferson or a Rousseau. What gave the 'sacred trust' teeth was the supervisory role of the international community, in particular the Principal Allied and Associated Powers, the main victors of the war — Britain, France, the United States, Italy and Japan (though there was the anomalous position of the USA which did not sign the peace treaty). The victors in this 'war to end war' made a solemn declaration that they would look after their charges. The black inhabitants of Namibia had good reason to understand the spirit of it. South Africa, for its part, ignored the obligations, enjoying only the fruits thereof. This was to settle white farmers on the land and exploit its great natural riches; instead of being educated, the people were turned into serfs, and Namibia was transformed into one of the most hopeless landscapes in the story of African colonization.

Much depended on who exercised the mandate. The other 'C' mandates, said to be the least developed of the German colonies inherited by the budding white Commonwealth, were New Guinea and Samoa. They have long since achieved independence from Australia and New Zealand. The world and the British government, which handed Namibia to the mercies of white South Africa, were unwilling or unable to enforce the promises.

The people had not forgotten. The 1924 annual report which South Africa was obliged to make to the Permanent Mandates Commission noted that:

> though in some parts of the Territory Natives, especially Herero, have evinced restlessness and assumed a truculent attitude, Magisterial [sic] reports indicate that generally speaking with the exception of the Bastards and Natives in the Rehoboth Gebied, the natives have been law-abiding and well behaved. [p. 16.]

The first dozen years of the mandate were bloodied by hopeless uprisings — Chief Mandume in 1922, the Bondelswartz people soon afterwards, the Basters in 1925, Chief Ipumbu of the Ukuambi in 1932. After that, the silence of the unheard scream.

NAMIBIA

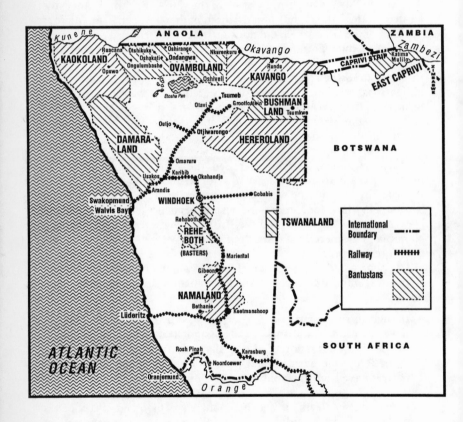

ANGOLA

Exile's return. What does the future hold for this child born in a camp in Angola?

1.
'Give us back a dwelling place' — Namibia 1945–80

With the Second World War over and the scourge of Hitler and the gas chambers banished from Europe, the conquering powers lost little time in launching a new supranational organization. They sought to avoid the mistakes of the old League of Nations. For the twice-defeated Germans there was no punitive Treaty of Versailles to sow the seeds of a Fourth Reich. Marshall Aid would turn West Germany into one of Europe's economic success stories.

For the people of Namibia, however, it soon became apparent that the great betrayal at Versailles, far from being remedied, was to be compounded. Field Marshall Jan Smuts, the South African prime minister, encouraged by the British Labour government of Clement Attlee, set about incorporating 'South-West' as a fifth province of the Union of South Africa. Smuts argued that the United Nations had not inherited the League's mandated territories and therefore South Africa should not be answerable to the new body's Trusteeship Committee. However, Britain, France and Belgium, which had also inherited German colonies after World War I, did accept the new dispensation.

In December 1945, the gun barrels still warm, Pretoria carried out a so-called incorporation 'consultation' with the territory's white and black leaders. The white legislative assembly duly chose the South African path. The decision for the black majority was left to the traditional tribal leaders. In Ovamboland the South African-employed kings and headmen were liable to arbitrary removal and deportation without the right of appeal, should they not toe the line. The government's report noted that, before making up their minds, tribal spokesmen wanted to know 'whether any change in the administration of the Territory would remove them from under the shadow of the Crown of King George of England.' (Dugard 1973, p. 110.) On being reassured, they voted 'yes' — even babes-in-arms were said to be in favour. South African officials and individual missionaries alike knew

1

the consultation to be a farce. Attlee, however, told the House of Commons he 'was satisfied as to the steps taken by the South African government to ascertain the wishes of the inhabitants.' (Hansard 427, col. 1659, 23.10.46.)

The Herero leaders, on the other hand, voted comprehensively 'no'. They were led inside Namibia by the venerable Chief Hosea Kutako who, as a teenager, had witnessed the arrival of the Germans in what was to become Windhoek. The Hereros, like the Namas hardly consulted, felt the injustice more than most. The 'Von Trotha survivors' had been waiting in Bechuanaland for 40 years to come home, while those living in Namibia had seen their fertile acres settled by Afrikaners, often poor whites barely able to eke out a living in their own country. Chief Hosea pinned his faith on the 'sacred trust' and asked the UN to conduct a referendum on the issue. South Africa, under the reputedly liberal Smuts and two years before the apartheid supremacists were voted in, refused. Nor would Smuts permit Herero spokesmen to travel to the United Nations to put their case.

Kutako, therefore, conducted a campaign by telegram. In this first concerted struggle to get a foot on the ladder of independence, Kutako had the support of other petitioners, among them the Ngwato chief in Bechuanaland, Tshekedi Khama, and the African National Congress president, Dr. A. B. Xuma. The words of the paramount chief of the Hereros, Frederick Maharero, were recorded in his Bechuanaland exile and reported to the Trusteeship Committee in New York.

> We gave our sons to the fight [2nd World War] and then we gave money to assist the King of England and the Allies to win the war . . . Now that the war has ended we should like that this country of South West Africa be given back to the African people and that it should not be incorporated into the Union of South Africa. [Scott 1958, p. 223.]

On 14 December 1946 the General Assembly voted to reject incorporation, recommending instead that 'SWA' be placed under the Trusteeship Committee (which had replaced the permanent mandate's committee of the League). The 37 states in favour included the United States, Canada and Belgium (and the then sole black independent African countries, Liberia and Ethiopia), while Britain, France and Australia were among the seven abstentions. No one voted for incorporation. To this day, white South Africans blame India or 'the communists and Third World' for the rejection. The passionate opposition led by Kutako had prevented 'South West' from being swallowed by its hungry neighbour. But if direct annexation had been denied Pretoria, the next best thing was incorporation by stealth. Smuts was voted out of office in May 1948. One of the first actions of his successors was to give white Namibians eight seats in the South African parliament.

The new government of Dr. Daniel Malan refused to furnish annual reports to the Trusteeship Committee detailing its contribution, if any, to black material and spiritual well-being; and so the service was provided by Chief Kutako. When he or members of his chief's council were refused permission to leave the territory, they were represented by the British Anglican priest, Michael Scott. It took three years to overcome objections, principally from Britain and South Africa, to Scott's testifying before the UN. Britain's delegates, Labour and Conservative, would complain that 'the correct procedure' had not been followed, or (once Scott was eventually allowed to appear) that 'a very dangerous precedent has been established.'

Kutako's aim, apart from the maintenance of the country's international status, was to reunify the Hereros in Namibia under Frederick Maharero. For those willing to listen, his simple prayer could only have advanced the cause — 'O Lord, help us who roam about. Help us who have been placed in Africa and have no dwelling place of our own. Give us back a dwelling place. O God, all power is yours in Heaven and Earth. Amen.' (Benson 1989, p. 59.) But the land they wanted to roam again was being grazed profitably by the white man's cattle and karakul sheep.

Kutako was by no means the only petitioner keeping the world informed of worsening conditions in Namibia. In 1957, Mburumba Kerina, a student at Lincoln University, became the first Namibian to appear before the UN. Two years later Jariretendu Kozonguizi left Namibia clandestinely as an emissary of the Herero chief's council. The solitary Herero and Nama petition in 1946 had grown to 120 by 1960.

Political Organisation

One of these petitioners was Father Theopil Hamutumbangela who, from his Anglican mission at Odibo in Ovamboland, had founded a movement called (in translation) 'The cry of the people is guided by God'. In 1954 he petitioned the UN on the strength of evidence collected from migrant workers. He was charged by South Africa, but his trial in the north created such a stir that it was postponed and he was transferred to Windhoek by a nervous white bishop. The priest's concern reflected the shift in resistance northwards, something which would one day lead to the end of colonial rule.

From the late 1940s, secure in their domination of the southern sub-continent, foreign industrialists turned greedily to South West Africa. The American control of the northern copper mining complex of

Tsumeb, the Oppenheimer family's limitless expanse of alluvial diamonds at the Orange River mouth, the fishing boats and canning factories, the karakul farms, all required black muscle to achieve 'El Dorado'. Poor pay, dangerous working conditions, isolation from family, an all-male environment, the paternalism of the mine and factory-owners and police harassment contrived to radicalize the workers of the mines and coastal towns. But organized resistance in these circumstances was fraught with difficulties. At the first sign of 'trouble', the mine or factory manager would telephone his golf-club friend, the local police chief. A good beating, deportation to Ovamboland, or a devastating fine was the invariable punishment. In one case, 54 contract workers who went on strike in Walvis Bay in June 1962 were fined R60, a crippling amount in those days.

Helao Shityuwete was born in Windhoek, but spent his formative years in Ovamboland. He recalls his recruitment at the SWANLA government–industry offices in Ondangua:

You would stand outside the building, and if picked out, had to strip to the waist and go inside. If you survived the next stage, you were sent to another room, took off the rest of your clothes, were made to bend down, while the doctor walked around examining. A stamped metal string was put round your neck. There were three categories, 'A', 'B', and 'C', and depending on which you were given, it was mining or stevedoring, heavy farm work, or domestic or light farm labour. [Interview with authors, 1988.]

The SWA Native Labour Association (SWANLA) was one step down from a slave market, where black muscle was bought for a period of 18 months. The 'servant' had no say over the type of work or his employer. No hours were specified — he had to 'render the master his service at all fair and reasonable times.' An attempt to change jobs or, worse, walking out of it, could lead to prison and a thrashing, sometimes with fatal results. The SWAPO veteran, Vinnia Ndadi, asked a 'master' for a wage increase. 'I bought you from SWANLA and brought you here,' he was told, 'so you'll do exactly what I tell you! And if you're a stupid kaffir and don't follow my orders, then I'll shoot you.' (Ndadi 1989, p. 37.)

Shityuwete arrived at Walvis Bay in 1958, the heyday of the fishing boom, as South African trawlers plundered the resources of the coastal waters. Only rarely were the huge profits of Cape Town-based entrepreneurs ploughed back to improve the living conditions of their employees. Shityuwete worked for Sturrock and Walker, loading and unloading ships at the docks.

The work was terribly hard. I lived in a compound belonging to the company. It was divided into cubicles, each with four cement bunks.

4

There were no wardrobes, and if you were lucky and got a bottom bunk, as I did, there was some space to put your belongings underneath. The people on top had to string their clothes onto a line.

It was in one of the coastal towns, Luderitz, that an unsuccessful attempt to unionize canning workers laid a stone on the path that would ultimately lead to national liberation. In 1952, Ray Alexander, a union organizer from Cape Town, set up a branch of the Food and Canning Workers in Luderitz. The police responded brusquely and the branch was broken up. Alexander being banned, returned to Cape Town. A brief report of her expulsion was clipped from a local newspaper by Andimba Toivo Ya Toivo, who filed it for future reference. Ya Toivo was unusual for a northerner; having served in the South African army in the war, rising to become corporal, he returned to school to enrol in standard 1 at the age of 23, worked on a Johannesburg gold mine, then as a clerk on a manganese mine. When he went to work on the railways in Cape Town, he sought out Ms Alexander and her husband, the radical professor of African studies at Cape Town University, Jack Simons. Soon a group of Ovambo workers and students were discussing the world of politics and the nature of Namibian society with Alexander, Ben Turok and others with ties to the underground South African Communist Party. It was these contacts which later led Prime Minister Johannes Vorster to declare that SWAPO had been born in sin, the brainchild of Cape Town communists.

That connection did exist, but the group also made enduring contacts with leaders of the then Liberal Party, men like Randolph Vigne, Peter Hjul and the late Patrick Duncan. Ya Toivo's group also numbered local African National Congress members among their friends. During the discussions on political action, the ANC had suggested setting up a branch in Namibia, but the idea was firmly rejected for the reason that a separate country should have a home-grown movement. Instead, in 1957, Ya Toivo and a group of Cape-based Namibians founded the Ovambo People's Congress (OPC).

Ya Toivo was expelled from Cape Town after security police discovered he had sent a tape-recorded message — hidden in a copy of *Gulliver's Travels* — to the United Nations in New York (First 1963, p. 194). News of the electronic message was broadcast over South African radio, to the intense interest of Namibian workers and the consternation of the authorities (Ndadi 1989, p. 69). On the eve of his departure, Ya Toivo met Kozonguizi, one of the promising Herero leaders, who was returning home after studying at Fort Hare University. They agreed to integrate the budding Herero and Ovambo movements, based on three congresses in the north (Ovambos), central (Damara and Herero) and south (Nama). Chief Kutako gave his blessing (First 1963,

p. 199). In April 1959, in Windhoek, Sam Nujoma and Jacob Kuhangua (one of the Cape Town group) founded the Ovambo People's Organization (OPO). 1959, like 1966, 1974 and 1979, was to be a year that Namibian nationalists, for good reason or bad, would remember.

Here was the first real attempt to find a political solution to the enormous injustice of being a black person in this white-ruled country. These family-minded men from Christian backgrounds were rebelling against a style of life which, for all their working days, gave them less time with their wives and children than that enjoyed by a petty criminal making regular forays to prison. Small wonder the OPO went down well with the fish and mine workers. A successful go-slow followed by a strike in a Walvis Bay fish cannery in January 1959 raised the confidence of contract workers in their collective power, and threw up grassroots leadership. They were an organization waiting for a party.

Helao Shityuwete recalls hearing about the OPO from his friend at Oceana Fishing, Vinnia Ndadi, who was in touch with Windhoek. Sam Nujoma came from Windhoek to address meetings in the main compounds. 'We called a meeting where it was agreed to organize every compound in Walvis Bay, nearly 40,000 people.' Shityuwete became secretary of several compounds, while Ndadi and Eneas Nanyemba (later military commander of PLAN — People's Liberation Army of Namibia) were in charge of the fish cannery workers. 'The response was tremendous. We held meetings in secret on Saturday or Sunday afternoons at one of the compounds, and hundreds came. Walvis Bay was a lively place then, with ships returning to port at all hours and shifts worked throughout the 24 hours.' The men returned to their homes, spread the word. Here Ya Toivo, a gifted organizer despite periodic house arrest in the kraal of the Ndonga chief Johannes Kambonde, figured largely in the OPO's success. Fresh workers set out for CDM (Consolidated Diamond Mines), Walvis Bay and Tsumeb ripe for recruitment into the organization.

SWANU

Running parallel with these developments was a political movement restricted to southerners — educated Hereros in the main. Founded in August 1959, the South West Africa National Union (SWANU) is the territory's longest surviving political party. The spur to Herero cultural resurgence came as early as 1923 when Chief Samuel Maharero, having died in exile, was ceremonially buried among his ancestors at Okahandja. The annual commemoration became a rallying point, providing a focus for the post-war demands of Herero leaders. Likewise, in the 1920s, Marcus Garvey's 'Universal Negro Improvement

Association' enjoyed a certain following in Namibia, and his call of 'Africa for the Africans' was seized on as a message of hope.

After the war, African Improvement Society night classes attracted blacks, again mainly Hereros, hungry for education. Several future SWANU and SWAPO leaders attended. It was 1948 before the first black matriculated (school-leaving certificate), but he had to go to South Africa, there being no secondary schools for black Namibians before the late 1950s. Even so, some attended South African universities in the 1950s, particularly Fort Hare, where many of southern and central Africa's future leaders had been and were being educated. This coincided with a period when thousands of Africans and Indians were being imprisoned for a 'defiance campaign' against apartheid. Inspired by the example, Kozonguizi, Mburumba Kerina and Zed Ngavirue launched the SWA Student Body (Dr. Ngavirue is today chairman of Rio Tinto Zinc's Rossing uranium mine). Back in SWA, Kozonguizi was invited to join the Herero Chief's Council, where he argued for a national organization to confront South African rule. The South West Africa Progressive Association followed, a cultural body with a political flavour, which was an attempt to break out of the chiefs' stranglehold. It briefly published Namibia's first newspaper, *South West News*, but soon collapsed (Katjavivi 1988, pp. 24–31).

Soon after the appearance of the OPO, the Herero group founded the SWA National Union (SWANU). There was no rivalry at first. Indeed, Nujoma was at one stage on the SWANU executive. For a while SWANU looked set to become the umbrella for other groups, including the OPO, which was already seeking links with non-Ovambos. That opportunity occurred in December 1959 with an event that was to transform the political climate.

Throughout South Africa the government had been 'cleansing' the cities and rural areas of black and mixed residential areas, expelling people who had lived there for generations to inaccessible wastelands downwind from the white suburbs. International status would not save Namibia from these 'tidying-up' operations in which land occupied or owned by blacks was erased from the register and given to white farmers or, in one case, incorporated into a game reserve. Windhoek's 'Old Location' was an eyesore to the white municipality, and a promising piece of real estate to boot. A new 'home' was designated for the blacks of Windhoek several miles out of town, with neighbourhoods segregated on ethnic — Ovambo, Herero, Damara, Nama — lines. Was it a cynic, or just a white unversed in the Herero language, who named it 'Katutura', meaning literally 'the place where we do not settle'?

The 89-year-old Kutako, Sam Nujoma and the Nama chief, Frederick Witbooi, joined forces to resist the expulsion, organizing the boycotting of buses and the despised beer hall where patrons were offered a home-made concoction, with profits going to the municipality. With tension mounting, white officials agreed to attend a meeting in the Old Location. As the crowd chanted 'We won't move', Nujoma turned to the officials to ask them, 'Why don't you move? You have shown you cannot rule us. Go back to South Africa and let us rule ourselves.' (Ya Otto 1981, p. 49.)

The climax came on 10 December 1959. Police were called in to break up a demonstration in which women, dressed in the cumbersome but picturesque Herero long dresses, were to the fore. The police officer gave the crowd five minutes to disperse. But there were no loudspeakers. Chief Kutako described the scene: 'Only those in front heard and when they tried to retreat, others from behind, curious, pushed forward. Five minutes up, the police fired. Not teargas but bullets.' (Benson 1989, p. 121.) Twelve protesters, mostly women, were killed. Today the Old Location has been transformed into the well-ordered white suburbs of Academia Extension and Pioneers' Park, numbering government officials and senior army officers among their residents. Their black maids bus in from Katutura.

SWAPO is born

One of Sam Nujoma's earliest memories is of war planes flying over to bomb the kraal of Ukuambi Chief Ipumbu, who had refused to submit to the authority of South Africa's native commissioner. It was 1932, and Nujoma was four years old. His traditional name, Shafiihuna, literally 'a time of trouble', may reflect the way his father saw the world at the time of his son's birth. His family lived in the remote Ongandjera region of western Ovamboland where his early years were spent herding the family cattle and goats. He eventually obtained a standard 6 certificate at night school, but missed out on secondary schooling. While working on the railways in Walvis Bay, a fellow worker was shipped home without compensation after a terrible accident. Already dismayed at the plight of migrant workers, the incident stirred him into political action. He was later sacked for trying to form a railway union, the first public indication of the considerable organizational abilities which have enabled him to survive almost three decades as the exiled president of SWAPO.

The shootings turned a protest movement into a revolutionary current. Petitions to the United Nations had been tried and found wanting. Kerina in New York and Nujoma lying low in Ovamboland saw the need for a national party. But SWANU was in disarray, with the chiefs not wishing to lose control to the militant young Hereros. The Chiefs' Council itself was also then in dispute over the designation of

Clemens Kapuuo as Hosea Kutako's successor.

The evolution from OPO to SWAPO was gradual, though the official version holds that the first 'congress' of the movement, in Ovamboland on 19 April 1960, elected Nujoma as president, with Nathaniel Maxuilili as acting president while he went abroad to address the United Nations. Little is known of the size of the meeting, or who attended. The doubling up of office bearers, home and abroad, was a shrewd move which left little room for usurpers. Ya Toivo was not at that first meeting. SWAPO's two major figures were not to meet until after Ya Toivo's release from prison a quarter of a century later. Nujoma and Kozonguizi, who was in New York representing the Herero chiefs, met in Monrovia and agreed on a merger. But the move was rejected back home. Katjavivi writes that SWAPO was not actually formed until June, when Nujoma was already abroad. Kerina in New York became chairman of the party.

As befitted its name, SWAPO's sights were no longer simply the improvement of the lot of the contract worker, but liberation from colonial rule. Its programme spoke of universal adult franchise, the unification of the country on non-racial lines, the removal of apartheid and bantu education, though the chiefs were promised a role in the future dispensation. Railways, mines, electrical and fishing industries were to be publicly owned, while foreign-owned land would be 'placed under the government in conformity with African communal ownership principles' (Katjavivi 1988, pp. 45–6). Though many pro-Western Third World governments would not have taken exception to these principles, in 1960 they alarmed the white colonists.

The SWAPO official history dismisses SWANU as possessing 'limited and sectional support, principally in the centre of Namibia and from students and teachers' (SWAPO 1981, p. 175). Randolph Vigne has written that 'SWANU was seen as sophisticated, perhaps elitist, and Peking-orientated; SWAPO as inexperienced, populist and non-aligned.' (Vigne 1987, p. 88.) In those early years it is well to recall that SWANU considered SWAPO to be too close to the Chief's Council, 'making a career of petitioning' and relying on getting freedom from abroad when it should come from the Namibian people themselves. When Kozonguizi broadcast on Radio Peking, SWAPO complained of his 'anti-imperialist tone'. The SWANU president accused SWAPO of a 'reformist approach'. There could never be peace, SWANU argued, 'until the white settlers' from South Africa had been removed — though Kozonguizi explained that 'settlers' excluded people born in the territory. The rhetoric got them nowhere. They were incapable of breaking out of the confines of the Herero tribe.

With much spadework already done, SWAPO got off to a running start. Indeed, it was instantly the largest political grouping in Namibia.

9

Northern villages were quickly won over to the cause. The one merit of the despised contract labour system was to allow SWAPO to spread its message throughout the country. The system of banishing upstart 'natives' to their kraals, to be watched over by the resident headmen, backfired more often than not. Ya-Toivo had a shop near the SWANLA recruiting office at Oluno where he could be sure of influencing the migrant workers.

The conservatism of the Ovambo traditional rulers meant that SWAPO had two revolutions on its hands. Some chiefs ruled their subjects like mediaeval despots, aided and abetted by South African native commissioners, pro-consuls who meddled and banished when the chiefs did not do their bidding. In 1963 the chiefs and the government got together to ban SWAPO meetings. In that year, Ruth First described men in Ovamboland and Okavangoland as being 'handcuffed' by slips of paper.

> They must have permits to seek work, permits to be in the areas for any purpose other than to seek work, service contracts to prove that they are working, passes to prove that they are schoolboys and too young to carry passes, certificates of registration authorizing residence in the area, permits to travel, tax receipts, exemptions from night curfew . . . they may move nowhere without joining the interminable queue at the government office for stamps of authority on their passes. No African in the Police Zone may buy a railway ticket without a pass issued by his employer or an authorised official. No African in a Reserve may leave it except by permit or in order to work for a white employer. Men have been reduced to mere labour units. [IDAF 1989, p. 32.]

These were the conditions that rendered every northern village and kraal ripe for SWAPO recruitment. Endola, a lively village a bare 20 kilometres from the Angolan border, was typical. It was founded in the mid-twenties by a Lutheran pastor, Simson Shituwa, one of the first Namibian blacks ordained by the Finnish missionaries. Then, as now, the people cultivated millet and tended their cattle and goats. By building a church, the missionaries provided a focus to an area of scattered homesteads. After the Second World War, white *algemene handelaars* (general dealers) arrived to exploit the cash brought back by the contract workers. New schools, synagogues (chapels), as well as market stalls and shops, contrived to make Endola, in the words of a former resident, 'a place of high-minded people who understood the political situation in their country.'

One day in the early 1960s Eliazar Tuhadeleni returned to Endola lugging a large church organ. Like many of the able-bodied men of Ovamboland, he was forced to earn his living far from home. But instead of the diamond mines or fish canning factories of his own country, he had gone further south to Cape Town to work as a dock labourer. He saved his money and went regularly to church. The gift he brought home for his fellow Lutherans earned him the nickname *Kaxumba kandola* — 'the organ of Endola'.

Tuhadeleni would play the organ during Sunday services, and afterwards young and old would gather to talk about the plight of their country. Once SWAPO had been launched, the Christian churches of the north became the debating chambers of the new movement. Occasionally a pastor or priest objected to the use of church premises for such dangerous talk, but they were few and far between. Although it was by no means unique in its enthusiasm, from Endola there emerged several prominent freedom fighters — Emmanuel Shifidi, John Shiponeni, Helao Shityuwete, the brothers Justus and Saloman Heita, and Kaxumba, all revered as heroes.

Tuhadeleni went on playing his medley of music, sacred and patriotic, until his arrest in 1967. Later his name was given to a trial which proclaimed the determination of the people of Namibia to shake themselves free of foreign domination. In less than ten years the resistance movement had progressed from a debating society to an organization capable of tying up Africa's most powerful army in one of the continent's longest wars.

Exile

By late 1960 Nujoma and a group of exiled comrades had set up external headquarters in Dar es Salaam, in the one-time German colony of Tanganyika. Here, as more young patriots left for exile, travelling through British Bechuanaland and pre-UDI Rhodesia, or more rarely through Portuguese Angola, the seminal decisions about the liberation struggle were taken.

For quite soon, SWAPO was faced with the agonizing but inevitable issue of armed struggle. It is difficult to know when exactly the leadership began to move away from peaceful protest at home as the main plank in its strategy. From the earliest discussions in Cape Town the 'barrel of a gun' would have been an option — in the forefront of the minds of some, morally unacceptable to others. Events in South Africa — the shootings at Sharpeville, which bore a remarkable similarity to the Old Location massacre, the banning of the African National Congress and the Pan-Africanist Congress, and the intensification of Prime Minister Hendrik Verwoerd's apartheid programme — all indicated clearly that Pretoria was not prepared to see reason over black demands. When, in 1961, South Africa was forced out of the

Commonwealth over its race policies, Namibia went out willy-nilly as well, a ward no longer of the British Queen but of the president of a new Afrikaner republic. In 1964, Pretoria published the Odendaal Commission's report advocating the division of Namibia into ten tribal bantustans with the white farmers and industrialists hanging on to all that was commercially worthwhile. The report was translated into law four years later as the Development of Self-Government for Native Nations in South West Africa Act.

The United Nations, legal guardian of the welfare of Namibia's blacks, seemed incapable of making inroads into Pretoria's occupation. Britain continued to speak with forked tongue. In 1958, Sir Charles Arden-Clarke, a former governor of the Gold Coast and now chair of the UN Good Offices Committee, suggested a partition plan — the fertile farmland and the mines to be swallowed by South Africa, the north administered by Pretoria as a trust territory. The plan came to nothing. But two years later, the UN's Committee on South West Africa, which had been critical of the Old Location shootings, was refused permission to visit the territory. The British government refused visas for them to go to Bechuanaland to talk to Namibian petitioners who had slipped out of the country and walked across the desert hoping to meet them, so the committee interviewed Namibian refugees elsewhere in Africa.

When, in 1962, a two-man delegation from the Special Committee for South West Africa was allowed in, they became a laughing stock, issuing contradictory reports amid suggestions in the local press that one of the two had been fulsomely plied with liquor. However, the final straw was the decision handed down by the International Court of Justice in July 1966 that it could not adjudicate on the legal status of Namibia on the grounds that the parties bringing the action had no standing. Liberia and Ethiopia, as former League members, had instituted proceedings four years previously. The president of the court, Sir Percy Spender of Australia, voted once in the seven-to-seven judgement, then exercised his casting vote in favour of South Africa.

Elsewhere on the colonized sub-continent nationalists had concluded that fine words and passive resistance would not lead to emancipation. In 1961 the FNLA began a war to liberate Angola, followed swiftly by the MPLA. In the same year, the ANC's *Umkhonto we Sizwe* (Spear of the Nation) and the Pan-Africanist Congress's Poqo (literally 'pure') took up arms against white rule. FRELIMO followed suit in 1964, while UDI in Rhodesia in 1965 triggered ZANU and ZAPU action against Ian Smith's 'rule of 1,000 years'.

In his 1967 Terrorism Trial speech, Andimba Ya Toivo would ask the poignant question: 'Is it surprising that in such times my countrymen have taken up arms? Violence is truly fearsome, but who would not defend his property and himself against a robber? And we believe that South Africa has robbed us of our country.' Ya Toivo described the interplay between external events and the grudging acceptance of the inevitability of an uprising. The suppression of the ANC and PAC:

> convinced me that we were too weak to face South Africa's force by waging battle. When some of my country's soldiers came back, I foresaw the trouble there would be for SWAPO, my people and me personally. I tried to do what I could to prevent my people from going into the bush. In my attempts I became unpopular with some of my people, but this, too, I was prepared to endure. Decisions of this kind are not easy to make. My organization could not work properly — it could not hold meetings. I had no answer to the question: 'Where has your non-violence got us?' Whilst the World Court judgement was pending, I at least had that to fall back on. When we failed, after years of waiting, I had no answer to give to my people.

Ya Toivo was sentenced to 20 years for his pains.

Of those who left Namibia, many hoped to complete their secondary schooling in a system other than bantu education, and equip themselves for a constructive role in an independent Namibia. Working in Windhoek, Helao Shityuwete was by now SWAPO secretary for northern affairs, but he still harboured ambitions to study abroad. Twice he walked and hitch-hiked hundreds of miles through the bush to the Angolan port of Lobito only to find his hopes of getting to the USA dashed by a shortage of money or by the war. Then he heard his old Walvis Bay friend, Vinnia Ndadi, broadcasting from Dar es Salaam on the Voice of Namibia. He tried a third time, crossing without documents into the newly-independent Botswana and, helped by the local SWAPO office in Francistown, travelled by bus through Zambia to Tanzania. That was 1964.

> As I wasn't on the executive, I knew nothing about preparations for the armed struggle until Nanyemba told me. They made me an offer. I could study or go for military training. The choice was mine entirely. There was no pressure. I chose the army. [Interview with author, 1988.]

His yearning for a formal education was subordinated to the needs of the struggle. Only after his release from prison 20 years later, was Shityuwete, by then in his late forties, able to further his studies in England.

Armed Struggle

One day in March 1962 Sam Nujoma appeared at the Mungurani camp in Dar es Salaam to brief SWAPO refugees about a trip he had just made to the United Nations and the Non-aligned Movement's summit in Belgrade. No one should have any illusions that the struggle would be other than long and bitter, he told them, and the Namibian people would have to bear the brunt of that struggle. His listeners clapped their hands in agreement, upon which the president asked for two volunteers to go back to Namibia 'to perform certain duties'. He waited ten minutes. Silence. He would not leave, he told them, until he had the volunteers. Finally Lucas Pohamba and Elia Muatale stepped forward. Two months later they were arrested in Windhoek, were gaoled for several months, then banished to Ovamboland under the eye of a chief. Now their mission could really begin. Over the next few years they sent out hundreds of volunteers for guerrilla training or further education (Wood 1988, p. 24). The majority went to Eastern bloc countries.

Years later, Andreas Shipanga put this dependence on the Eastern bloc in context. SWAPO leaders had first approached the West, and chiefly the United States, for help.

> Either . . . because of grave naïveté or some strange illusion, the first rounds we made in Dar es Salaam were to knock on the doors of Western embassies. We really believed that it would be possible to convince the Western democracies that our right to self-determination and our struggle against South African rule was noble, just and worthy of their support.

They met with 'hostility and contempt'. South Africa's 'propaganda division had done its homework', Shipanga complained. 'No black who talks about oppression and injustice is his own man — behind him must be the Russians.' (*Dateline: Namibia* 3, 1982.)

The decision to launch an armed struggle was taken in 1962, and military training began soon after. At first the recruits went to Ghana, Egypt or Algeria, the latter fresh from its long struggle against French colonialism. They received eight months basic instruction in small arms, explosives, mines, radio communications and politics. Others went to the Soviet Union for specialized instruction. China and North Korea were added to the list by 1965.

SWAPO's military effort received a tremendous boost with the establishment in 1963 of the Organization of African Unity. The OAU's Co-ordination Committee for the Liberation of Africa collected obligatory contributions from its members. In 1965, the Namibians received £20,000 in assistance, to be equally divided between SWAPO and SWANU. But as SWANU was not willing to take up arms, the money was not released to them. SWANU then disappeared from the international stage. SWAPO, however, was accorded recognition as a 'liberation movement' and opened offices in Lusaka, Cairo and London.

By mid-1965 the first batch of trained men were returning to their headquarters at Kongwa, Tanzania. But before the shooting started, Nujoma had one last non-violent hand to play. He and Lucas Pohamba (by then back in exile) flew into Windhoek on 20 March 1966 in a chartered plane. Arrested at the airport, they were put back on the plane at gun point. Through this action, SWAPO's leaders had disproved South Africa's claim that the nationalists were in exile of their own choice, able to return whenever they wished.

Now the external leadership would brook no delay in sending the troops in. A few weeks later Shityuwete was one in a group of nine which crossed from Zambia into the Caprivi Strip hoping to work their way back into Ovamboland. SWAPO's alliance with the Caprivi African National Union (CANU) facilitated the first stage of their passage. But in Kavango they were intercepted by the police. 'Our mission was not to engage in military activity but rather to organize and prepare for the time when it would become necessary.' Others did get through and established a guerrilla training camp at Omgulumbashe, near where Ovamboland runs into the arid Kaokoveld (between the village of Okayoko and the Finnish mission settlement at Okwaludhi). The South African minister of police told parliament in 1966 that the first group carried 'Russian-manufactured sub-machine guns, automatic pistols and thousands of rounds of ammunition', and had set up an underground hideout in an isolated, dense forest where they trained the locals in guerrilla warfare (SAIRR 1967, p. 59).

According to Ya Toivo their sudden arrival caused anxiety to Namibian political leaders in both Windhoek and the north, and was exacerbated by the problems of communicating with the men in the bush. But the South Africans, having captured the Shityuwete group, and no doubt helped by informers in the area of the training camp, were soon aware of the threat. In the weeks that followed, the guerrillas went into action against several police camps. The internal leadership wanted more time to educate the locals in preparation for the fighting.

On 18 July 1966 SWAPO headquarters in Dar es Salaam declared: 'We have no alternative but to rise in arms and bring about our own liberation. The supreme test must be faced and we must at once begin to cross the many rivers of blood on our march towards freedom. And as sure as night follows day, victory will be ours.' (Weaver in Totemeyer et al., 1987, p. 240.) SWAPO annually marks the launch of the 'Revolutionary Armed Struggle' on 26 August 1966, the day of a shoot-out with the colonial authorities in which Omgulumbashe camp was scattered. Two of the camp's occupants were killed and several captured. Some, however, escaped. One of these was Eliazar Tuhadeleni. Seeing him disappear behind an anthill, the police gave chase only to find a large bird which fluttered its wings and slowly flew off, a fact which gave rise to a certain myth about Tuhadeleni. It did not last as he was eventually caught. More guerrillas were captured, the movement's political leadership inside Namibia — Ya Toivo, Johnny Otto, Nathaniel Maxuilili, Jason Mutumbulua — were arrested; eventually as many as 100 men, though some allege it could have been 250, were spirited away to prison in Pretoria. There they were held under South Africa's 180-day detention law, not applicable to Namibia. Perhaps inspired by these events, the UN General Assembly voted decisively to revoke the Mandate. South Africa and Portugal voted against; General De Gaulle's France, Malawi and Harold Wilson's Labour government in Britain abstained; all the rest, including the American Johnson administration, voted in favour.

The Pretoria Trial

The mini-invasion shook the government's complacency. Deputy Police Minister S. L. Muller announced that 'the communistic alliance had sent about 2,000 trainee terrorists out of the country.' Several hundred 'terrorists' were in transit camps in Tanzania and Zambia en route to the Republic (SAIRR 1966, p. 54). A fortnight after Omgulumbashe, Prime Minister Verwoerd was assassinated. His successor, Justice Minister and war-time pro-Nazi internee Johannes Vorster, prepared a show trial. Parliament hurriedly enacted the Terrorism Act, with terms retroactive to 1962 so as to cover the activities of the Namibian detainees from the earliest preparations for the uprising. Here was a novel method of 'crime' prevention — arrest the suspects, beat and torture them, find out exactly what they have done, then draft an appropriate statute to cover those actions, not illegal at the time they happened. Piet Pelser, the new justice minister, admitted that the Act was 'of a very far-reaching nature.' Asked why he had not used the existing Suppression of Communism Act, draconian by any standards, he explained that the authorities were no longer dealing with 'Red ideology' but with 'Red arms' (SAIRR 1967, p. 61).

The Terrorism Act was promulgated on 21 July 1966. Next morning 37 of the Namibian detainees were formally charged. They were the first Namibian freedom fighters to be brought to the attention of the public, though the case evoked little interest in South Africa. No relative or friend of any of the men was able to travel to Pretoria to view the proceedings. These early leaders of SWAPO were labelled variously as bloodthirsty terrorists, Marxist revolutionaries, godless killers, and misguided dreamers. It is instructive to find out something of their background.

Eliazar Tuhadeleni, the first accused, was by then a married man of 50 with seven children. His formal education had been limited to a few years at a Lutheran primary school, and regular Sunday Bible classes. The son of a tribal councillor, he was a man of both inherited and natural influence far beyond his village. His attorney, Joel Carlson, described his tortured feelings as they prepared for the Terrorism trial.

> One morning, speaking through one of the teachers, he took me aside to tell me that the guilt of all the defendants was on him. He wanted to take the blame for all of them and he was prepared to be hanged immediately. He asked me to tell this to the security police so that, having hanged him, they would then free the innocent men among the thirty-seven. He insisted that this was the Christian way and that he was prepared to carry his cross. Eliazar would quote at length from the Bible as he talked to me, giving me the number of chapters and verses that explained more articulately than he could his point of view on any matter. [Carlson 1973, pp. 171–2.]

Others of the accused included teachers, subsistence farmers, shopkeepers, but mostly they were migrant manual workers. There were grandfathers in their sixties — Ndjaula Shaningwa, aged 59, father of nine, 'no education' (according to an International Commission of Jurists report), who had fired a barrage of feathered bows at the South African helicopters as they swooped on the guerrilla camp. Of the 37, 32 were practising Christians — mostly Lutherans, but Anglican and Roman Catholic as well. Johnny Otto, then SWAPO's secretary for foreign affairs, was a bible study teacher, while the organization's acting secretary-general, Nathaniel Maxuilili, was a lay preacher. Others had a knowledge of the Scriptures which belied their limited formal education. The three or four 'pagans' among them were simply men too old to have been taken in hand by the missionaries. Very few had, like Shityuwete, lost their belief in God.

Soon after making contact with his clients, they pressed Carlson to arrange a church service. Bishop Pakendorf, of the Transvaal Lutherans, was asked by the Lutheran World Federation (LWF) in Geneva to contact the prisoners, but he refused because they were politicals. Pakendorf was at that time also president of the Evangelical Lutheran Churches in Southern Africa, which then included Namibia. The Lutheran bishop in Northern Namibia, Leonard Auala, was refused permission to visit. It took three months for Carlson to find a willing white Ovambo-speaking pastor in Pretoria. The service was held in a corrugated iron shed in the prison precincts. As the pastor led the men in prayer in Afrikaans, the watching policemen, sten guns in hand, clustered in curiosity.

The dominie's voice rose in strong but clear tones and the police recognised the prayers. One by one they removed their hats and standing at ease, their guns in front of them, their hats on the butts of the guns, they bowed their heads as they listened to the dominie's fervent words. The prayers ended and as they sang a hymn, all thirty-seven voices reverberated through the courtyard. Their voices, deep and melodious, seemed to echo on and on. Even the policemen were visibly moved; the language spoken was their own, the prayers were familiar. Suddenly, for a moment, they saw the prisoners in the iron shed as Christians and fellow men. . . . [Carlson 1973, p. 189.]

On Robben Island, the Namibian compound always tried to obtain a priest for Sunday services. White preachers from a wide range of denominations, including a rabbi and an imam, would make the uncomfortable sea crossing from Cape Town. When the last of the 'Tuhadeleni' politicals were released in 1985, most came out more radical, but still God-fearing.

What turned these (and other law-abiding Namibians) to armed revolution was not a desire to be violent for violence's sake, nor to set up a Stalinist-style republic. Their very humanity, a sense of fair play which permeated their daily lives and which was strengthened by northern European missionaries expounding the Judeo-Christian ethic of the equality of humankind, drove them to seek a desperate solution. Of these first 37 men arraigned on charges relating to their desire to free their country, only six were accused of actual physical attacks. Others were said to have intimidated government-appointed chiefs and headmen, while most were charged with receiving military training either at home or abroad. As the International Commission of Jurists report pointed out, 'it was never made very clear in the prosecution or judgement as to which defendants were guilty of which overt acts.' (Falk, 1968, p. 5.)

There is no denying that the intention of all but a handful of the prisoners was to engage in an armed struggle. But the inherent injustice of the hearing, 'confessions' battered out of them by police during months in solitary confinement, the retroactive nature of the law, the refusal of the judge to allow them to be tried in their own country, all served to confirm South Africa's determination to move not an inch out of its colony. The judge rejected defence counsel's argument that, since the revocation of the Mandate, South African laws no longer applied in Namibia. Ya Toivo spoke for all the accused when he told the judge:

My Lord, we find ourselves here in a foreign country, convicted under laws made by people whom we have always considered as foreigners. We find ourselves tried by a judge who is not our countryman and who has not shared our background. Had we been tried by our equals, it would not have been necessary to have any discussion of our grievances. They would have been known to those who judge us.

Twenty of the accused were sent to prison for the rest of their natural lives. Nine were given 20 years, and the remainder received lighter sentences.

Courts, Churches, Unions and Chiefs

They were the first martyrs of the revolution. By putting them on public trial far away from home, the Vorster government intended that they and their cause be forgotten by a world with more pressing matters. In South Africa the imprisonment of the ANC leadership at the Rivonia trial in 1963 dampened real resistance for a decade before the children of Soweto rebelled. For Namibians, the Pretoria trial was both a shattering blow and an inspiration. The solid foundation laid in the early years was the springboard for a substantial expansion in membership. South Africa's military build-up, and the brutalities inevitably visited upon the civilian population, provided a recurring reminder of what the *ovamati* (our boys) were fighting for. Scattered guerrilla attacks continued in Ovamboland and in the Caprivi Strip. On 18 May 1967, SWAPO suffered a grievous setback when its military commander, Thomas Hainyeko, was killed in a boat on the Zambezi river while on a mission in Caprivi. South Africa took revenge for a guerrilla attack on a military camp in 1968 by killing 63 peasants. When freedom fighters were put on trial in Windhoek for the first time (July 1969), blacks crowded the public galleries. The next trial was held in secret (SWAPO 1981, p. 178).

SWAPO's at-home military training was a serious undertaking, but it was inhibited by a shortage of arms and ammunition and the need to keep the secret from government spies. The 'weapon' was usually carved out of wood with a piece of piping shoved in as the barrel. One such, belonging to an accused who did not go abroad for his training, is buried to this day in a field near Ongwediva.

SWAPO took stock at a Consultative Congress in Tanga, Tanzania in late 1969. Some delegates came from Namibia. Special interest sections for women, elders and 'youth' — members between six and 35 — were set up. The Youth League was to shake up Namibian politics in ways not always comfortable for the leadership. Soon afterwards, the National Union of Namibian Workers (NUNW) was launched.

19

Then came the first good news from a world body since the vote, more than 20 years before, against incorporation. In June 1971, the Hague court ruled that South Africa was in illegal occupation of Namibia, and should get out forthwith. People danced for joy in the locations (townships), but South Africa vowed to 'continue to govern South West Africa as in the past.' Despite the brave words, the opinion rather than the 1966 revocation would weigh heavily on the juridically-minded South African government. It also had a startling impact on the churches. Namibia is one of Africa's most Christian countries. As many as three out of four of its people are Lutheran, Catholic, Anglican or African Methodist Episcopal (AME). The Finnish Lutherans, who, in the late 19th century, began their work in the north, were different from other missionaries in that their country had no colonial ambitions. In 1963, a Namibian, Leonard Auala, became moderator, and then bishop of the newly-independent Ovambo–Kavango Lutheran church in the north. His election coincided with the rise of nationalism. In 1968 a joint Anglican, Lutheran and Catholic delegation protested to the South African police commander in northern Namibia against the torture of detainees.

Now the Hague 'Opinion' spurred the Lutheran bishops into drawing up an open letter to Prime Minister Vorster denouncing apartheid and making a telling comparison between South African policy and practice and the Universal Declaration of Human Rights. One Sunday morning the pastoral letter was read in every black Lutheran parish in the land, so that its content reached half Namibia's population. Roman Catholic, Anglican and AME parishes followed suit. The effect of the dignified demand for freedom was to ally the churches unequivocally alongside SWAPO in the struggle for freedom.

Most of all, the 'opinion' fired the students of the Youth League. They demonstrated and many were expelled from schools in the north. Within months, they had become clerks, interpreters, white collar workers in Walvis Bay and other strategic centres. Soon the contract workers were agitating for better pay and work conditions, but most of all for an end to their migrant labour status. Their anger boiled over when Jannie de Wet (Commissioner General of the Indigenous People of South West Africa) made a public statement denying that the system was 'a form of slavery'. It was, he said, a purely voluntary arrangement and men who objected did not have to enter into contracts (SAIRR 1972, p. 432). The strike that followed threw the mines, transport system and municipalities into disarray. Almost three-quarters of the non-farming workforce were sent back north. There were cases of farm workers, the most isolated, under-paid and brutalized stratum, downing tools and making their way home. The strikers faced a variety of pressures — police batons, the trickery of the mine-owners, chiefs brought down to harangue them into submission. They held firm. 'Scab' replacements were difficult to find.

South Africa was shaken by the skilful organization of the strike. In Ovamboland, Johannes Nangutuuala headed a strike committee which on 10 January 1972 held a meeting where 3,500 people demanded comprehensive reforms. Police reinforcements were sent in as whites were threatened by a breakdown of food and essential services. In the end, the strikers won some changes, but the system remained intact. SWANLA recruitment was replaced by a network of labour bureaux run by the bantustans. 'Master and servant' became 'employer and employee', working hours were to be agreed on, and it would be possible to change jobs. Wages improved, but more enduring was the awakened sense of power in a country massively dependent on labour-intensive industry. The resurgence of union activity in the late 1980s has its roots in the actions of these migrant workers.

Disgusted at the brutal government reaction, many of the 20,000 sacked workers crossed into exile, swelling guerrilla ranks. They faced an exacting journey to Zambia, with the west of the country wide open to South African special operations. In Angola, the Portuguese regime of Marcelo Caetano collaborated with its like-minded allies in providing intelligence and manpower to combat respective revolutionary threats. But the tide was turning as SWAPO's ally, the MPLA, made inroads along the escape route of southern Angola.

By early 1972, the north was in a state of insurrection, the temperature in the colonial hothouse stoked by fuels of many sorts. With SWAPO Youth League activity increasing in the wake of the strike, the government promulgated Proclamations R17 and R26, measures equivalent to martial law. It became an offence to say or do anything likely to have the effect of undermining the authority of the state, the Ovambo government, officials of these bodies, or a chief or headman. Persons suspected of committing any offence, or intending to do so, or having information relating to an offence, could be arrested without warrant and detained for questioning until the authorities were satisfied that they had fully and truthfully answered all relevant questions put to them (SAIRR, 1972, pp. 439–40). Now, with SWAPO meetings effectively banned, hundreds of their followers in detention, and the arrival of a substantial military contingent from the Republic, reports of violence against civilians increased — a phenomenon which continued for the next seventeen years.

The 1972 strike moved the Security Council to call on the secretary-general, Kurt Waldheim, to start negotiations on self-determination. After visiting Namibia and meeting Vorster, he said the main stumbling-block to a solution was the interpretation of the terms 'self-determination and independence'. For the United Nations, it meant independence for the whole territory, whereas Vorster wanted 'independence' for the various population groups. Since 1968, each of the seven Ovambo tribal authorities had been represented by six members in an appointed legislative council. Now, in 1973, elections were to be held for Ovambo and Kavango legislative assemblies, with the aim of drawing SWAPO's sting. Participation was restricted to Chief Filemon Elifas's Ovambo Independence Party. Elifas was duly elected 'leader' of the Ovambo people on a 2.5% poll, the lowest recorded percentage poll in any election anywhere in the world.

The dismal result was largely the result of the political work of the SWAPO Youth League (SYL). The Leaguers, whose ages ranged from mid-teens to mid-thirties, had roots going back to the 1950s, when Namibian students in South Africa came under the influence of the African National Congress. As in the Republic, bantu education in Namibia turned well-behaved children into radicals. On one celebrated occasion, the students of Augustineum College marched the 40 miles from Okahandja to Windhoek to present their grievances to the authorities. So, when the 1969 SWAPO congress created the Youth League, it simply coralled a generation that was raring to break out of the starting pens. At times the SWAPO elders were to find the language and actions of the League rather too strident for comfort. 'When a Namibian youth is not fighting for a better education he is found engaged in a battle against the bosses, foremen and even boss-boys in the work place,' ran the SYL manifesto.

> He is also found either battling or running for his life in the street, where the fascist police are harassing the population. When expelled from work, or from school, a Namibian youth finds work for himself to survive, and most of his time is devoted to the struggle for the emancipation of his people . . .' [*Action on Namibia*, Spring 1988.]

The League also mobilized and sent out recruits for PLAN. In Namibia, the most accurate guide to an organization's success was the level of police interest. In 1973, the SYL leader, Jerry Ekandjo, and a group of activists were convicted of 'sabotage', which in Pretoria-speak amounted to making fiery speeches at a meeting in Ovamboland. Within months, the Special Branch had skimmed off the leadership and deposited them with the Pretoria trialists on Robben Island. When, in June 1974, the League's acting-secretary, Joseph Taapopi, was sentenced to two years on the Island (after being charged with 'incitement to murder, public violence and arson' for writing to Nujoma calling for PLAN to liberate Namibia) he reacted jauntily: 'I am off to college. There I will meet our head boy Ja-Toivo.' [Soggot 1986, p. 95.]

If this period in Namibia's unhappy history saw a quantum leap in official violence, it also marked the introduction of what is perhaps an even more craven practice — the use of blacks to do the white 'baas's' dirty work. Elifas was the archetypal tribal chief — conservative, autocratic, happy to go along with a government which pandered to his dignity and paid him for it — the sort of man to whom SWAPO, and more especially the young Turks of the League, was anathema. While indirect rule might have worked well enough in some colonial systems —at least the Emirs of Northern Nigeria had enjoyed the confidence of their subjects — the people of Ovambo were in no mood for subjection. In 1973 the South African police began to hand over 'Swapos' to the various tribal councils. After a cursory hearing, men and women were publicly flogged by Ovambo headmen with an *epokolos*, the two-foot long central rib of the makalani palm. Elifas and his 'court', which included women, and a white policeman seated in a chair for comfort, watched with relish the acting out of a barbarism worthy of a mediaeval European king. The victims, respected members of the community, fathers, teachers, nurses, were flogged on bare buttocks, 15, 20, in one case, 28 times. Nangutuuala, the strike leader and founder of the small Democratic Cooperative Party (Demcop), had pleaded with Elifas not to accept self-government. In public at Ondangwa he received 21 strokes on his bare buttocks (SAIRR 1973, p. 390). These were not 'canings' familiar to generations of English public schoolboys. Administered by drunken headmen, the blows fell sometimes on thighs or the spine, leaving open flesh wounds which turned septic.

And the trial? In one case a SWAPO shirt, coloured red, blue and green, was taken as confirmation of guilt. A nurse, asked why she had joined SWAPO, replied that 'it struggles for our betterment'. Two hundred spectators watched the punishment for that reply. The public flogging of women is unknown in Ovambo society. Pretoria did nothing, other than to explain that Ovamboland was now self-governing. It was not for South Africa to interfere in the affairs of a sovereign state. The floggings were belatedly halted by the South African courts after the intervention of Auala, the Anglican bishop, Richard Wood, and Thomas Kamati of the Youth League. Six years later, when the government set up Koevoet, the makalani episode would seem by comparison like a children's rough-'n'-tumble. But the government had tested the water and uncovered a small minority of northerners willing to take sides against SWAPO. Two years after the floggings, Elifas was assassinated.

The Coup in Portugal

On 24 April 1974, Portuguese junior officers, their country no longer able to sustain a far-flung and disaffected empire, staged a *golpe do estado*. Within days, the young officers announced that all of Portuguese

23

Africa would become independent. The repercussions were felt thousands of miles away on Angola's border with Namibia. Portuguese soldiers, who only days before had collaborated with South Africa in hunting down and handing over captured guerrillas, now viewed the struggle with disinterest.

The precipitate Portuguese withdrawal from Angola, leading to a left-wing government in the space of 18 months, created opportunities and obstacles. It was a watershed period for southern Africa, obliging all parties to review their regional strategies. South Africa initiated a more interventionist policy, only to come to grief on the outskirts of Luanda. For SWAPO, it was a time of hope. In all the arenas of struggle —diplomacy, the battlefield, among the enthusiasts at home — the nationalists appeared to be in the ascendant and Pretoria in retreat.

By 1975, all of Africa, save Rhodesia and Namibia, had been decolonized. In most cases, Britain and France had strengthened economic links with their former colonies. But the European powers had invariably resisted demands for self-government where there was a settler community. Algeria was one of these. Frenchmen, even left-wingers, saw their maghrebian colony as an integral part of France. The cry *Algérie Francaise* had its echo in *Suidwes in ons s'n*. This fantasy of Namibia as a fifth province was shared by all South African whites, English and Afrikaner. There was a similarity, too, in the roles of the soldiers. The French army had returned from the debacle in Indo-China determined that it not be repeated in Algeria. It needed a resolute and far-seeing statesman, himself a military man, to take on both the army and the settlers and extricate France from a 'no-win' situation. Vorster's actions for a time gave the impression that he would eventually quit Namibia. But he was no De Gaulle; and he was a man of the police, not the army.

Yet from 1974, perceptive whites should have known there was no avoiding the eventual independence of Namibia. The decisiveness of the Hague Court's 'opinion', followed by the devastating suddenness of the Lisbon coup, should have persuaded them that something new had to be paraded before the international community. But 'South-West' was nowhere near ready for the only independence that Pretoria would contemplate. Five decades of creeping incorporation had turned it into a de facto province of the Republic, superficially as South African as the Cape or Transvaal. Dependence on outsiders was well-nigh total. The machinery of state and business belonged to non-Namibians. Bantustan 'self-government' remained the favoured policy, and though the Ovambo elections had been a disaster, Vorster was not abandoning it. But now he embarked on another, more traditional neo-colonial course. South Africa's first initiative after the Portuguese coup was to call a constitutional conference to 'settle the country's future'. Each tribe would send a delegation. SWAPO dismissed the talks out of hand, not the least because it was only open to Pretoria's tribal appointees. But Chief Kapuuo of the Hereros accepted, and thereby bestowed on it an element of respectability. Kozonguizi, another one-time opponent of Pretoria, returned from exile as legal adviser to Kapuuo's delegation.

The delegates met in September 1975 in the Turnhalle, a German gymnasium hall in downtown Windhoek. The Broederbond, ideological backbone of Afrikaner nationalism, had worked out the scheme carefully. But the sight of dyed-in-the-wool Afrikaner nationalists sitting round the table with blacks impressed few people, for the show was run by the white National Party of SWA and South African government officials. Delegates argued heatedly about integrating public libraries and municipal swimming pools. Two years later, the conference agreed on a 'Final Concept' for the establishment of an interim government and a plan to create three layers or tiers of administrative authority, a device to retain budgetary and political power in white hands. To the South African government, the 'Turnhalle' was projected as a formula representative of all the Namibian people.

Meanwhile, in January 1975, South Africa tried once again to corral the voters of Ovamboland. Once again SWAPO boycotted. This time the ground was thoroughly prepared, with voting over five days. The electorate, 'captive' of the chiefs and headmen, were told that if they did not vote, land would not be made available for ploughing; one witness alleged 'the old, blind and disabled, as well as mentally retarded people, who receive pensions from the government, were told they would lose their pensions.' (Katjavivi 1988, p. 76) Teachers and nurses were threatened with dismissal; the special branch, tribal police, and government officials, armed with the emergency regulations, patrolled, while the army and air force put on a show of strength. SWAPO could not repeat its successful boycott of two years before. Many teachers had by now fled, while the youth leaders were in prison. The poll in Ovamboland rose to 70 per cent. Outside Ovamboland, in the south, free from coercion, a mere 4.2 per cent of eligible Ovambos cast their vote. The government could now boast that 55 per cent of 'the Ovambo nation' had given their imprimatur to the bantustan concept. Chief Minister Filemon Elifas saw it as 'a vote of confidence in himself and his government, and as a mandate for action against certain individuals, including churchmen, on grounds of incitement.' (Totemeyer 1978, p. 108.) Pretoria now had two options, both racial: the naked bantustans of 'separate development', as in the Republic, and the undisguised ethnicity of the Turnhalle.

War in Angola

The prospect of Marxist governments in Angola and Mozambique galvanized South Africa. For 25 years white racists had forecast the imminent onslaught of the red menace and here, as if in a self-fulfilling wish, was the real thing on their doorstep. To the east, Mozambique, having warded off an attempted settler uprising, had become independent on 25 June 1975, and the FRELIMO government was nationalizing land, schools, hospitals, businesses and property, provoking a huge Portuguese exodus to South Africa and Europe. Though Mozambique was considerably more relevant to South Africa than Angola, Pretoria did not then intervene directly. Yet Angola, far away and always beyond Pretoria's economic orbit, was fair game.

When the Portuguese soldiers laid down their arms, Angola's political inheritance was by no means clear. There was still a chance that the MPLA, the best organized and most determined of the contenders to take over the government, could be kept out. It was not simply that they were 'Marxist'. More critically, they were, of the three nationalist movements, the most likely to provide safe passage to SWAPO. But the South African government was divided over the political dangers of intervention. The military (SADF), led by Defence Minister P. W. Botha, were in no doubt that they could install a friendly government in Luanda before independence on 11 November 1985. Vorster, and his security adviser, Hendrik van den Bergh, were concerned at the international ramifications.

US Secretary of State Henry Kissinger provided the moral support and the CIA personnel that Vorster needed. For several years America had been arming the rival FNLA, and its military advisers were thick on the Angolan ground. The SADF hurriedly co-opted an FNLA detachment on the run from the MPLA, and a San (Bushmen) battalion which a year before had been fighting for the Portuguese. In late October 1975 they combined with South African troops in an unexpected invasion which swept through southern Angola, until halted by tough Cuban–MPLA resistance (and unfordable rivers) on the road to Luanda. Thanks to maximum censorship, South Africa was the one country ignorant of the fact that its army was at war several hundred miles inside Angola. As the black troops, which by now included UNITA, bore the brunt of casualties, few white lives had to be accounted for. Once Kissinger's clandestine manoeuvres were exposed, the Senate voted the Clark Amendment, outlawing the arming of parties to the conflict. (It was repealed in the first Reagan–Bush administration.)

South Africa's invasion and ignominious withdrawal had far-reaching consequences. A white officer described the escapade as 'our Bay of Pigs', but it was a disaster more in diplomatic than military terms.

The SADF was not defeated, only checked, by the Cuban–MPLA army. But perceptions count for much in these circumstances. To the blacks of the sub-continent, the 'Boer' soldiers were coming home because they could not stand the shooting. As would happen again 12 years later at Cuito Cuanavale, South Africa discovered to its chagrin that in this kind of game, not winning was tantamount to losing. It certainly acted as an inspirational factor in the Soweto schoolchildren's rebellion five months later, an event which would lead to Vorster's political demise. Curiously, the prestige of P. W. Botha, who pressed most heavily for intervention, was not damaged. The Organization of African Unity, having been split down the middle over which of the contending movements to back, opted for the MPLA once the others were shown to be fighting alongside the apartheid army. The large Cuban army presence, a direct reaction to South Africa's invasion, would later be used as pretext by Washington and Pretoria to delay Namibian independence.

Once the intervention in Angola turned sour, it was clear that the guerrilla threat inside Namibia could only multiply. South Africa built up its manpower and weaponry to a level that would soon make Namibia the most militarized country on earth (100,000 Security Force personnel to fewer than 1,500,000 people). In 1973, when the army took over border security from the police, there were but four security force bases in Ovamboland. A decade later there were 80. The war saw an abrupt escalation of the SADF establishment from 16,000 to more than 50,000. The Permanent Force underwent a sizeable expansion, in numbers and quality of training, but most were conscripts. Full conscription had been introduced in 1967, with nine months national service for every white male school-leaver, including Namibians. It was extended to twelve months in 1972, and to two years in 1977, by which time Namibia — or the intentionally hazy 'border' — began to weigh heavily on the emotions of white parents. Recruits received both conventional and counter-insurgency training. After national service, they automatically became members of the Citizen Force, to be called up annually for camps ranging from one to three months. These tributes were a bone of contention, interfering with studies and work. But though the pay was low, one in five patriotic industrialists, including famous foreign firms, made up the salaries of absent employees (Cawthra 1986, p. 84, citing Magnus Malan).

Even before the guerrilla war began in 1966, the military had been in occupation of the Caprivi Strip, the narrow stretch of Namibia jutting into south central Africa. This was a breach of article 4 of the Mandate which stipulated that 'no military or naval base shall be established or fortifications erected in the territory.' The breach was widened still further with the placement in Caprivi of a black territorial force, as the Mandate prohibited 'the military training of the natives, other than for . . . internal police and the local defence of the territory.'

By then, however, the stretched white resources of the SADF needed supplementing. In the midst of the Angolan war, '1 Ovambo Battalion' (later called '101 Bn') came into existence. The unit's role was depicted by its insignia — an eagle clasping a Kalashnikov in its claws. The mercenaries' magazine *Soldier of Fortune* (February 1989) disclosed that 'urbanised Ovambos, who have usually lost most of these tribal skills (that is, tracking and bush survival) are rarely selected.' Until the appearance of Koevoet three years later, the battalion was the main 'reaction force' inside Namibia. At the outset, it seems they were genuine trackers and did not bully local people. As to why they joined, *Soldier of Fortune* noted the incentive of a wage which, by late 1988, was R700 per month, greatly in excess of that of unskilled labourers.

For reasons of diplomacy white troops could not in the late 1970s pursue guerrillas into southern Angola. There was another consideration: cross-border action meant deaths and injuries and embarrassing funerals in the cities and towns back home. The solution was to transform the FNLA mercenaries into 32 Battalion, a fully-fledged unit of the SADF. They were installed at Buffalo base in the Caprivi Strip, hence their other title, Buffalo Battalion. With families living in a nearby village, they had little choice but to accept their hosts' 'invitation' to continue making war. Responsible for the unit was Colonel Jan Breytenbach (ironically, brother of the anti-apartheid writer, Breyten), and it was officered by mercenaries — French veterans of Algeria, Americans from Vietnam, Rhodesians, Britons, white Angolans, and Portuguese-speaking SADF regulars.

For years Buffalo's existence remained a secret, though it may have numbered as many as 9,000 troops, six times the size of a normal battalion. Officially it was fighting SWAPO, and as such was the 'blood brother' of UNITA, South Africa's other surrogate force, which had the Angolan army in its sights. But Buffalo's secondary role became known in 1980 when a British mercenary, Trevor Edwards, told his story to the London *Guardian*. He described a systematic policy of striking at both civilian and military targets, gunning down men, women, children and livestock, burning homes, schools and fields. 'Dressed in unmarked camouflage uniforms, under strict orders to carry no documents of any type, and using East European weapons, they move into Angola for sweeps through groups of villages. White officers and NCOs black their faces [29.1.81]'. The exposé changed little: after lying low for a while, the battalion resumed its activities with even greater ferocity. The battalion's colours were sponsored by Volkskas Bank Insurance group, a pillar of Afrikaner business. In 1985 it was reported that the unit had lost almost 200 men, mostly with Portuguese–African names.

The first black unit in Namibia had been recruited from amongst Angolan San (Bushmen) in 1974. In a war fought exclusively in the bush, their prowess at tracking added substantially to the war effort. However, for the San people this transition from nomadic hunter–gatherer to comparatively well-heeled regular soldier has been disastrous. Breytenbach (1986, p. 8) describes his first contact:

> I spotted a dozen or so Bushmen, impassively staring to their front, showing no interest in the proceedings whatsoever. They were, obviously, former Portuguese *flechas* (indigenous guerrilla-hunters employed by the secret police, PIDE) who had joined the enemy they had once hunted so successfully. There was no other way for them or their families. The FNLA cause held no attraction for them whatsoever.

So now the army ranged the operational area, hunting guerrillas and attempting to bend the minds of its inhabitants. But to little avail. As early as 1976, South Africa was receiving a taste of the new breed of guerrilla. In that one year SWAPO carried out three times as many raids as in the previous ten years. Senior SADF officers were forced to admit that 'the enemy' had improved his fighting ability and 'would not simply go away.' (Interview with Herbstein, Ondangwa, 1976.)

Hard pressed, from 1978 the army began to operate more and more across the border as the war was exported to southern Angola, while the police and ethnic militia took over much of the counter-insurgency role from the army in the north.

The Gang of Five

Having withdrawn the Mandate in October 1966, the United Nations lacked the muscle to enforce its writ. Thereafter, the Security Council voted a succession of resolutions, each recalling previously disregarded resolutions, calling on South Africa to 'withdraw its presence from the territory', concluding with a warning that it (the Security Council) remained 'actively seized of the matter'. Britain and France invariably abstained, rendering the motions even more ineffectual. In the first six years of the seventies, Britain and America three times vetoed mandatory economic sanctions in the Security Council, and France twice. They argued that both the armed struggle and economic sanctions would endanger Western investment and strategic interests, put whites and blacks at physical risk and, they insisted, would not work. On the other hand, their industrialists and traders continued to benefit from the expansion of the South African and Namibian economies. The UN Council for South West Africa (later 'Namibia') was created in 1967 as a

29

stop-gap administration for Namibia until independence. Had the United States government of Lyndon Johnson lent its prestige to the birth of the UN Council by becoming a member, South Africa might have taken it seriously. But it did not and a plane-load of council officials which flew into Windhoek were unceremoniously sent back to Lusaka. In 1974, the Council issued a decree warning multinational companies against exploiting Namibia's natural resources. It was ignored by Western mining houses and Soviet fishing boats alike.

A series of events, none directly related to Namibia, led to some action by the West. In November 1977, Britain and the US allowed the Security Council to vote a mandatory arms embargo against the Republic. The occasion for the unprecedented non-use of the habitual Western veto was the death in a Pretoria police cell of the black political leader, Steve Biko, and the banning of a string of church and black consciousness organizations. Observers have noted that the West normally acts in concert against South Africa on the 'easy' issue of abrogation of human rights, when public opinion, outraged by scenes on television, demands action. Rarely has the West taken effective measures on race laws or Namibian independence.

The presence of Cuban troops in Angola also set the alarm bells ringing in Washington. Whatever the Ford and Carter administrations' views on SWAPO and Namibian independence, these were over-shadowed by the American obsession with Fidel Castro. Carter's secretary of state, Cyrus Vance, had to manage the Cuba–South Africa balancing act. He wrote of this period:

> The more intense the conflict in Namibia became the greater the risk that the South Africans would carry the war more deeply into Angola, thus increasing the possibility that the Cubans would be engaged directly in the fighting. If a Cuban–South African conflict spilled over into Rhodesia, as we believe(d) it could, there would be a war along race lines in southern Africa in which we would be virtually powerless to prevent immense damage to American political, economic and strategic interests . . . Without a strategy for achieving Namibian independence, the Western nations would soon be faced with the dilemma of how to respond to African demands for mandatory sanctions against South Africa. If there were no credible negotiating initiative the Africans would be able to force a Security Council vote. We would then either damage our relations with black Africa by vetoing the resolution . . . or, by approving it, destroy the negotiating process and harm important Western interests [pp. 274–5.]

A contact group of five Western nations (United States, Britain, France, plus Canada and West Germany, members of the Security Council at the time) was established in April 1977. All had substantial business interests in Namibia. They asked for 'one last chance' to persuade Pretoria to leave the territory.

The 'Gang of Five', as they were soon irreverently named, held separate meetings with the Vorster government and SWAPO, then recognized as the two main parties to the conflict — unlike the position a decade later when SWAPO was excluded from the negotiating process with tragic consequences. The Americans and British took the lead in the negotiations. They enlisted Zambia, Tanzania, Angola and other Frontline States to reassure and persuade SWAPO. The negotiators had inherited a Security Council resolution (no. 385) which, when voted in 1976, reflected South Africa's weakened bargaining position. But now the Five produced a watered-down plan altogether less favourable to SWAPO. Under '385' the pre-independence election process was to be run by the United Nations. The modified plan left it almost entirely in the hands of Pretoria, which would draw up voters' rolls, manage the elections, monitor through their own police, repeal security and apartheid laws, and leave the UN relegated to a supervisory role.

Resolution 385 had included Walvis Bay as part of Namibian territory. The enclave, being part of the British Cape Province from 1878, was inherited by South Africa at Union in 1910. But since 1922 it had been administered as an integral part of 'South-West'. Then, as South Africa's grip on Namibia was loosened, Walvis Bay was taken back into the Cape administration. So, by this quirk of colonialism, Namibia's sole deep-water port, major railhead, centre of the fishing industry, and home for South African army and naval bases, became a dagger pointed at the heart of the new country. To placate SWAPO and the United Nations, the West in 1978 sponsored a resolution declaring that Namibia's territorial integrity 'must be assured through the reintegration of Walvis Bay . . .' and that 'South Africa must not use Walvis Bay in any manner prejudicial to the independence of Namibia or the viability of its economy.' There were no coercive provisions in the event of South Africa violating the understanding.

On 25 April 1978, Vorster formally accepted the Western proposals (later to become UNSC Resolution 435). Nine days later, South African paratroopers dropped onto a SWAPO refugee settlement at Cassinga, 200 kilometres inside Angola, and perpetrated the bloodiest massacre of the war, shooting over 600 unarmed men, women and children, as well as a handful of PLAN guards. For South Africa, Operation Reindeer was a successful shoot-up at a 'terrorist' camp. In fact, 61 Mechanized Battalion did attack PLAN's Vietnam base just across the border on the same day, but here too unarmed refugees were shot in cold blood.

Secretary of State Vance, who was deeply committed to the settlement, later declared: 'Given the size of the attack and the prior intelligence work and military planning it required, it seemed that Pretoria must have been preparing the raid even as Vorster was agreeing to our clarified proposal.' (1983, p. 305.) This penchant for signalling your real intentions by a separate but warlike act was repeated in May 1986 — as the Commonwealth Eminent Persons Group were holding top-level talks in Pretoria about apartheid, the South African airforce bombed neighbouring Commonwealth capital cities.

A military insider has written that 'Reindeer' (the SADF code name) was the idea of General Constand Viljoen, chief of the army. Soldiers and politicans meeting at Vorster's seaside cottage the previous December heard that military contacts with SWAPO were averaging 100 a month. There were said to be 2,000 'insurgents' in Angola, with another 1,400 opposite Caprivi in Zambia. (Steenkamp 1983, pp. 5–6). So Cassinga was not a simple act of defiance. It had both diplomatic and military aims. Pretoria wanted SWAPO to reject the Western plan. In addition, P. W. Botha, though not yet prime minister, had signalled a new policy of driving the enemy northwards, hoping to isolate them from their catchment areas. The army now undertook an unbroken series of large-scale operations, ranging from a semi-permanent occupation of thousands of square miles of Angola, to hot pursuit. A secret, undeclared war was launched against the civilian population of that country. Tens of thousands of Angolans would die, destruction valued in billions of dollars would be wrought, with the ostensible aim of keeping SWAPO out of Namibia.

SWAPO put aside its severe reservations about Walvis Bay and Cassinga and accepted the UN plan. But now (1978), to the dismay of Pretoria's western sponsors, 'internal elections' were called. The Democratic Turnhalle Alliance (DTA), a loose coalition of white and conservative black parties, led by Dirk Mudge, a breakaway from the National Party, duly won a majority of the votes amidst well authenticated allegations of 'ruthless coercion'. Thousands of Angolan refugees and South African expatriates voted. People unable to produce a registration card in the weeks before the election were deemed to be SWAPO or one of the other boycotting parties, suffering harassment from headmen and soldiers. No voters' roll was published. In some polling stations, electoral officers filled in 90 per cent of the voting slips. (Ellis 1979).

With the 'Muldergate' information scandal revealing the unauthorized use of public funds at the highest level of government, Johannes Vorster resigned. On 20 September 1978 Pieter Willem Botha, whose initials and quick temper had earned him the nickname 'Piet Wapen' (Pete Weapon), became Prime Minister. The army was now in complete control. Within a few months Margaret Thatcher was prime minister of Britain; the election of Ronald Reagan to the US presidency followed.

Both looked kindly on white rule in South Africa and this constellation of events was to have a dramatic and tragic effect on south western Africa.

2.

Partners in Liberation:
SWAPO and the Churches

Within weeks of the 1974 Portuguese coup, a group of youth leaguers tested the water in southern Angola. The Portuguese soldiers and the PIDE secret police were gone. Word went back that the coast was clear. By the end of 1974, the refugee exodus from Namibia had swollen to 4,000. They were teachers, church workers, nurses, civil servants, police, bank clerks, school children, people who had been flogged, who feared detention, who could no longer stomach bantu education. SWAPO sent representatives to the Angolan border town of Pereira d'Eca (now Ngiva) to ensure that UNITA did not recruit the new arrivals. They were then bussed to a station on the Benguela railway, from where they travelled by train through Zaire to Zambia.

In 1973 SWAPO's army was named the People's Liberation Army of Namibia (PLAN), reflecting its designation by the United Nations as 'sole and authentic representative of the Namibian people'. Its political wing was rebaptized SWAPO of Namibia, the handy acronym surviving despite its overtones of the *ancien régime*. The very term Namibia, reflecting the harsh and beautiful desert in which only the toughest species survive, was a spiritual break with the dependency inherent in the colonial designation, South West Africa. A Military Council was set up to 'discuss . . . past experiences, arising from both successes and setbacks encountered by the freedom fighters in different parts of the country.' (Katjavivi 1988, p. 90.)

SWAPO moved its head office from Zambia to Luanda and military headquarters to the southern Angolan city of Lubango, formerly Sa da Bandeira. Concurrently, any visions of a clear run across the border for returning guerrillas was blurred by the defection of UNITA under its opportunistic founder Jonas Savimbi. In colonial times, UNITA and SWAPO, drawing members from the Kwanyamas astride the border, had existed harmoniously. Often, they had worked together on the mines. But when Savimibi went to war with the new Angolan government, the Ovambo 'cousins' turned angrily on one another.

What had been up to then a low-key guerrilla or 'bush' war, as the South Africans derisively described it, now intensified. Extra money was available, with the OAU's Liberation Fund relieved of the need to finance anti-Portuguese movements. More East bloc arms were offered, and Western, in particular non-military Scandinavian, government aid supported refugee settlements and scholarship programmes.

For each recruit to the armed struggle, dozens more joined or identified with SWAPO inside the country. It was fast becoming a national movement in every sense of the word. As early as 1973, the Namibian specialist, Gerhard Tötemeyer, estimated SWAPO's following in Ovamboland at 60 per cent, and 40 per cent in the country as a whole. (Interview with authors, 9.5.89). By 1976, the organization claimed a two-thirds national following, with active branches in most towns and villages in the territory, and 80 per cent support in Windhoek. In that year, a pro-government newspaper, *Die Suidwester*, printed on a commercial basis 10,000 stickers for SWAPO, for sale at 25c. A repeat order followed within a month.

In those days it cost R2.50c to join SWAPO, with an annual subscription of R1.00 in the towns and 0.50c in the rural areas. The traditional South African *braaivleis* (barbecue) was a popular way of raising money and of nurturing a community spirit. Unlike its counterparts in the Republic, SWAPO was not (nor has it ever been) legally banned. Pretoria was no doubt inhibited by the contested status of the colony and the potentially negative international repercussions of giving it the 'ANC treatment', a rare case of where the spirit of the Mandate still wielded an influence. However, from 1973 the Ovambo chiefs constantly used their emergency powers to prohibit SWAPO's meetings and rallies. Likewise, whosoever identified openly with SWAPO, whether ordinary member or the leadership, courted harassment, arrest and torture. The experience of Axel Johannes illustrates the brutality and intimidation then directed at SWAPO members.

Johannes first knew injustice when his father, having spoken out against the South Africa occupation, was beaten up by tribal chiefs and exiled to the Kaokoveld. The young Axel joined the Ovambo People's Organization as a teenager in 1959. He was imprisoned for the first time in 1964, and then, with the launch of the armed struggle two years later, his role as a SWAPO youth organizer led to arrest and several months in solitary confinement in Pretoria with the treason trialists. Eventually the police were persuaded that he was a minor and the charges were withdrawn. A third bout of detention (three months this time) followed the crackdown after the 1972 contract workers' strike. He was not charged. Soon afterwards, together with several SWAPO leaders, he was detained under the Terrorism Act. In six months 'solitary', Johannes was repeatedly tortured. Released eventually on bail, he was later acquitted of assisting people to leave Namibia illegally. In August 1975 he was arrested again, along with most of the party leadership, after the assassination of Ovambo Chief Minister Elifas. 'I went 14 days and nights without sleep. The police sat around and would throw a bucket of water on me . . . I was crying. They were just laughing: "Ask SWAPO, ask Sam Nujoma to come and help you, where is he?"' (IDAF 1981, p. 6.) Seven months later he had still not been charged. In March 1976, he was gaoled for a year for refusing to testify in a Supreme Court trial of SWAPO comrades accused of the Elifas murder. After his 'release', he was escorted to Ovamboland (where he did not live), re-arrested and detained yet again under Section 6 of the Terrorism Act. Once again he was released after being fined R50 for refusing to testify against another comrade.

The assassination in 1978 of the Herero leader, Clemens Kapuuo, offered further opportunities for persecuting SWAPO, and Johannes in particular. Lacking real evidence, the police were desperate to link Johannes to the pistol used in the killing, though on the day of the murder he had been hundreds of miles away addressing a meeting in Tsumeb. The police walked him along a dry river bed, and when he was unable to locate the imaginary weapon, they hung him by his handcuffs on the branch of a tree and levered him off the ground. He then 'confessed' to burying the pistol in the sand. He was let down and began digging in the sand. The police forced him into the hole, covering his whole body, including his head, with sand. Police stood on top. He later signed a prepared 'confession'. It was palpably bogus and he was not charged.

In London in 1979, on his first visit abroad, Johannes was asked why he was returning to Namibia. Half-seriously, he explained: 'I go to prison while the others get on with the political work.' Sure enough, soon after his return he was behind bars again. Rarely charged, his only conviction has been for refusing to testify. After each brutal bout of ill-treatment, Johannes would decide to leave the country. But 'then people come to greet me . . . we organize a public meeting. I'm on the stage and I see the crowd — a very big crowd — I can't leave.' (*Anti-Apartheid News*, May 1979.) Finally, in 1980, his political mobility restricted by house arrest, he went into exile. SWAPO internal lost an inspiring leader.

SWAPO's 'un-banned' status in Namibia has spawned something of a myth, one encouraged by the authorities and not contradicted by SWAPO at home, that there were two distinct organizations. Thus, the internal leadership could not be held responsible for the accelerating guerrilla war. Dan Tjongarero, SWAPO spokesperson in Windhoek, explained that there were two wings with the same aims and objectives, 'only the means are different'. Another SWAPO leader in Swakopmund, Pastor Festus Naholo, suggested there was just one SWAPO, 'but we don't know what the external link is up to.' He added, a shade blithely, that 'SWAPO has repeatedly condemned violence. Our struggle is by peaceful means. We don't know who is responsible for the recent attacks in Namibia.' (Herbstein interview, May 1976.)

Another illusion diligently fostered by Pretoria was that SWAPO's guerrillas were insurgents from outside, as if their umbilical cord with Namibia had been severed. They were depicted as mere adjuncts of other forces. The PLAN magazine, *The Combatant* (August 1983), asked SWAPO's Comrade Kalenga why South Africa insisted on the myth that there were Cubans and Russians among SWAPO's ranks.

> 'Guilt-feeling,' he replied. 'They are ashamed to admit they are only fighting Namibians, while they have mercenaries from all sick Western countries, immigrants who come to work in South Africa plus our misguided brothers. They take the story further by saying we wear FAPLA [Angolan army] uniforms. This is to justify the wearing of SWAPO uniforms by their Koevoets [false guerrillas]. If a landmine explodes deep inside Namibia, Pretoria vulgarly puts the blame on Angola. The whole thing is to get a pretext for attacking Angola and to belittle us.

The fact is, trained guerrillas also lived inside the country, taught in schools or worked by day in government offices; they met at night, collecting arms from a cache to go out on a mission. There was no need for them to go back to Angola. Unlike the South African military machine, PLAN has always been an exclusively Namibian force. No mercenaries, no bantustan contingents, not even South African 'volunteers'.

Divide and Rule

In the propaganda war South Africa has long attempted to categorize SWAPO as exclusively Ovambo in order to dispute its claim to be a national party, and to marginalize the aims and achievements of the freedom fighters. It is true that SWAPO has a membership preponderance of Ovambos, but then they do account for at least half the country's population. Their territory has been at the heart of the ideological and military battleground and Ovambos have borne the brunt of the illegal occupation. Ovambo men have endured the hardship of living away from home for much of their working lives. Likewise, going into exile has been logistically easier for an Ovambo, being close to the border, and speaking the language of southern Angola and possibly, if of the Kwanyama clan, having relatives there.

But SWAPO's aspirations have always been national rather than tribal, harmonizing rather than accentuating the differences between people. This is reflected in its constitution, in the language of its representatives and the ethnic make-up of its leadership. From the beginning, non-Ovambos have held high office. Hage Geingob (Damara) opened the SWAPO bureau in New York in 1973, and then became director of the United Nations Institute for Namibia in Lusaka. Theo-Ben Gurirab, secretary for foreign relations, and Moses Garoeb, administrative secretary, are also both Damaras. David Merero (national chairman) and Karikutuke Tjiriange (legal affairs secretary) are both Herero.

The internal executive of 14, before being decimated by the arrests that followed the Elifas assassination in August 1975, comprised five Ovambos, a Baster, a coloured woman and seven Hereros. The ethnic mix has not varied markedly over the years, with the Nama chief, Rev. Hendrik Witbooi, as SWAPO's influential vice-president, and non-Ovambos Dan Tjongarero, Nico Bessenger and a white lawyer, Anton Lubowski, among the best-known local officers in Windhoek.

South Africa was, however, somewhat successful in its attempts at divide and rule. It is a sad irony that the Hereros, primary victims of an earlier war of liberation, should be the instrument of this policy. The *New York Times* (11.8.82) noted that 'the breach between the Ovambos and Hereros represents the major failure for the insurgents in their effort to build a national base — and the major success for South Africa in trying to prevent that.' It was, as we have seen, Hosea Kutako who set in motion the struggle for independence. The agenda was narrower then, aimed at reversing the injustices of his people, though he expanded his horizons in his later years. But the Hereros, decimated by the Germans and scattered by the South Africans, simply did not possess the numbers or the geo-strategic base to spearhead a second armed struggle.

For a while SWAPO, SWANU and the Chiefs Council worked together inside Namibia. Beyond the stable confines of SWAPO, however, territorial politics has been a bewildering honeycomb of factions, tribal schisms, nine-day wonders, one-person planks. In 1971 the National Convention came into being, aimed at uniting the people in their fight for 'total and complete' freedom and independence. Along with SWAPO, it included Clemens Kapuuo's National Unity of Democratic Organizations (NUDO), a front for the Herero chiefs, though the Chiefs Council was also separately represented; SWANU, then headed by the allegedly Maoist Gerson Veii; the Volksparty of Rehoboth; the Nama–Damara Voice of the People and other Damara and Nama factions.

Clemens Kapuuo was elected leader of the Convention. He had succeeded Hosea Kutako as chief of the Hereros and had been forced out of the teaching profession for his opposition to the government. He expected the Convention to take a front seat. But with its international standing, its guerrilla army and cadres of activists at home, SWAPO was not going to be hemmed in by a collection of small talking shops. When SWAPO quit the Convention in 1974, criticizing Kapuuo in the process, bitter animosities surfaced.

'The Ovambos, who are today represented by SWAPO . . . did not take part in the war against the Germans,' Kapuuo said in a statement. SWAPO was:

> an Ovambo political organization because about 99 per cent of its members are Ovambos. . . . South Africa did not deprive the Ovambos of their lands. . . . For the tribes of the central and southern parts of South West Africa who have suffered terribly for more than 70 years under the German and South African governments, their lands and their rights are very dear to them, and they cannot and will never allow their lands and their future to be decided by a political organization of just one tribe which was not elected by them. [Katjavivi 1988, p. 93.]

The Chiefs Council was now about to link up with Hosea Kutako's great enemy, the white colonizers. The Kapuuo pendulum had swung across the spectrum. Now his solution was a Namibia divided in two, echoing the new Ovambo chief minister, the defrocked pastor Cornelius Ndjoba, who had proposed that Ovamboland be hived off and joined with Angolan Ovambos as an independent nation. Parts of the National Convention followed Kapuuo into the National Convention of Namibia, others aligned themselves with SWAPO in the Namibia National Convention. In April 1977, one of the major Herero clans represented by the Association for the Preservation of the Tjamuaha/Maharero Royal House, with an estimated 17,000 members, pledged its membership to SWAPO. Though not every individual clansman and woman would vote for the movement in an election, it once again pointed up Herero divisions.

The shooting of Clemens Kapuuo in 1978 denied South Africa the last internal indigenous leader of any standing, even though his tribalistic outburst had considerably marginalized him. No one was ever charged for this murder, though we know from Axel Johannes that the police were desperate to assign responsibility to SWAPO — which has always denied it. It is possible that the assassins were tribal rivals but, at the time, Kapuuo's NUDO vigilantes were conducting a bullying campaign against SWAPO, in the black areas of Windhoek, such that its Herero supporters had to move to the Ovambo section for their own safety. The police stood by and did nothing. The likeliest explanation is that Kapuuo was assassinated by angry SWAPO supporters, with or without a direct order from the leadership. The argument that the police, acting as *agents provocateurs*, killed him in order to lay the blame on SWAPO is unconvincing because, to many, it would have been seen as an acceptable act of self-defence. In addition, Pretoria needed Kapuuo for, if as seemed possible at the time, it resorted to a unilateral declaration of independence, he was the only possible black prime minister of any legitimacy.

The Guerrillas

The refugees who left Namibia were housed in camps in Zambia, and later in Angola. These were ordinary people driven to arms by desperation rather than visions of heroic deeds. Among them were some made homeless when the army cleared homesteads and villages for free-fire zones along the border. Others, like the 'ice-cream man' had gone south from Okalongo, Ovamboland in 1976 'to search for work which can feed my family.' He had become an ice-cream salesman, 'cycling the whole day long in search of buyers who were usually only children. My pay depended on how well I sell. 20 cents from each rand is mine. If I'm lucky I may sell ice-cream for about R4 to R7 a day.' Unless, that is, you are 'the victim of an accident, which may break the container of ice-cream, or of tricky kids who may rob you. Whatever happens, they subtract from your meagre salary.' In seven years, the ice-cream man sent no money home. 'I came to realize that I'm only wasting my time and decided to join the freedom fighters fighting for a better Namibia . . .'

A second man, in his mid-30s, had organized a strike at the Tsumeb copper smelters:

> The Boers simply dismissed us saying there are enough 'natives' idling around to substitute. 'Go and demand higher salaries from your Sam Nujoma.' Since then I stayed in northern Namibia where I was having no work except to be a punching bag of the Boer boys in uniform. From one hell to another . . . it is just too much. I decided to be a freedom fighter in order to give them a taste of their own medicine. [*The Combatant*, March 1983.]

High school teenagers offered a larger recruiting pool than contract workers. They found bantu education intolerable, their parents were harassed at home, often brothers or sisters were already in exile. A few went for personal reasons, to join a girl or boyfriend, or on the spur of the moment with classmates who were setting off. But most were political activists, and hence government targets. When the army or police set up a base down the road from a school, lobbed shells or sprayed bullets all around, turned a blind eye to men molesting schoolgirls in their dormitories, beat up the boys in the playground, the incentive to leave was not hard to find.

For most, exile was a commitment to offer oneself to the liberation army. If at least 18 years old, and with some secondary schooling completed, one might soon find oneself undergoing military training. This was eventually provided in Angola by Cuban, Angolan, East European and SWAPO instructors, with specialist training for some at Chinese or Russian military academies. Equipment was Soviet, Czech, Yugoslav, East German — the AK 47, the Soviet POMz-type mines, SA-7 surface-to-air missiles, Maharav pistols, heavy machine guns, grenade launchers, armour-piercing anti-tank rockets.

Guerrillas also received lessons in ideology, intended to reinforce motivation for those faced with a well-armed, well-heeled, numerically superior standing army. It was also a preparation for the less publicized but seminal function of the freedom fighter, to make contact with the people back home, keep them informed about the aims and success of the struggle, recruit them in their turn. To PLAN's chief political commissar, *nom-de-plume* 'Comrade Lumumba', political education was of fundamental importance:

> It must be filled with concrete content, it should be of class character, be based on the irreconcilable hatred against class enemies, capitalist and imperialist . . . A PLAN combatant [must] be first and foremost a political activist and then an armed militant. Therefore the raising of our political consciousness and ideological level is the basis and soul of our people's army in order to direct and strengthen the class position of our combatants in the interests of the toiling and exploited, but fighting people of Namibia. [*The Combatant*, July 1986.]

Guerrillas had to be unusually fit, for this was a rural battleground, often in open country, with escape, following detection, only on foot. Carrying heavy armoury, long-distance jogging was an essential requirement. Setting out from forward camps in southern Angola, the guerrilla had several obstacles to negotiate en route to the war zone. Buffalo Battalion waited to intercept, then came the kilometre-wide free-fire zone created by South Africa along much of the Ovambo–Okavango border. Police and military bases dotted the map of the north like an outbreak of measles. Yet most travellers crossed with comparative ease, a clear example of the maxim of the guerrilla swimming like a fish in the sea. Canoes would be available for river crossings, the burnt vegetation regrew quickly and, most of all, friends abounded.

In a rare guerrilla trial in Windhoek, one of the accused gave an inkling of how the 'bed-and-breakfast' chain operated. Guerrillas, having crossed the border:

> ... were now in the Ovambo-speaking region, and villagers gave them water and food. The villagers knew some of the men in the group. They left early the next morning and walked the whole day. That night they arrived at another village where once more its residents provided them with nourishment and water. From there, on the third day, they trekked on foot to yet another village which was reached by nightfall, and once more nourishment was provided by local people. [*Windhoek Observer*, n.d.]

The SADF and the local press would portray these incursions as suicide missions, with the 'insurgents' facing automatic elimination or ignominious retreat back to where they came from. Such portrayals were untrue, for throughout the war the border was a SWAPO motorway. Cadres crossed it constantly with messages, with weaponry, for social visits, for recruitment, and, of course, to fight.

Not too much is at present known to outsiders about SWAPO's style of operation. We know that the guerrillas tried to avoid pitched battles with the larger enemy forces. *The Combatant* provided occasional glimpses of the guerrilla at work. Idealized, perhaps, but that is nothing new in war reporting by interested parties. A description from 1983 begins:

> For Mokahonde it was a long cruel day. His throat was burning, the body exhausted, the feet paining, the skin burnt and scratched. If only I can rest a few minutes and drink water, he thought. But he could not for he knew rest will lead to sleep . . . And this he could not afford. The enemy was everywhere . . .

Three combatants were guarding a section of the road two miles from where comrades were preparing a major action. They mined the road, then waited with two RPG-7 rocket launchers and an AK-47 sub-machine gun:

> Not long and then they heard the droning of an oncoming enemy convoy. The order was that nobody should pass. The forces were unequal. Three guerrillas against one truck full of racists, two armoured personnel carriers and one Land Rover. The guerrillas placed their rockets in various positions, in order to be able to shift position quickly and even to create the impression there were many raiders. Mokahonde kept his breath as the truck with enemy soldiers reached the mark . . . and pressed the button. An explosion rocked the truck and there was flesh in the air. The rocket whistled furiously

from the hill to the dark-green target . . . and finding it, exploded as if in anger. The APC [armoured personnel carrier] stood ablaze. As more rockets flew down, Mokahonde pressed again the buttons of the remote controlled mines, maximizing the chaos among the racists. The enemy too was determined and was now coming up the slope. One boer started to fire a mortar from near the burning vehicle. Soon one guerrilla, Ananias, got hurt. A fragment pierced his thigh, leaving a deep wound from which blood flowed profusely. The other comrade was already out of sight and Mokahonde darted from rock to rock till he reached the wounded warrior. It looked bad. He opened his arms, welcoming his life-long friend. He embraced Mokahonde briefly but tightly and said, 'There is no more time . . . leave me here and continue as always. I'm to die . . . I feel proud . . . Now go.' He turned the RPG-7 and immediately opened fire on the few oncoming racist troops. As they took cover, Mokahonde hurriedly took two hand-grenades from his belt, then whispered, 'Take this. Never surrender' . . . Later he heard from a distance a single pistol bullet, and he cried. It was Ananias who had shot himself. [*The Combatant* April 1983.]

While they often made uncomplimentary claims about the guerrillas, the South Africans interestingly never described them as cowards. If an ambush did not work, it was known the guerrilla would stand and fight, withdrawing only if tactically convenient.

There is a Kwanyama tradition of suicide in order to avoid capture, or of allowing your enemy to kill you because you refuse to be driven from a spot, so that then your spirit can go free. One guerrilla, described as 'a brave man' by a police inquest witness, blew himself up with his last grenade after wounding several policemen. The incident took place on a white-owned farm near Tsumeb in 1983 (Windhoek Observer, 6.8.83).

Shoot-outs with the police or army were the dramatic moments of the war. Equally effective, in a land where the dirt road is more common than a concrete or macadamized surface, was the landmine. Early every morning the army had to sweep the roads, in particular the link between the southern Ovamboland 'border' post at Oshivello with Ondangwa and the gravel road to the border at Oshikango. The South Africans railed against the use of these devices, an indication that they made life uncomfortable for the security forces. But though the guerrillas always attempted to lay mines where they thought military vehicles or so-called 'puppets' would pass, there was an inevitable element of indiscriminateness in their targetting. PLAN's deputy chief of engineering and demolition explained the dependence on mines as being 'designed to cope with the situation in which the enemy is infinitely superior in relation to every conventional factor of warfare.' (*The Combatant*, July

1986). It is also certainly the case that, where innocent people were victims of mines, they had been planted by the army in order to discredit SWAPO. Locals understood, whenever the radio announced that the mine was 'of Russian manufacture', that the army possessed weapons captured from PLAN. That was the local consensus when, in June 1982, a Lutheran pastor and four members of his family were killed in an explosion on a narrow track north of Oshakati.

Almost as unsettling for South Africa was the tactic of assassinating collaborators — two Ovambo chief ministers (Elifas and Ndjoba), traditional chiefs, headmen, paid and honorary informers, bantustan councillors, San trackers, soldiers from 101 Ovambo battalion, and Koevoet constables. Members of their families were also sometimes viewed as legitimate targets. In military terms, there was a grim logic to the SWAPO campaign. They were not simply ill-tempered reprisals, justified by the maxim 'my enemy's friend is my enemy'. Traditional chiefs, and especially those whose authoritarian manner was challenged by a new generation of northerners, sided openly with the government. They were viewed as 'quislings'. The homes of chiefs and headmen, defended by tribal policemen, were not the 'soft targets' of government propaganda, though here the innocent could be hurt too. The mortar and grenade attack on the kraal of deputy headman Sakaria Shilongo in December 1981 was a case in point. The headman grabbed one of his children and fled, together with some of his ten bodyguards. Watching his huts go up in flames, he heard the attackers 'bursting out in song, singing "Namibia is our land"'. He escaped, but eight others perished — two special constables, the girlfriend of a special constable, a 19-year-old woman, three small children and an old man.

Each year of the war, the post-Christmas period, when heavy rains bogged down pursuers, produced an escalated rate of guerrilla infiltration. By mid-1976, PLAN units were operating south of the police line separating the black reserves from the white farms. Occasionally, white farmers, members of their families or servants, were killed. Towns in the 'triangle of death' — Tsumeb, Grootfontein, Otavi — would call out the commandos of the area task force, white Namibians who had completed their national service. On one occasion, the SADF magazine *Paratus* reported the guerrillas posed such a threat that the northern town of Outjo was put on a war footing. The commandant, Stoffel Rothman, said that almost all the white males in the district, the majority of women and even blacks were members of the unit. Rothman revealed that as soon as 'terrorist activity' began, SADF and police units were deployed on each farm. Outlying farmers were linked into MARNET (for Military Area Radio Network), a border defence-alert system provided by the British firm Marconi (Cawthra 1986, p. 232). Despite their fortresses, many white families put black foremen in charge of their farms and left to live in town.

'Total Onslaught'

By 1978 Prime Minister Vorster had run out of steam, devoid of ideas to deal with the swirl of events at home and abroad. He was a man of the police, and the pressure within and without South Africa had grown beyond the capabilites of a branch of state far to the right in terms of membership and with a low calibre leadership. Vorster also had an intense personal dislike for Sam Nujoma, manifested in repeated statements about SWAPO being the creation of communists. This precluded any hope of a settlement between the two sides. So the advent of P. W. Botha at a time of declining white fortunes at home (PLAN's success, the Soweto uprising, the fiasco of 'Muldergate'*) and abroad (the UN arms resolution, Angolan and Mozambican independence, the imminent end of white rule in Rhodesia and the Commonwealth's Gleneagles Agreement which tightened the sports boycott) demanded a change of presentation, possibly of direction as well. White South Africa saw itself standing alone, without true friends, the Soviet wolf at the door baying to enter. Many of the generals were intelligent men, with degrees in military science and a knowledge of the wider world. The army, navy and air force, which now reflected, through the universal call-up, a cross-section of white male opinion, was the natural vehicle for a fresh approach.

In March 1975, a defence white paper first broached the new philosophy. 'Defence strategy embraces much more than military strategy. It involves economy, ideology, technology, and even social matters and can therefore only be meaningful and valid if proper account is taken of these other spheres.' The solution, it suggested, was to 'muster all [our] activities — political, economic, diplomatic and military [in a] total national strategy.' So now the idea was not simply to counter a perceived communist threat with nasty words and brutal deeds — these would continue in abundance — but to offer the benefits of free enterprise to all members of society and all states in the region. The government's response was enunciated by an industrial–military complex of businessmen, generals and backed by the *verligte* (enlightened) wing of the ruling party. Botha, 'the forceful managing director' (Grundy 1986, p. 34) held high-profile meetings with leaders of the nation's white business community, who complained that the restrictions of apartheid were a hindrance to accumulation of yet greater profits. In the Republic, black trade unions were permitted to organize within a legal framework, while efforts were made to encourage a black middle class, which, in protecting its own interests, the argument went, would constitute a buffer against the masses. Urban Africans were granted permanent residence in the urban areas, and the chance of

---

* A corruption scandal catering around the propaganda activities of the Department of Information which resulted in the resignation of the Minister and Transvaal Party Leader, Dr. Connie Mulder.

owning their homes. Other changes, part of the 'reform' package of Botha's early years, saw an end to a few of the more indefensible practices of 'petty apartheid'. But the infrastructure of the apartheid state remained intact, and black dissent was, if anything, put down more ruthlessly by the police.

These developments were introduced through the State Security Council (SSC), a cabinet committee which grew to be more powerful than the cabinet itself, headed by P. W. Botha and dominated by the SADF and the several cabinet members — defence, justice, law and order — charged with security. The council's full-time secretariat had a strong military bias, with 70 per cent of its personnel drawn from the SADF, 20 per cent from the National Intelligence Secretariat, formerly BOSS, and the remainder from Foreign Affairs (Swilling and Phillips 1988, p. 15). In this way the SSC became both source and executor of 'total strategy', through an octupus-like National Security Management System of regional and local committees, which intruded more than ever into the life of the citizen. In order to achieve this Orwellian control, the centralization of South Africa was accompanied by an intensive militarization. The terms 'total onslaught' and 'total strategy' became lodestars of South African life, mouthed in Parliament, on television and at festivals commemorating victories over blacks and Britons.

General Magnus Malan, chief of the SADF (later defence minister), was the son of a one-time chairman of the Afrikaner banking house, Volkskas. In his early career he had been on attachment to the French forces in Algeria and studied at the US Army Command and General Staff College. He was a powerful advocate of the new policy and, in a sense, Namibia was its laboratory. Here the 'total strategy' was to be used to prepare the way for the neo-colonial state. Windhoek became the headquarters of one of the eleven regional Joint Management Centres. Cosmetic change became the order of the day, enough hopefully to bolster Pretoria's chosen local political vehicle, the DTA, but not too much to frighten the whites. The pass laws and the prohibitions on inter-racial sex and marriage were repealed, residential areas and some hotels and restaurants were opened to all races, though many continued to have 'Whites only' signs. An elaborate 'Winning Hearts and Minds' (WHAM) campaign was launched in the north, extolling the benefits of capitalism and denigrating SWAPO as communist and un-Christian.

The external ambitions of 'total strategy' centred on the so-called Constellation of Southern African States (CONSAS), which would bring the countries of the sub-continent into a loose trading alliance dominated by the Republic's economy. Through this mechanism, South Africa's neighbours would be 'encouraged' to desist from aiding and comforting the liberation movements. In CONSAS, a pliant, independent

Namibia would give South African business and diplomats the coveted beachhead into black Africa. But SWAPO and the Angolan government were barriers to be overcome. Then the election of Robert Mugabe's ZANU in Zimbabwe's independence elections in 1980 further upset these plans. P. W. Botha, putting the 'carrot' of 'total strategy' aside, set about destabilizing regimes which did not toe his line. Mozambique's rail link to Zimbabwe was cut by the Renamo bandits in the pay of Pretoria, the Lesotho government was pressured and eventually ousted, regional capitals bombed. On the western flank of the sub-continent, the 'stick' entailed the devastation of southern Angola and the attempted pacification of northern Namibia by Koevoet counter-insurgency police.

The Rough and the Smooth

The vilification of SWAPO was an essential element in South Africa's plans. As far as the colony's whites were concerned, this presented few problems, given the wide gulf in perceptions between themselves and blacks. Sentencing two farm labourers to death in the Windhoek Supreme Court in 1980 for aiding guerrillas (no-one was killed), Judge Hans Strydom, an old-fashioned white of Afrikaner descent, described SWAPO's objectives as 'detestable'. It wanted a political order, he said, which 'promised no good for the country.' (*Focus* 32, Jan. 1981).

SWAPO's links with communist countries were no secret. In waging a life and death struggle with a ruthless regime, there was little room for sentimentality, for questioning the motives of one's armourers. The West refused to grant the only sort of help that would shift South Africa out of the colony, although the Nordic countries were the source of extensive aid to the Angolan and Zambian refugee camps. Aid came too from the World Council of Churches and Lutheran World Federation. The camps operated under the wing of the UN High Commission for Refugees.

The largest Namibian settlement abroad was in Angola's Kwanza Sul province, 250 kilometres south east of Luanda. Its 19 camps were strung out over a wide area of palm groves and coffee plantations. Some 57% of its 45,000 residents were children, another 29% women, while many of rest were older men. Among these 'elders' were 'scouts' who, having done reconnaissance work for the guerrillas in Namibia, were forced to flee when they came under suspicion. Support groups in Europe were reminded of their existence by requests for pipes. But it was the young on whom love and attention was lavished. As time went by, more and more were born abroad, while others hardly remembered what home was like. It was essential to foster a community spirit in exile. The trenches all around them were a reminder that South Africa might attempt another Cassinga.

More positively, community medicine reduced the infant mortality rate to 25 per 1,000 live births, compared with 200 per 1,000 in Namibia that same year. The Under-Fives Team checked nutritional status and vaccinated 90 per cent of under fives against tuberculosis, polio, diphtheria and measles. Four hospitals served the camps, and there was a special programme for soldiers disabled in the war, while the 800-bed military hospital outside Lubango staffed by Cuban and East German doctors was said to be the finest medical facility in Angola. The AIDS scare led to a joint SWAPO Health Department–WHO education campaign.

Education in exile was a powerful magnet for the shoolchildren at home. Sometimes whole classes left at a time, needing special attention. Some 1,500 Namibians were placed on the Cuban *Isla de Juventud* (Island of Youth) at secondary schools named after Hosea Kutako and Hendrik Witbooi. Others were in Zambia, Ghana, Nigeria, Sierra Leone, Cameroons, and at a technical school in the Congo. SWAPO also ran a small settlement and school in the German Democratic Republic for children of guerrillas killed in the war, as well as sons and daughters of SWAPO leaders, including Mrs. Nujoma, a school teacher, who taught there, and the couple's three sons.

Hundreds of Namibians have gone to Western colleges and universities on government, church and NGO scholarships. Namibians studied medicine in the Soviet Union and Romania, social work in Poland, dentistry and engineering (women as well) in East Germany. The UN Institute for Namibia (UNIN) in Lusaka began in 1976 to train exiled Namibians for the day when they would participate in the administration of their country.

The Angolan camps had few secondary schools, but huge kindergartens and primary schools, the largest housing 3,361 pupils between six and 13 years of age. Now for the first time Namibians were taught a non-South African version of their history. Lessons were in English, the language SWAPO wanted for Namibia. No doubt some lessons were couched in the language of Marxism, but reports from camp schools indicate that it formed a small part of instruction. There is no doubt that exiled children will return home better educated than had they stayed. They could attend church Sunday school, and there were meetings where they discussed Namibian culture, current affairs and the future political dispensation. These were conducted by political commissars, who might well have been on a leadership course in East Germany featuring administration and Marxist ideology.

In 1974, in co-operation with SWAPO, the Namibian churches set up a special ministry for exiles. Priests from the Anglican, Lutheran and

Roman Catholic churches were placed in the refugee settlements. Bishops and pastors made regular visits from Namibia. Father Gerhard Heimerikx, chaplain to SWAPO's Zambian camps, reported on a visit to Kwanza-Sul in 1987 that he served holy communion in 12 camps and baptized 252 new Christians, mostly children. He found that many Christians had their own Bibles, hymn and prayer books. But pastoral duties were in the hands of two elderly Namibians, a Lutheran, Nathanael Nghatanga, aged 87, and an Anglican, George Shameulu, aged 62, and they had only one car between them. 'May the Lord give them long lives to carry out these essential tasks,' said Heimerikx.

> When I see the Namibians living together in harmony in exile it reminds me of the passage in Acts, Chapter 4, 32–37 about how the first Christians lived together. 'No one said that any of his belongings was his own, but they all shared with one another everything that they had. . . .' [NCC, Dec. 1987.]

With a 50–60% adult illiteracy rate, Kwanza-Sul offered night school classes to remedy the deficiencies of colonial education. Adults could learn trades in tailoring and weaving, vehicle maintenance, brick laying, carpentery, joinery, fitting and shoemaking. Trade unionists, through the external wing of the National Union of Namibian Workers, prepared for a new labour dispensation on their return home. On the other hand, the camps never became even remotely self-sufficient in food. There were farms with poultry, goats, pigs, and maize was grown, but nowhere near sufficient in a climate and soil blessed for growing things. SWAPO blamed the insufficiency of cultivable land, but the dependency on food aid worried camp administrators.

The charge of a communist SWAPO seems hardly to have been justified by its style of life abroad. Perhaps the movement's rhetoric sometimes led to this misunderstanding. In its 1976 constitution it described itself as 'a national liberation movement rallying together, on the basis of free and voluntary association, all freedom-inspired sons and daughters of the Namibian people . . . a vanguard party of the oppressed and exploited people of Namibia.' It promised to 'unite all the people of Namibia, irrespective of race, religion, sex or ethnic group. . . .' Economic policy would entail 'effective control over the means of production and distribution . . . and social ownership of all the resources of the country.' Enlarging on the constitution, the political programme pledged SWAPO to 'unite all Namibian people, particularly the working class, the peasantry and progressive intellectuals, into a vanguard party capable of safeguarding national independence and of building a classless, unexploitative society based on the ideals and principles of scientific socialism.' (Vigne 1987.)

The rhetoric of the 1970s has since given way to more sober reflections on economic possibilities. But the language of revolution is a vital element in buoying the spirit (the 1976 constitution states that SWAPO members had an obligation to 'act in the spirit of self-sacrifice, dedication and boundless commitment to the cause of national and social liberation.') But to white Namibians, it conjured up the anti-Christ. SWAPO gladly formed part of the world-wide masonry of liberation movements — ANC, PLO, Polisario, each offering fraternal inspiration to the other, often amounting to no more than vague promises — and left-wing regimes facing Western-sponsored counter-revolutionaries — Nicaraguan Sandinistas, FRELIMO in Mozambique, the beleaguered government in Luanda. The Russian October Revolution is annually the subject of admiring comment in the SWAPO literature. There are hiccoughs in the line-up. The Eritreans, who have fought longer than anyone in Africa to establish national sovereignty, and who might be thought of as soul brothers to the Namibians, are officially taboo because they are at war with an Ethiopia aided by the Soviet Union and Cuba.

The Churches

Whatever the public affiliations of SWAPO, or its financial supporters, or its arms suppliers, it made little difference to most people in Namibia. Faced with the constant litany that SWAPO was communist and terrorist while South Africa was Christian, democratic, capitalist and aligned with the freedom-loving West, Namibians did not confuse propaganda with reality.

So the people of Namibia did not tremble at the constant accusation that SWAPO was communist. To them SWAPO was a liberator. Those who saw the organization this way included the majority of the Christian churches, three out of every four Namibians. Lutheran Bishop Kleopas Dumeni, leader of the largest church in the territory, repeatedly told Western critics:

I know that the South African government makes propaganda that they are fighting against Communism. It is propaganda! Who is SWAPO? Let me tell you. SWAPO are members, men and women, daughters and sons of our families, members of our churches. I said churches, regardless of denomination. Baptized, confirmed, married, with rights in their parishes — they are Christians . . . the question is why they left the country. Precisely because of the hardships of the war situation, apartheid, separate development and injustice. And that is what is not Christian — it is against the whole of Christianity. [*Dateline: Namibia* 3, 1982.]

Christianity, in a comparatively short time, has become an important part of the culture of Namibia. A large majority of the people are devout to an extent long lost in the secularized world of Europe and North America. Their faith touches on many aspects of their daily lives. The Bible is the 'Word of God', prayers are said at meals and, in front of the fire in the evening, stories are told from the Old and New Testaments, along with tales of life before the white man came. It was the sort of background that led them to say 'no' to apartheid, and to give birth to a home-grown, church-based liberation movement not imposed by revolutionaries from afar. As a result, the Church has been a formidable force in the struggle for independence.

Before the white man came, the nomadic San, the Namas, Hereros, Damaras, the Ovambos and Okavangos of the north, had developed their own cultures, with economic and justice systems. They were not constantly at war with one another, as some colonial writers insisted, certainly no more than European colonizers were with their own neighbours. A mid-19th century German missionary described the people of the north as numerous and peace-loving, 'making gardens and fields and also wearing clothes.' These were animists, heathens in Christian terms, who practised monogamy, polygamy, or polyandry, killed twins and handicapped babies at birth, and treated women as chattels or with reverence, depending on local custom. Their language was not written down, but they were wise in the ways of hunting, food gathering, farming, herding, smelting of iron and copper — all dependent on the traditions of their community.

The missionaries who came to Namibia were, to a large extent, the advance guard of empire. After benign visits from London Missionary Society clergy based in the Cape Colony, German Protestant missionaries moved into the central region and soon became the purveyors of Christianity and manufactured goods. One man of God operated a gun-running syndicate in the years before the Herero and Nama wars. Heinz Hunke, a German Catholic priest, noted that the German annexation and military occupation were called for and effectively prepared by missionaries, and the colonial wars fought with the assistance and blessing of the mission staff. 'The racial legislation and the slave-like labour system' introduced by the Germans:

> . . . met with the explicit consensus of the Christian missionaries who were the first to profit by the military pacification, the social uprootedness of the 'natives', their concentration on urban locations or in rural reserves. While their social assistance work was the beginning of Christianizing the country, cheap African labour was necessary for the running of church institutions: farms, hospitals and schools. [*Action on Namibia*, Summer 1988.]

While German missionaries concentrated on the central and southern regions of 'Sudwest-Afrika', they invited the Lutheran Finnish Missionary Society to work in the relatively unknown north. The Finns were not colonizers, and while they sometimes exhibited the same superior attitudes towards the 'natives' as their southern cousins, their mission was geared more to spreading the Christian faith through education and medical assistance, than to commercial or political control. The Finns arrived in the north in 1870, and the first converts were baptized in 1883. It was not easy work, as exhibited by their encounters with the Ukwanyama King Mweshipandeka who permitted the missionaries to teach him but not his subjects. A modern historian and activist, Dr. Abisai Shejavali, says that the king was 'not at all concerned about his soul's salvation; he only wanted the missionaries as his servants. . . .'

But the Finnish Lutherans worked hard, with what in retrospect seems to have been a great love for the people of Ovamboland. A woman doctor, Selma Rainia, founded the mission hospital at Onandjokwe in 1908. The nurses training college which started there in 1930 became a driving force in the emancipation of Namibian women. 'The death rate of infants was reduced and the power of malaria checked,' writes Shejavali. Meanwhile, a theological seminary had been set up at Oniipa, with the first Namibian pastors ordained in 1925, long before other missions permitted such active participation by blacks.

German-based Roman Catholic mission orders started work in Namibia in the last years of the 19th century, but Anglican mission activity was negligible until after the fall of the German Protectorate in 1915. Both Anglican and Roman Catholics were given conditional permission by the South African administration in SWA to work in Ovamboland if they promised in writing 'to support and promote government policy and encourage the Ovambo people to work in the south as migrant labourers. . . .' (Nambala 1987, vol. I.) Both groups built schools and hospitals, and generally imposed the values of European civilization along with the claims of the Christian faith.

Mission work was not universally appreciated. Shejavali recalls the strong opposition to Christianity in many places in the north. 'Those who accepted the word of the Cross were mocked, despised and persecuted, and there were those, too, who bore in their bodies wounds for Christ's sake.' Yet the aims of the missionaries, to spread the Gospel to every village and household in the north, have been realized more completely in Namibia than anywhere else in Africa.

One remarkable aspect of the spread of Christianity in Namibia was the absence of the Afrikaner's state religion, the Dutch Reformed Church. The DRC might have been expected to seek converts in the 'fifth province' when it had mission stations as far north as the Sudan.

But in 1920 it had signed an agreement with the Finnish and German mission agencies not to undertake mission work among blacks in 'South West' for 50 years. The reasons are not clear, but a cynic might suggest that in this case, at least, South Africa carried out its League of Nations civilizing mandate — by keeping its racist version of Christianity out of the territory.

World War II disrupted European domination of the churches in Namibia. German missionaries were interned, while Finns found it impossible to travel to Africa. Local Christians took over greater responsibilities. While the Finnish Mission had ordained Namibians in the 1920s, German Protestants did not permit this until 1949. By then, a large number of their followers, rejecting these racist practices, had left to join the African Methodist Episcopal Church, an American-based church started by freed slaves in Philadelphia in 1787.

In those post-war years, the yearning for self-determination came to the surface in ever more powerful waves. The missions were caught up in the current, and one by one the churches became more or less independent — still in need of funds and teachers from overseas churches, but now increasingly they determined which teachers were to be invited and how the funds should be spent. First the Finnish Lutheran (1960), then the German Lutheran (1972), then the Roman Catholic (1979) and the Anglican (1981) mission churches elected Namibian clergy as their leaders.

But radical changes within the church were not wholly explained by the colour of the bishop's skin. Many foreign clergy, Anglicans in particular, identified with the people and were duly punished for their troubles. Michael Scott was deported after being enlisted by Kutako to inform the United Nations about Namibia. In 1968 a joint Anglican, Lutheran and Catholic delegation protested to the South African police commander in northern Namibia against the torture of detainees, an action for which the Anglican bishop, Robert Mize, an American, was deported. When the British-born Bishop of Damaraland, Colin Winter, was deported in 1972 for his open opposition to apartheid in Namibia, he continued his ministry as Bishop-In-Exile, informing the world about South Africa's largely unknown colony.

But the single most important act of the Christian church in Namibia came from the black leadership.

On 21 June, 1971, theological students at the Lutheran seminary at Ojtimbingwe heard via the BBC that the International Court of Justice had ruled in favour of the United Nations, ordering South Africa to quit Namibia immediately. Rejoicing, the students asked, then demanded of, their missionary professors an understanding of this event in light of the faith. Told that there was none, that the ruling was only political, the students walked out of class. Led by Zephania Kameeta, later to be both

53

imprisoned and elected deputy bishop of his church, the students drafted a statement of their own understanding of oppression, using the Universal Declaration of Human Rights as the touchstone. The boards of the two Lutheran churches, from the north and the south, were meeting together at the time. The students sent their essay to the meeting, and after long discussion, it became an open letter to Prime Minister B. J. Vorster:

> We believe that South Africa in its attempts to develop South West Africa has failed to take cognizance of Human Rights . . . the non-white population is continuously being slighted and intimidated in their daily lives. Our people are not free . . . By the Group Areas Legislation the people are denied the right of free movement and accommodation . . . people are not free to express or publish their thoughts or opinions . . . the use of voting rights should also be allowed to the non-white population . . . the right to a free choice of profession is hindered . . . the contract system breaks up a healthy family life . . . the Church board's urgent wish is . . . that Human Rights be put into operation and that South West Africa may become a self-sufficient and independent State.

Signed by Bishop Leonard Auala and Moderator Paul Gowaseb on June 30, 1971, the letter was a direct challenge to the authorities in Pretoria. This was not just another crank appeal from powerless individuals. As the writers asserted to Vorster, they represented between them 'the majority of the indigenous population of South West Africa.' The largest Christian church in the colony had placed its moral and theological weight behind the independence call of the South West Africa People's Organization. To evade postal censorship, the letter was delivered by hand to every Lutheran congregation, with instructions that it be read aloud at the next Sunday morning service. In this way, one half of the country heard that their plight was the result of a deprivation of human rights, and that Christians could, based on their faith in a just God, demand both humane treatment and independence. Alongside the launch of the armed struggle, that date, June 30, 1971, is one of the most memorable in Namibia's anti-colonial history.

Certain that a white man had been behind the open letter, South Africa deported a Finnish missionary, Mikko Ihamaki.

Unlike South Africa, where many white Christians have supported radical action against apartheid, the struggle in Namibia developed mainly along racial lines. As Hunke points out, 'the division over the understanding of freedom, justice, human dignity runs totally according to the racial barriers within the churches and across confessional lines. . . . The confrontation is between White Catholics, Anglicans, Lutherans, and Black Catholics, Anglicans and Lutherans.' (Hunke in Wood 88, p. 630.)

In 1978, the better to address the problems of society with a unified voice, the major denominations formed a common agency, the Council of Churches in Namibia (CCN). The same year, the Catholic Hunke, the Anglican Fr. Ed Murrow and Justin Ellis, administrator of the Christian Centre, were deported for publicly challenging Pretoria's intimidation and torture. Through the council, the churches set up programmes to provide legal aid for political prisoners and assistance for their families. There were English adult literacy classes and university scholarships for black students to study abroad. Lutherans, Roman Catholics, Anglicans, Methodists — they became a formidable ecumenical consortium able to confront the occupying ruler with a clear, unified voice. Church schools and hospitals offered teaching and medical care, but a focus for independence as well.

Two twice-monthly newspapers, the Catholic *Omukuni* and the Lutheran *Omukwetu*, written in Kwanyama and Ndonga, reported the facts of the war frankly and bravely in the face of threats and harassment. At the headquarters of the northern Lutheran church in Oniipa, a printing complex produced Sunday school material, pamphlets, textbooks, as well as *Omukwetu*. One night in November 1980, an explosion reduced the print shop to a mass of rubble and twisted girders. An army patrol had been seen earlier that evening dropping off soldiers. The blast was heard 18 miles away. The police, called on the radio, did not show up till the next morning. The army, which had mounted dozens of raids on the nearby Lutheran-run hospital from their nearby bases, disappeared for two days. When they did arrive, it was to search the church compound for 'terrorists'. The press was out of commission for a while, but the church raised more funds from its German and Scandinavian sources. There were no arrests. A year later the seminary at Odibo, headquarters of the Anglican church, was demolished by an expertly planted device, illustrating, as one cynic suggested, that the South Africans were nothing if not ecumenical in their targetting.

Congregations at prayer were often surrounded by the military. At one such event, Bishop Kleopas Dumeni was conducting a children's service when two unmarked army trucks drove up, discharging black troops with a white commander. Dumeni tells the story:

I greeted them in Afrikaans, '*Goeie môre*' [good morning]. '*Môre*' [morning], they answered. 'Who is your Chief? I want to talk to him.' One of them said, '*Dis ek*' [It's me]. Then I said: 'I plead with you, could you please retreat to a distance from the church for a while, for we are busy with the worship service and the people are so scared to see you surrounding the Church like that.' The commander's answer was: 'We are following the footprints of SWAPO. Why are the people afraid? We are at war, and we are fighting for you. I have seven comrades killed by SWAPO.' He spoke angrily and ordered me to shut up immediately. I answered: 'You are representing a government which claims to be a subscriber to the principles of the freedom of religion, therefore it will be better if you can let us continue with our service in peace.' He then retorted: 'Go into the church right now. *Ek moer jou, jou kak*' [I'll kill you, you shit]. I can shoot all these people dead. It is the Ovambo government which has given me the order to do that.'

In the event, 600–700 worshippers were forced out of the church building, women and children were separated. The men were taken away one by one to be interrogated and beaten. 'Some of the women started to cry, when they saw that the men were really badly beaten,' wrote Dumeni.

The soldiers then ordered the men to move further behind the walls of the church . . . where they were beaten and kicked with boots. All these things were done before our very eyes. All lasted for about an hour. After they have finished beating up people, the soldiers left. Even though some were obliged to go home on account of injuries, most of the people were fortunately able and ready to continue with our worship service. [*Dateline: Namibia*, June 18, 1982.]

Every Sunday, across the country, and not only in the north, priests and pastors preached against both personal sin and the occupation, citing biblical chapter and verse. These sermons ranged from the intellectual heights of Zephania Kameeta to village catechists echoing the Old Testament prophets. They could also do it with humour. Pastor Matti Amadhila, Bishop Dumeni's assistant, used the I Kings story of King Ahab's desire for the vineyard of Naboth in a sermon at Westminster Abbey on Cassinga Day, 1988. In the tale, King Ahab wanted the vineyard, but Naboth refused to give it to him, saying the land was his from his ancestors. Queen Jezebel conspired on behalf of her husband, framed Naboth, and had him stoned as a traitor. King Ahab got the vineyard. Pastor Amadhila likened South Africa to the King, with Namibia the stolen vineyard. 'For many of us in Namibia today,' he said, 'we feel very much like the family of Naboth.' Amadhila cast Britain and the West in the role of Jezebel. The allusion to Margaret Thatcher was barely disguised. '. . . willing to conspire with the evil one, provide money to keep the apartheid machine going, participate in the murder of our children.' (NCC, 4 May 88.)

The churches counted on their ties with overseas Christians to exert pressure on South Africa to abide by international law. The response from around the world has been an important ingredient in the struggle between Pretoria and the United Nations. Governments of countries with trading and cultural ties with the Republic have sometimes been persuaded by their own churches' members to enforce arms and trade boycotts of South Africa.

In November 1986, Namibia's four leading bishops, and the CCN general secretary, Abishai Shejevali, took part in an ecumenical consultation in Hanover, West Germany, after which the delegates dispersed to European and North American capitals, carrying at the highest level a message which was not palatable to the South Africans. Simultaneously a 63-year-old Lutheran pastor, Gabriel Amupolo, was killed at his home at Othika, ten miles from Oshakati. The military authorities announced that three insurgents had arrived at the pastor's home and shot him in the head with a Tokarev pistol. The incident, suggested the military, marked the 'start of an intensified campaign of intimidation aimed at central Ovambo where 50 per cent of the Ovambo people live.'

Pastor Amupolo was a clever choice for a target. In the 1970s he had been a member of the Ovambo bantustan administration, so that there might have been a presumption that SWAPO had gunned down a collaborator. But he had been out of politics for a long while. His family doubted the explanation. South African-made cartridge shells were found near the body. At his funeral, Assistant Bishop Matti Amadhila told 4,000 mourners that 'the mood of the people was that the South African radio was wrong, they don't believe SWAPO killed him,' (*Windhoek Advertiser*, 27.11.86.) while Dr. Shejavali was sure the pastor was killed to discredit the churches by seeming to ally them with the armed struggle.

The churches' ability to make known the story of the occupation to a wider audience has been facilitated by the Namibia Communications Centre (NCC), an international news service opened in London in 1984. Constantly circumventing South African censorship, the Centre is funded by Protestant and Catholic churches in Europe and North America and despatches regular mailing to over 2,000 clients throughout the world. Some of these news gatherers are church officials (including bishops) and lay workers 'on the ground' in the war zone. Without these dog-collar reporters, Namibia would have been a closed book to the outside world. Namibia is a graphic example of the people attempting to counter a powerful propaganda machine by simply telling the story of their everyday lives.

While the Christians of Namibia tend to be conservative when discussing the historical basis of the Bible or Christian tradition, they are radical when it comes to applying their orthodox faith to the political situation of the day. In southern Africa, this contextual theology is at the heart of the opposition to apartheid. It takes the Scriptures very seriously, looking at the liberating themes of both the Old and New Testaments as calls to faith and action today. One might say, as did Anglican Bishop James Kauluma in a letter to *The Times* (London, 20.1.84), that this is in fact the historical faith. Quoting Martin Luther, Kauluma said, 'if you preach the Gospel in all aspects with the exception of those issues which deal specifically with your time, you are not preaching the Gospel at all.' The Roman Catholic bishop, Bonifatius Haushiku, told an ecumenical gathering in West Germany, 'Christ was hanged as a criminal because he spoke up for the oppressed and downtrodden . . . He spoke up for the poor. But that death which seemed to be a criminal's death was the founding of salvation and liberation for the entire human race, for you and me.'

South Africa's persistent criticism of the Namibian churches centres on the refusal to condemn 'violence'. The Dutch Reformed Church, many clergymen from the white wings of the Western church and members of the SADF Chaplains Corps have no hesitation in giving their blessing to South Africa's war against the people of Namibia. But 'violence' perpetrated by black freedom fighters troubled not only President Botha, but Western leaders like George Bush as well as churchmen in developed countries who sanction force to preserve the status quo. Namibian church leaders have spoken out repeatedly against violence, the violent illegal occupation of their nation by the South Africans. But when it comes to the war for their liberation, Zephania Kameeta asks, 'Is it violence to stop the thieves and robbers from wounding and beating the innocent man?'

Exilitis

Inevitably, like any exile-based liberation movement, SWAPO has suffered internal traumas. Many of the youth leaguers who arrived in Zambia after April 1974 were anxious to return quickly to give South Africa a taste of its own medicine. After all, it was they who had started things moving inside. They complained that their work was not recognized, openly criticizing Nujoma and other leaders, alleging incompetence and corruption. The SYL were joined by Andreas Shipanga, part of the OPC founder group in Cape Town, once representative in Cairo, now in the key post of secretary for information and publicity. Early in 1976 the dissidents took over SWAPO's central base in Zambia. Officials from the OAU office in Zambia intervened, persuading them to meet SWAPO leaders in Lusaka. There they were disarmed. Angry at what was perceived as a trick, 50 PLAN guerrillas left camp intending to release them. The Zambian army intervened, and some dissidents were said to have been killed. All this was happening when Zambia was under constant threat from Rhodesian Special Forces.

Reports circulated of there being at least 1,000 PLAN guerrillas in detention in Zambia. Some were eventually allowed to leave Zambia for exile elsewhere, others were 'reintegrated' into the fold. But Shipanga, Solomon Mifima (also an OPC veteran and labour secretary at the time), and nine others, mostly youth leaguers, were detained in Tanzania. The bitterest outcome of those days was the ease with which South Africa attacked two PLAN bases in western Zambia, killing 24. The rebels, SWAPO alleged, had provided the enemy with a layout of the camps. Two years later SWAPO reluctantly released the faction, following an international campaign which reflected the flamboyant Shipanga's connections in Africa and Europe. He returned to Namibia, but his SWAPO–D (for Democrats) party, despite — or perhaps because of — receiving all the advantages that the South Arican regime could bestow on a prodigal son, failed to light a political beacon.

The other notable SWAPO expulsion was the extrovert Caprivian, Mishake Muyongo. In 1964, with Caprivi a stepping stone on the tortuous route from Tanzania to Ovamboland, SWAPO and CANU merged. CANU's Brendan Simbwaye became vice-president of the new organization and, when he was arrested, Muyongo stood in as acting vice-president. The union was never perfect. Caprivi's importance for SWAPO waned with Angolan independence. In 1980, Muyongo was expelled for reviving CANU. SWAPO's first serious loss had been the former vice president, Louis Nelengani, who was expelled for turning state witness at the Pretoria trial.

SWAPO has shown itself capable of recovering from its crises. The 'affaire Shipanga' was followed by the most successful period, in diplomatic and military terms, in SWAPO's history, with PLAN embarking on the successful military operations of the late 1970s. Ten white soldiers died in a single attack on the Caprivian capital, Katima Mulilo, in August 1978. Foreign Minister Pik Botha in a letter to the UN Security Council in March 1979 listed SWAPO's 'disturbing increase in violent activities' in the first two months of 1979: 'seventeen cases of sabotage of power, telecommunication and water installations; 9 incidents of abduction of members of the civilian population, 324 landmine incidents, 15 cases of intimidation resulting in the death of 3 black leaders.'

The contradictory voices emanating from South Africa can now be seen to be part of the waiting game of Controlled Change. Just as SWAPO had a multi-pronged strategy, so did Pretoria. In the war, it was Namibianizing apace, pushing its forces more regularly into Angola and essaying, however, gauchely, the art of public relations. Internally, the Turnhalle party, the DTA, was the ploy to wean blacks away from revolution. Turnhalle figures, projected as the real voices of Namibia, were flown around the world in a vain search for a government, any government, which would say a good word about the 'internal solution'.

Already Namibians were getting a taste of a nasty South African policy initiative, the counter-insurgency 'police' constables of Koevoet.

3.
The Crowbar

In the early months of 1980 rumours of a death squad began to circulate in Ovamboland. The South Africans, it was said, had trained a group of thugs to assassinate prominent Ovambos. Then in May 1980, Levi Kamangwa, an official of the Ovambo administration, was injured in a motor accident and died soon afterwards in the Oshakati State Hospital. At first the corpse was mistakenly thought to be that of a guerrilla leader. Then, in his pocket was found a list of names of prominent northern Namibian personalities, religious leaders, businessmen, teachers, Ovambo administration officials and tribal politicians.

A nurse handed the list to the church authorities, so that soon afterwards the news — though not the names — appeared in *Omukwetu*, the Lutheran newspaper published in the Ndonga language. With the security police on his tracks, the editor, Ambrosius Amutenja fled to Angola. From there, Sam Nujoma publicized the allegations on a Radio Luanda broadcast beamed to Namibia, while the *Windhoek Observer* (7.6.80) named some of the 50 'targetted for assassination'. Among them was Bishop Kleopas Dumeni, head of the Evangelical Lutheran Church, the country's largest denomination.

The newspaper talked of an extermination squad of 40 whites and 50 blacks operating under various code names. Apart from Koevoet (pronounced coo-foot, Afrikaans for crowbar), there was Cold Feet, One Way, and Unit K (K for Kill). The aim of the squad, it suggested, was to eliminate support for SWAPO before the holding of internationally supervised elections under the aegis of the United Nations.

With the appearance of the *Observer* report, Administrator-General Gerrit Viljoen issued a strenuous denial. A 'libellous lie' was being spread by 'malicious rumour', said the one-time Broederbond leader. This type of journalism 'could not but play directly into the hands of SWAPO, which is the source of the lie,' and which had spread the rumour to cover up its own plans to assassinate its adversaries. But it was no rumour.

Two of those on Kamangwa's list had already been dealt with. One was David Sheehama, a respected businessman, colleague of the founders of SWAPO when a contract labourer and no doubt suspected of funding it from the profits of his busy supermarkets across the north. In the early hours of 14 March 1980, two black men armed with AK-47s entered his flat above one of his shops, ostensibly looking for money. In those days AK-47 meant 'terrorist'. A witness reported the intruders' strange behaviour in not bothering to keep their voices down. They shot Sheehama, then turned their guns on his wife. She survived, though wounded several times. The shopping complex was burnt to the ground, and Sheehama's tractor, trucks, his Mercedes Benz and Ford Granada, sprayed with bullets. Radio Wambo blamed SWAPO. Those were the days before it became well known that the South African government was engaged in assassinating its opponents. Some SWAPO supporters had an uneasy feeling the radio report might be true.

The attack took place under the noses of the normally ubiquitous South African security forces, but they seemed unwilling to track down the assailants. Mrs Sheehama had seen one of them, a 'policeman', in the supermarket the previous afternoon. When a white police officer arrived to investigate, he had no camera. Constable William Campbell of the security police called later with a camera, but by now it was too dark to take pictures. Still, he had no doubt, he told the inquest, that 'SWAPO terrorists' were the killers. The Ondangwa magistrate, Mr. D. Bennett, agreed — Sheehama was probably murdered by 'insurgents'.

The second listed victim was an Oshakati baker, Mateus Elago, blown up by a mine planted under his car. In Ondangwa, a mine was found on the spot where another named target, furniture stores owner Eliakim Prince Shumi, normally parked his car. The mine was said to have been of South African manufacture. Shumi had made no secret of his sympathy for the struggle. Eliakim Namundjebo and Simon Nambili, both supermarket owners, were already in detention when their homes were bombed. Why, it was asked, would SWAPO blow up houses of people held by the police. Even before the death list was made public, several of those still to be dealt with had fled the country.

They were wise. The dean of the western diocese of the Lutheran Church, Mika Iilonga, was on the list. That he was a marked man was evidenced by a brief period of detention in 1980. On 8 January 1982, the 50-year-old pastor drove in a small truck to Lutheran headquarters at Oniipa to pick up food and material for drought-stricken parishioners. He knew it was safe, for at daylight the army had mineswept the gravel road. Returning at 5pm that afternoon, his van hit a mine, killing two passengers outright. With an army outpost close by it would have been impossible for the guerrillas to have planted mines during the day. Ignoring pleas to take Iilonga to a nearby hospital, the soldiers moved him to their outpost with assurances that a helicopter would fly him to the hospital. The soldiers tried to make the dying man sign a statement blaming SWAPO for the mine. He refused. They were no more successful in persuading Mrs. Iilonga to sign. The helicopter arrived at 10pm, by which time Iilonga was dead.

The veteran correspondent of the *Los Angeles Times*, Jack Foisey, visited the area two days later, and reported that both Namibian and Finnish missionaries 'believe that some of the misfortunes that beset Lutheran activists like Iilonga are South African created. They suspect that some mines are detonated on command of the South Africans.' (*Dateline: Namibia* 3, 1982.)

On the death list were people who at first glance might have seemed hostile to the nationalist struggle. As a minister in the Ovambo cabinet, Frans Indongo was a natural guerrilla target. Even so, he was still a popular personality around Oshakati. With South Africa's resources it would have been an easy matter to stage-manage his demise to make it look as though SWAPO were the killers. Okavango ministers and Ovambo legislative members were similar cases. The death of popular churchmen could be couched in the context of rumours about SWAPO's anti-religious strain. As for the businessmen, they depended on government for provisions, licenses to sell liquor, and transport. The Koevoet list, then, was a clever device to discredit SWAPO, while at the same time eliminating its covert supporters. General Charles Lloyd, a former chief of the Namibian territorial force, and then secretary of the State Security Council, confirmed years later that it was 'part of the security forces strategy to remove the enemy leaders, to take them away from the masses, so that you can inform them [the masses] and convey to them the real situation.' (*Weekly Mail*, 23.6.89.)

Unexplained disappearances were nothing new in northern Namibia. Detainees were held incommunicado under security laws which placed the police under no obligation to inform families. They might eventually be freed. But there was always the chance of elimination on the spot, or, if they were thought to have useful information, of being disposed of during or after interrogation. Two years before Koevoet's appearance, a SWAPO supporter described the fate of a missing person.

> One woman told us that the soldiers went to her home and took her husband to their camp. The soldiers laughed and said to her, 'Didn't your husband go home? We sent him yesterday.' As she was leaving the camp, a black worker told her of having seen the South African soldiers kill her husband the previous night, wind his body in socks soaked in petrol and burn it. [*Focus* 32, Jan–Feb 1981, p. 3.]

By 1981 the secret of Koevoet was out. These were not 'bobbies in the bush', but bogus policemen trained in the art of ambushing, tracking, bush survival and murder. The dirty task of causing enemies to disappear had been assigned to a specially groomed squad. Its formal title was the cumbersome Special Operations K Unit of the South African Security Police, alternatively COIN, for Counter-Insurgency Unit, but its founder, Brigadier Hans Dreyer, personally preferred the Koevoet pseudonym. Law and Order Minister Louis le Grange encouraged the name by describing it as 'the crowbar which prises terrorists out of the bushveld like nails from rotten wood.'

Off duty, members of Koevoet wore T-shirts proclaiming 'Murder is our business — and business is good.' For once, South African propaganda had the ring of truth. Of all the armed units employed to retain Pretoria's grip on Namibia, none has been more controversial than Koevoet. While 100,000 army regulars were in Namibia engaged in a seemingly endless war against SWAPO, it was Koevoet's white officers and black constables, numbering no more than 3,000, who spearheaded a campaign of terror against the Ovambo and Okavango people, achieving a kill ratio of twenty-five to one by comparison with the army. Ordinary black policemen were terrified of them, while the army was said to be jealous of their success. Some Koevoet victims were indeed SWAPO freedom fighters, but they were also the elderly, young children, housewives, villagers going about their lawful business, shot in cold blood or victims of casual acts of brutality.

Koevoet's activities have been raised at the United Nations, decried by Amnesty International, tut-tutted over by the opposition in the Cape Town parliament. The South West African Bar Council, though dominated by Afrikaner lawyers not known for their radical behaviour, have seen fit to castigate 'some members' of the unit for using 'the conditions of war as an excuse' for murder, assault, rape and robbery. Despite growing controversy and public concern, the South African government continued for five years to deny the very existence of the unit. It was not until 1984 that Minister Le Grange admitted in parliament that it had been operative since January 1979, confirming the accuracy of Moses Garoeb's (administrative secretary of SWAPO in Luanda) disclosure to the press in 1979 of the existence of a secret 'assassination squad'.

'Sterk' Hans Dreyer

The man chosen to set up Koevoet was one of South Africa's most experienced counter-insurgents, 'Sterk' (Afrikaans for 'strong') Hans Dreyer, Chief of the Security Police in Natal. From Natal Dreyer had been able to study the *modus operandi* of the Flechas (Portuguese for arrows) in neighbouring Mozambique. This was a black unit run by

PIDE, the Portuguese secret police, to hunt and eliminate guerrillas. Files discovered at PIDE headquarters in Lisbon after the April 1974 coup contained reports of regular meetings between the heads of the South African, Rhodesian and Portuguese security police. The exchange of information on anti-guerrilla combat techniques was of special interest to South Africa. With the collapse of Portuguese rule in Mozambique, the Flecha commanding officer, Oscar Cardozo, with many of his white and black troops, fled into Rhodesia. There they were taken under the wing of Ron Reid Daly, founder of Rhodesia's equivalent to the Flechas, the Selous Scouts. As with the Flechas, the Scouts had a dual role — the elimination of freedom fighters and the gathering of intelligence. In reality, they could do exactly as they liked. For them, the law was of minimal concern.

Dreyer's other strand of crucial experience was to have served with the South African Police (SAP) contingent in Rhodesia. When, in 1967, Joshua Nkomo's ZAPU guerrillas invaded north-western Rhodesia from Zambia, they were accompanied by *Umkhonto we Sizwe* units (the ANC's military wing) heading for South Africa. In response to a call for help from the Rhodesian leader, Ian Smith, Vorster sent a contingent of police which ultimately numbered 4,000 men.

In his book *Selous Scouts, Top Secret War* (1982), Reid Daly provides numerous insights into the operation of irregular units. Both Koevoet and the Scouts were police, not army, units. Reid Daly writes that:

> Military Intelligence could never have tackled the task . . . they did not have the means of being in contact with the country's grass roots . . . they were geared towards conventional rather than unconventional war tasks. [Here was] a terrorist insurgency — a civil war where no battle lines were drawn. The only people who could have their finger on the information pulse of a civilian population . . . where every next man could be an enemy or an enemy sympathiser . . . was the civil police force spearheaded by the Special Branch (p. 23).

The conventional army chiefs distrusted two key Selous activities which were to become staples of Koevoet. The first was what Reid Daly calls pseudo operations. Selous Scouts would go into villages impersonating freedom fighters and, if the welcome was warm, inflict vicious punishment on their hosts. The Rhodesian generals were also suspicious of 'turning terrs', that is, incorporating captured freedom fighters into the scouts' ranks and using them for counter-insurgency. Of the army's generals, Reid Daly wrote: 'Their logic . . . demanded that all captured enemies should be knocked on the head and killed.' By the end of the war, the scouts had 'turned the best part of a thousand' men from the liberation armies (p. 62.) 'It was only the newly captured terrorists who could keep the teams up to date with the constantly changing

65

picture of what was happening in the enemy's camp to enable us to get, and then to stay, ahead.' (p. 40.) In the same way, 'turned' SWAPO guerrillas were a key component in the Koevoet operation.

Koevoet was born in the greatest secrecy. More than likely the idea for a force of this kind came from Vorster himself, given his many years as minister of police and his close association with the contingent in Rhodesia. It was 1978. P. W. Botha was defence minister, and Ian Smith still ran Rhodesia, albeit through a black surrogate, Bishop Abel Muzorewa. General Magnus Malan, SADF chief, instructed the police to set up a Selous Scouts type operation, its role, in the words of a later law and order minister, Louis le Grange, 'to act as the eyes and ears of, and to collect information for, the military.'

It is important to establish the declared official aims and pattern of Koevoet policing which the government did not mind being made public. In the debate in parliament in May 1984, Le Grange took the opportunity 'to place full particulars' about the unit on record:

> . . . so that there need be no further misunderstanding about Koevoet and its involvement. SWAPO had succeeded by means of intimidation, propaganda and family ties existing between them and the local population, in maintaining a permanent presence in Owambo [South African spelling for the Ovambo bantustan]. The population was intimidated and influenced to such an extent that the rendering of assistance to SWAPO occurred on a large scale.

Le Grange talked of sabotage, murder, abduction, land-mine attacks and ambushing forming part of the daily intimidation. Spies came and went, he said, and the guerrillas were even getting down to the white south, there to commit acts of sabotage.

> As . . . the ordinary conventional methods of warfare appeared to be ineffective in combating terrorism in Owambo and the rest of South West Africa, it was decided after consultation between the SA Defence Force, which at that stage was engaging in the struggle on its own, and the SA Police, to form a special unit to gather information and make it possible for the security forces to track down and wipe out terrorist gangs. We did not simply send a unit of the SA Police to the operational area arbitrarily. It was a calculated operation at the request of the SA Defence Force as a result of the problems which I have sketched. With the passage of time it became apparent that the initial basis on which the unit had come into existence, and according to which it would transmit all information it obtained about terrorist movements to the combat units of the security forces while the latter would carry out the pursuit operations, gave rise to problems in

practice. In many cases the unit had to follow the tracks of terrorists across a vast expanse of territory, and when the unit ultimately succeeded in tracking down the terrorists, the long distances, impassable routes and dense undergrowth made it impossible for the combat units of the security forces to mount their attacks in time, with the result that the terrorists got away. [So] the unit in due course . . . began to operate as a combat unit, together with the rest of the security forces. [Quotes from Le Grange from *Hansard*, 2.5.84, cols. 5613/4.]

That was the last time the government allowed Koevoet to be debated in parliament.

Those early days were described in the semi-official South African magazine, *Armed Forces*.

Once the final arrangements had been made between the SAP and the SADF, Dreyer was allowed to pick five of his men to accompany him and was sent to Owambo, arriving on 11 January 1979 in a small convoy of two police cars, two *bakkies* [vans] and some private vehicles. Arriving in the area more or less 'cold', the new team was greatly assisted by the local security police chief who had earlier been Dreyer's second-in-command in Natal. The first three months were spent with the local security police and with the Recces, absorbing background information and studying the situation. The next step saw them drive around much of the region . . . building a mental picture to go with the maps and files. [*Armed Forces* Dec/Jan 1984, p. 7.]

Already operating in the territory was a group of Ovambos trained by the white police intelligence unit. This group of comparatively well educated men had done a number of jobs for the South Africans at a time when they were losing their grip. They distributed a newspaper called *Eume* ('Friend') and showed propaganda films at schools and *cuca* shops. They also trained bodyguards for pro-South African chiefs and headmen who might be targets for the guerrillas. The guards were nicknamed *makakunya*, literally 'bone-pickers and bloodsuckers', a universal term for anyone fighting for the South Africans. This group and the men they trained were the earliest Koevoet recruits.

Dreyer claims to have captured the first insurgent in May 1979, and that he 'proved a highly valuable source', allowing Koevoet to 'greatly flush out the existing information on SWAPO organization and activities.' (p. 7.)

In the beginning it seems that Operation K, as it was at first known, was genuinely concerned with looking for clues and apprehending wrongdoers. The police were put on to political murders and sabotage cases, and behaved more or less as criminal investigation officers. This training programme for special constables took Dreyer away from a 'purely Scouts type of pseudo operation as originally foreseen, towards the Flecha concept of utilizing local personnel and former insurgents. [*Armed Forces* Dec/Jan 1984, p. 8.] Very soon 64 Ovambos had been chosen from the special constables and by June 1979 the first Koevoet fighting group, called Zulu Foxtrot, was set up, headed by 10 white South Africans. According to American journalist Jim Hooper, its 'first major success' came in 1979 when 12 guerrillas, said to have killed four people on white farms south of the Etosha game park, were killed (1988, p. 110).

Koevoet's 300 white officers were almost all South African policemen. They numbered members of the special branch which, for two decades, had bludgeoned a bloody path through South Africa's own resistance movements. Koevoet fell directly under the jurisdiction of the Security Branch. Dreyer's early deputies included white Rhodesian Selous officers as well as members of the now disbanded South African police unit which had served in Rhodesia. One of them, Frans Conradie, described as a legend in his obituary in the police magazine *Servamus* (November 1983) had been a counter-insurgent in the late 1960s when South Africa set up an observation post in the Caprivi Strip.

Namibian whites did join Koevoet, but in insignificant numbers. With barely 60,000 in Namibia, the country's white manpower resources were heavily stretched. In 1981, as part of the show of turning over responsibility to 'South Westers', an 'own government police service for South West Africa was instituted', called SWAPOL. The first annual report noted in a show of defiant complacency that in the field of crime there were generally 'no unusual trends and the situation is well under control.' It did mention that, with the need to maintain the internal security of the territory 'of prime importance to the Force', an anti-insurgent unit was established immediately. This unit, it explained, was functioning so efficiently that it was considered to be justifiable.

In South Africa, white Koevoet officers were recruited informally, often by word of mouth. An officer serving in Namibia might well recommend to a colleague back home a six-month or year's stint in the far north-west of the empire. Indeed, those with a historical perspective might have seen themselves as something of a praetorian guard defending a prized African possession from communism. Nurtured on the theory and practice of *baasskap* (literally, 'masterliness'), fed a diet of 'commie onslaught' propaganda, what better way to serve the motherland? Eugene Terre Blanche, leader of the Afrikaner Resistance Movement (AWB), has estimated that 80 per cent of all white police and the lower ranks of the armed services are AWB sympathizers. (*Financial*

Times, 24.11.88.) The police are often drawn from the economically poorer ranks of white South African society and feel threatened by the rise of black nationalism. Among them are those who feel hemmed in by even the modest restraints of South African custom relating to the treatment of political prisoners.

These days a growing number of South African police, civil and security, black and white, have counter-insurgency experience, as they attempt to plug the ANC guerrilla tide inside the 'white' cities and across several thousand miles of permeable border. But northern Namibia, criss-crossed by SWAPO soldiers and inhabited by a population offering them safe passage, posed a special dilemma for the security forces. Koevoet recruits attended the police counter-insurgency training course at Maleoskop, near Groblersdal, Eastern Transvaal. The syllabus was indistinguishable from army infantry units, with instruction in 'patrolling, battle-craft, ambushes, counter-ambushing, road movement, attacks on enemy bases, follow-up and mopping-up operations, forward air control, anti-riot procedures, urban terrorism and terrorist tactics.' (*Resister* 37, p. 18, April 1985.) It is unlikely that the course referred to the 1984 United Nations Convention against Torture and Other Cruel, Inhuman or Degrading Treatment or Punishment, which has still to be signed by South Africa. Article 10 of the Convention calls for signatories to:

> ensure that education and information regarding the prohibition against torture are fully included in the training of law enforcement personnel, civil or military, medical personnel, public officials and other persons who may be involved in the custody, interrogation or treatment of any individual subjected to any form of arrest, detention or imprisonment.

Namibianization of the War

The precedent of blacks fighting for whites against other blacks is well established in colonial Africa. The British employed Fingo against Xhosa in the 19th century 'pacification' of the Eastern Cape. In Kenya, Senegal and Mozambique, as well as elsewhere, indigenous black troops were pitted against rebellious fellow-countrymen. Without the King's African Rifles, Ian Smith's UDI would certainly have collapsed years earlier.

The Koevoet operation could not have got off the ground without its black component. White officers spoke no local languages. Nor would they have been able to unravel the intricate family, clan and religious connections so different from the European experience. The exercise of terror had to be backed by an understanding of local culture and daily life. But why did blacks join, be it Koevoet, the territorial force, or any of the units whose sole aim was the strangulation of one of Africa's most respected freedom movements?

Namibia has the highest ratio of settled refugees in the world — one to 28, compared to the next highest, Australia, at one to 125. Few were allowed to live in the south so that the ratio in the north of Namibia will have been substantially higher. 'Refugees, or immigrants, as the South Africans call them,' notes an American academic, 'are renowned for their political docility and support of the host regime. Indeed, do they have much choice in this matter?' (Gordon 1988, pp. 22–3.) Koevoet attracted veterans of the unsuccessful UNITA Angolan liberation movement. They may have been Kwanyamas from the Angolan side, speaking the same language as their clansmen south of the border. (Only one-third of the Kwanyamas live in Namibia.) There were also a sprinkling of the black Angolans who fought in the Portuguese Special Groups (GE) and Flechas against the black nationalist armies. Few options offered themselves to these desperate men other than that of being sent back to fight SWAPO. Even if they no longer had the heart for combat, they had to pay the price for being black exiles in South Africa's orbit. Many came out with parents, wives and children.

A rare Koevoet defector to go public recounted how he was abducted from his village in southern Angola by UNITA and taken to a Koevoet base near Oshakati.

> I was happy when I heard that I could get a job as a policeman, because I hated the idea of being jobless, but it also became very clear to me what kind of a policeman they had in mind for me . . . I had no choice. My colleagues repeatedly warned me that if one resigns, then you are in trouble, be it from Koevoet or from civilians.[*Namibian*, 7.10.88.]

When he defected five years later, Constable Mweulyato Jonas Kemanya said many of his colleagues wanted to quit, but feared reprisals against themselves and their families.

Brigadier Dreyer claims to have enlisted large numbers of 'turned' guerrillas. With disarming candour he has also declared, 'We don't need to take prisoners. This is a war.' The word volunteer has little meaning to a prisoner for whom the alternative is to be shot on the spot or battered to death for refusing to divulge the whereabouts of comrades. Undoubtedly former guerrillas worked for Koevoet. They have testified in court cases. But the exact number was almost certainly inflated as part of the propaganda war. The London *Observer*'s Zimbabwe correspondent, the late Godwin Matatu, was told at a military briefing that half the unit were guerrillas who had been turned (4.12.83). On the other hand, a South African journalist reported that 'each fighting unit of about 40 men will usually have a former terrorist in its ranks.' (*Scope,* 25.1.85, p. 13.) But Jim Hooper, the only journalist to have lived with Koevoet, was told that the unit had '40 or 50 ex-terrs'. (p. 108). In part, South Africa also exaggerated the 'turned' factor to mask Koevoet's dependence on Angolans. Koevoet recruited almost exclusively from among Ovambos, north and south of the border, and from the less numerous Kavangos. In theory blacks from other ethnic groups, even from South Africa, could apply, but they would not be accepted. A journalist close to the SADF explained that the applicant would have to be exceptionally good 'to make up for the distrust a foreign black face causes in tribal areas where white faces are more easily accepted.' (*Armed Forces,* Dec/Jan 1984, p. 13.)

Unlike their white counterparts, black Koevoet constables were not generally recruited through the conventional police or security network. Those who started as home guards were posted to the kraals of black 'leaders'. Their numbers were so great they were more like military camps than kraals, often with more guards than resident civilians. A posse would accompany the protected man when he travelled around. Any lad of 16 could apply for the job, receive 16 weeks drill and counter-insurgency training, and then expect to be on duty 24 hours a day.

These *makakunya* might then graduate into the more peripatetic and better paid world of Koevoet. It is clear that Koevoet attracted the ill-educated and the illiterate, people on whom the hold of the established churches had wavered, or relatives of those already compromised by their support for the regime. But such a recruit would have to understand English or Afrikaans in order to communicate with his white officer. They used to say in Ovamboland that a criminal record was a useful recommendation for a potential recruit. Philip Shilongo, priest at the Odibo Anglican mission, explained that the South Africans recruited 'these foolish idiots, give them salaries and tins of beef and they do damage wherever they go.' It must be said, however, that the vast majority of unschooled Namibians and non-Christians, and those supposedly tainted by a kraal connection with the colonial administration, did not join the enemy.

A consideration of those who did showed there were not too many genuine volunteers among them. Poverty and unemployment were powerful recruiting sergeants. The better educated northerners were employed as teachers and nurses, or had clerical jobs in the bantustan administrations. Ovambo workers have long been the country's sweated backbone, their remitted wages topping up the meagre pickings of subsistence farming. The drought of the early 1980s may have driven some into Koevoet or the army, but the primary targets were early school-leavers (and there are many) and the rural and urban jobless. The average age of a black Koevoet in 1983 was between 23 to 24, with some

71

apparently recruited before they were 18. The northern economy was turned upside down by the war. Once dependent on agriculture and mining revenues, it came to be dominated by the military and the ethnic bureaucracy. In Kavango, the SADF accounted for over two-fifths of buying power. It would not have been much less in Ovamboland, probably considerably more in Caprivi. This war economy created a climate which, like a magnet, drew in the poor, the hungry and the ill-prepared. So the SADF's average monthly wage of R600 was a princely sum. It was also an indication that the regime had to pay considerably 'over the odds' to buy a man's soul. The blacks, Namibians among them, who volunteered to fight for South Africa in two world wars were not so well rewarded.

Radio Wambo, local mouthpiece of the South African Broadcasting Corporation, would announce that the South West Africa Territorial Force (SWATF) and the police were recruiting. The station would drive home the message of the battle against 'communism, atheism, terrorism'. Though many schools refused Defence Force offers of educational activities, the army sometimes gained entrance to show films and take pupils and teachers on a ride in the most up-to-date military vehicle. White national service schoolteachers helped SWATF recruiting — at one stage, 40 per cent of the staff at Ongwediva's teacher training college were soldiers. This classroom propaganda was the main reason why Peter Kalangula's bantustan administration expelled all SADF teachers from Ovambo schools.

The perks made it attractive to join Koevoet and difficult to leave, even beyond the grave. South African insurance companies offered life policies which left a widow with more money than she could ever have dreamt of. The *Windhoek Observer* (11.4.87) detailed the inventories of deceased estates filed with the Master of the Supreme Court. In one case, the mother of a dead coloured SWATF rifleman from Outjo inherited R104,000 derived entirely from two policies with SANLAM, the Broederbond-founded insurance company. Black Angolans in 32 Battalion who 'died in a contact with hostile forces,' would normally leave assets of R10,000, 'being the proceeds of an insurance policy.'

It should be remembered that Koevoet never numbered more than 3,000 blacks against a population in the north of more than 600,000. South Africa may, as it used to claim, have turned away applicants. But the figures should be compared with the 80,000 exiles, largely from the north, who made the more dangerous, and less lucrative, decision to resist. So much for the myth that the north was rife with collaborators.

Extermination

Koevoet's two publicly avowed roles — avowed, that is, by South Africa — were extermination and interrogation-on-the-run. There was a third, never stated publicly: the spreading of maximum terror so as to discourage the civilian population from offering food, drink and an instructive send-off to 'terrorists'. The authorities were placed in the peculiar position of wanting the world outside the war zone to know as little as possible about Koevoet, while leaving no doubt in the minds of the local population that they were at the mercy of a band of ruthless men.

For most of the war, PLAN sent its cadres in quietly, secreting them across the border to lie low until the time was ripe for a strike. Small groups criss-crossed the border with impunity. By February the sub-tropical rains would provide verdurous cover to men on the move, especially in the thick woods of Kavango and eastern Ovamboland. This was the time for dramatic, almost provocative, invasions by groups of 50 men and more. Now the security blanket would spread over a vast area of southern Angola, the war zone, and white farms to the south. Army leave was cancelled, farmers primed their automatic weapons and instructed their black 'boys' to report the presence of suspicious visitors. Amongst these farmers, it had the frenetic build-up of a rugby test match. The body-count machine was plugged in. If the guerrillas were cornered, the white tribe celebrated another successful man-hunt. After a guerrilla attack on a farm north of Tsumeb, a farmer's wife said: 'I am a fatalist. I don't think God could be that unfair to let me die at the hands of a black man'. (*Argus*, 14.1.84.) If the prey, or some of them, got through to the so-called triangle of death between the white towns of Otavi, Grootfontein and Tsumeb, or even further south to Windhoek and Walvis Bay, the story would die out — until the travellers surfaced to attack a Casspir (armoured personnel carrier) or a white farm.

Let us follow a Koevoet team in its most conventional guise, hunter–exterminator. The unit had headquarters in three regions of the north: Opuwo, in the vast, empty expanses of the Kaokoveld; Rundu, the Kavango capital; and Oshakati. Permanent bases and temporary encampments, some shared with the regular police or army, were strung along the border and 'red' areas. At any one time half of Koevoet's strength would be on a fortnight's patrol. Each group was prefixed with the name Zulu — Zulu Alpha, Zulu Whisky, Zulu Bravo. Inter-group rivalry was strong. Groups were said to be unwilling to pass on too much 'for fear of the rivals accumulating more contacts at the end of the year.' (Hooper 1988, p. 104.)

Koevoet's means of conveyance was the towering Casspir, weighing eleven tons, steel-plated against mines, with room for ten men and their weapons. A machine-gun was mounted on the roof of the driver's cab. The men carried South African-made R5 semi-automatic rifles, with grenade launchers and 60 mm mortars as support weapons. The Casspir was capable of travelling at speed over the roughest terrain. A patrol consisted of four Casspirs, a supply truck and a fuel bowser, also cushioned against mines. The 40 men in each *span* (team) included three white officers, and, if available, a recently 'turned' freedom fighter (or 'terr' in SADF-speak) to provide up-to-date local intelligence and offer insights as to how his former comrades might react in combat. There were also said to be 'skilled interrogators as well as specialists in extermination.' (Court testimony, Hamukwaya inquest, Windhoek, 1983.) The trackers, Ovambo herdsmen or bushmen (San), led the way in the penultimate act of the chase, closing in for a shoot-out with the 'terrs'.

The groups roamed the 'red area', where a contact was likeliest, directed by headquarters in Oshakati, which monitored around the clock. At night the patrol turned in at a police or army base, or slept in the wild, feeding out of 'rat packs' of canned food, packet soup, chocolate bars, tea, coffee, powdered raspberry-flavoured milkshakes and an orange drink mixed with tepid water tapped from the Casspir's tank. This high-energy diet might be enhanced by the meat of a cow found grazing in the bush. Springbok, kudu, eland, the large game which once roamed the veld in abundance, have been thinned out by South African soldiers and officials.

The airforce played a key role in the hunt. Spotter planes patrolled incessantly, watching for the tell-tale signs. *Flight International* magazine's reporter, Herman Potgieter, flew on a recce. His pilot, Dave, described it as 'like being a cop on the beat', getting to know your area, and picking up anything unusual. It would be quite normal for them to see a kraal where three women were pounding mealies (corn). 'If you see five doing it, then I'd get the Koevoet team to check it out. They could just be having a feast or celebration, but it might mean that they are having to feed a SWAPO team.' Normally the people being watched did not seem too bothered. But, said Dave, 'if they look up a lot or scurry around, then just maybe they are nervous, so we'll check it out.'

SWAPO, in turn, responded accordingly and effectively to the increasing battery of forces and tactics arraigned against it. Despite all the vigilance, the first intimation that guerrillas were active in an area was often shells raining down on the kraal of an unpopular headman. A journalist reported that 'the days of picking up insurgent's tracks by chance are long gone. They have learned not to wear boots with a readily identifiable sole pattern, using *tackies* [sneakers], shoes or commercially available boots instead. Some even go barefoot on occasion.' Once the tell-tale spoor was sorted out of the general mass of innocent tracks 'littering Owambo', the chase was on. The trackers walked or ran in front of the Casspirs.

> The trackers' ability is amazing. One pointed out a typical spoor to me, where a dead leaf had flipped over. How could he tell? All the other leaves had a few grains of sand on them, this one did not. The trackers literally run along the spoor in line-abreast formation, yelling directions and clues to each other. When the team in use gets tired, a new team takes up the spoor as the first team boards its Casspir to rest. In this way the SWAPO are kept on the move and tire, thus making mistakes. The trackers do not. [*Flight International* 19.)

Tracking could last for days — the longest distance a spoor was followed without interruption was 185 kilometres (115 miles), and across the 'cut line' (border) into Angola.

If the indications were that only a few guerrillas lay ahead, one or more Casspirs would be sent in for the shoot-out. A larger group, and other Koevoet units might go in. When the spoor was '30 minutes old', two Alouette helicopters joined the hunt, ranging ahead of the Koevoet patrol. On being run down, the guerrillas would either 'surrender, fight or run for it'. If they split and ran, life again became difficult for their pursuers. 'Their camouflage techniques are extremely good,' one pilot noted. A Koevoet commander complained in a 1983 court case that 'these people are being specifically trained in anti-tracking. They wiped out tracks, retraced tracks, changed footwear. . . . They have the ability to vanish without trace.' (*Windhoek Advertiser*, 20.10.83.)

Armed Forces (Dec/Jan 1989) described 'the most successful single contract of Operation K by early 1984 which saw the demise of 34 out of 34 insurgents.' (p. 12.) The security police had located the spoor of a large group of insurgents, and was joined by a Koevoet team patrolling nearby.

> The insurgents had in the meantime become aware of the two security police Casspirs following them. Being in rather greater strength, they were so sure of themselves that they took to leaving taunting notes on their tracks. As soon as they found what they considered to be a suitable ambush site, they settled down to wait for their pursuers. Not long after this, they realized that there were more than two vehicles involved and — rightly suspecting the worst — broke off the ambush and attempted to flee the area. By now, a spotter aircraft and two Alouettes had arrived to assist in locating them and controlling the contact. One of the Alouettes had barely arrived when it spotted the insurgents breaking cover only 300 metres ahead of the pursuing police. The contact followed immediately and was also joined by

other Koevoet fighting groups that had been following events on the radio as they neared the area. The action lasted some 40 minutes over an area of roughly 2,000 metres radius and ended with 34 insurgent bodies being collected and no spoor found leaving the area. [p. 12.]

In the aftermath of a PLAN–Koevoet shoot-out there was never independent confirmation of how many had died or been taken prisoner, if any. The deaths were not reported to the civil police. Hooper (1988) described the bodies being 'stripped of equipment and left where they have fallen.' (p. 82.) A Koevoet officer confirmed in a Supreme Court trial that post-mortem examinations were not held on dead guerrillas. For some, there might be a momentary reprieve. After a contact, Hooper was surprised to see a prisoner. 'He was stripped to his shorts and his wrists were tied tightly behind him with strips of bark. Sweating heavily, his chest still heaved from the chase. He looked terribly frightened. They must have killed the other one to make this one talk, I thought.' (p. 148.) There are reports of at least 20 camps along the border where, according to a former South African conscript, information is squeezed out of them and 'if they say nothing they are killed'. (*Observer* 7.3.82.)

There was money in corpses and accompanying booty. Special constables were paid *kopgeld* (literally, head money) for every guerrilla brought in, dead or alive. The amount ranged between R2,000 and R20,000. Captured weapons were rewarded on a sliding scale of lethality. The Southern African Catholic Bishops Conference reported in 1985 that Namibians, in or out of uniform, were being offered R20,000 for informing on the presence of SWAPO fighters in the neighbourhood (*Rand Daily Mail*, 28.1.85). The war was being privatized.

For years there were unconfirmed reports of Casspirs driving through the north parading captured corpses. The authorities were aghast. 'A Christian organization, like the South African Defence Force,' said a police spokesman, 'would not publicly exhibit the enemy's dead.' His SWATF counterpart warned that 'if anyone did such a thing, he would be prosecuted.' In December 1986 a wisely anonymous photographer snapped a Casspir draped with the bodies of two dead guerrillas on a gloating, whooping drive through an Ovambo village. The ghoulish scene was reproduced in *The Namibian* (16.1.87), captioned 'Parade of Death'. The newspaper was promptly banned by the South African Directorate of Publications on the grounds that the picture was 'a threat to state security, the general welfare and the good order of the territory.'

For once the censors were right. But the banning came too late to prevent the newspaper being widely distributed, and, after a court appeal, it was allowed back on sale a week late. The picture was reproduced in magazines and newspapers around the world. Police public relations now explained that the bodies were on their way to the mortuary in Oshakati. Why had they not been carried inside the vehicle? 'The Casspir only has room for 12 people. There was not enough space for the bodies as well as the soldiers, boxes of ammunition and rifles.' For the people of the north it was 'old hat'. Reports of corpse parades flooded in to church and newspaper offices.

The 'body-count' briefing was a crude but much-loved method of telling the world that the war was being won. The *Voice of America* used it with telling, but inaccurate, effect in Vietnam. The SADF claimed to kill hundreds of 'terrorists' a year. Local newspapers, unable or unwilling to make independent checks, would report that the 'headquarters of the Armed Forces in Windhoek today announced that since the start of the year (it is now June) 322 SWAPO insurgents have been killed in actions with the Armed Forces.' The Windhoek Bar Council in a memo to an official enquiry commented that Koevoet 'may enable the security forces to kill more terrorists, but certainly more civilians [as well].' One example: a young woman, the daughter of a headman, eating her lunch in a millet field, was killed by a passing army Casspir. The vehicles, retreating after a shoot-out with guerrillas, then drove through the homestead fence, killed two elderly sisters, while three other people were injured. Who is to say that these innocent bystanders were not counted as 'enemy kills'? (*NCC* 25.3.87.)

Not all guerrillas were killed instantly. A PLAN officer or a guerrilla who looked as though he might have information was handed over to the security police for interrogation, where they still faced the prospect of unofficial execution. Koevoet's regime of extermination and interrogation was backed up by a panoply of security laws which has made South Africa the envy of dictators around the world. The Terrorism Act, although repealed in South Africa, remained in force in its colony, where it was a considerable prop to the legal system. Under Section 6, a person suspected of 'participation in terrorist activities' could be arrested on the say-so of a senior police officer. Detainees could be, were, held indefinitely, without access to lawyer, family or priest.

Proclamation AG 26 of 1978 (Detention for the Prevention of Political Violence and Intimidation) was used by the Security Police for putting SWAPO leaders out of the way for an indefinite period. In the war zone, the security forces favoured Proclamation AG 9 of 1977 which replaced the bantustan emergency regulations. AG 9 gave the AG (Administrator-General) the power to declare most of the inhabited area of Namibia security districts. Though not creating any serious offences, the measure was invaluable in allowing a non-commissioned officer to arrest, without the need for a warrant, any person suspected of having committed an offence at any time, or, if that was not sufficient, any person 'who is in possession of information relating to the committing of any offence by any person.' A place of detention was wherever it was most convenient — a river bank, the back of a van. Soon after the formation of Koevoet, lawyers located the Osiri camp, 100 miles north of Windhoek, where inmates were held in tiny corrugated iron cages, and were blindfolded in the presence of their interrogators. (Weaver memo to authors, November 1983.) The detainee was then questioned about the offence, or intended offence. Though the period of detention was limited to 30 days, the order would simply be renewed when it expired. In 1986, the Windhoek Supreme Court ruled that the detainee should be allowed to make adequate representations before the detention was renewed for a further 30 days. The government avoided that hurdle by thereafter detaining the prisoner under the Terrorism Act.

In the matter of Koevoet's battle casualties, the public was left largely in the dark. Inquests were held into the deaths of all Namibian members of the armed forces. Reporters, however, had to dig out the records of magistrates sitting in the war zone in conditions tantamount to secret sessions. Occasional newspaper reports provided a sketchy picture of the hazards facing Koevoet. Mines did the most damage. A typically brief account in *The Namibian* (14.11.86) had a Koevoet 'span' on the track of guerrillas; there was 'a loud explosion' and two men, Simon Shindele and Simon Toivo, 'did not stand up'. In the same report mention was made of an Ernesto Hishitivale who died when his tracking group was attacked from a millet field with small-arms and RPG-7 rockets. Portuguese first names reflected the prominence of Angolan refugees in the firing line. Constable Armada da Batista, aged 30, of Zulu Hotel was blown up by a mine on patrol in the Onhunda region. (*Windhoek Observer*, 22.11.86). An inquest reported two men, Theodor Mathias, aged 22, and Kanungipe Tjimbua, being thrown off their Casspir after an explosion in which four linked anti-vehicle mines were detonated. (*Windhoek Observer*, 22.5.85).

As with the *maquis* (resistance) in German-occupied France in World War Two, police working for the enemy were considered to be collaborators and were never able to relax. The Namibian guerrillas had at their disposal an extensive Ovambo grapevine, which made it imperative for Koevoet constables to be on their guard 24 hours a day. The execution of an off-duty constable, revealed in an inquest court in Rundu, illustrates the role of family ties in the conflict. Three armed guerrillas, dressed in olive green battle fatigues, came to a village to inquire about special constable Josef Kambodja. One of the three was engaged to the sister of a teenaged girl who just then happened to be grinding wheat. The men walked over to a fireplace and spoke in calm fashion to a resident of the hamlet. The girl heard a burst of fire. Kambodja's body lay at the entrance to a kraal. The villagers were called together and told to inform the armed forces that the execution was the work of SWAPO.

The state public prosecutor disclosed in a murder trial that in 1982 alone, 45 off-duty Koevoet constables had been 'murdered in cold blood by terrorists'. Since 1978, a total of 198 had died in this way. The unique disclosure, intended to explain why off-duty special constables had to be heavily armed 24 hours a day, was never updated. But the numbers must have risen substantially afterwards, as the Koevoet establishment was at this time increased from 2,000 to 3,000. These deaths were presumably incorporated into the figures for terrorist murders of 'innocent and unarmed civilians'.

The Law

No neutral eye-witness account exists of what happened to captured guerrillas. We do know, from evidence in a 1984 Windhoek Supreme Court trial, how the army handled Namibian prisoners. A black soldier was charged with murdering one of his men in an argument at a liquor store in Kavango. He had, he said under cross-examination, seen people shot between the eyes. 'I have seen this when we have captured SWAPO terrorists and when our commanding officer says "you must shoot them", usually we aimed like that, that was how we shot.' (Weaver in Totemeyer et al, 1987, p. 253.)

Police methods in dealing with political activists were the subject of a Cape court case when a journalist, Tony Weaver, was charged under the Police Act with unlawfully broadcasting 'untrue' matters on the BBC. Weaver had claimed that seven men, said by the authorities to be African National Congress guerrillas, were shot by the police in cold blood in a Cape Town black township, after which weapons were planted on the bodies to justify the deed. Medical evidence showed that six of them had been shot in the head at close range, giving the lie to the police story of a gun battle. The charges were withdrawn and the police launched an internal inquiry. In line with the practice of their colleagues in Namibia, the seven deaths were likely to have figured in the periodic body count (SAIRR 1988 pp. 834–5).

As for Koevoet, it can be said with some certainty that they were not in the habit of taking prisoners. If the oath of secrecy they swore on joining the unit had one moment in mind, it was to keep them silent over the cold-blooded slayings of disarmed guerrillas. Even Dreyer's on-the-record statements were ambivalent. His unit's 'main task is to locate terrorists infiltrating into the territory and to destroy them.' This involved 'the gathering of information, and obliteration based on collated intelligence.' A blunter Koevoet officer admitted that 'we have told our men we are not interested in captures. Killing is the name of the game . . .'

Section 30 of the 1957 South African Defence Act grants absolute immunity to members of the security forces for murder, assault and other criminal behaviour if 'done *bona fide* for the purpose of or in connection with the prevention or suppression of terrorism in any operational area.' Imagine then the last stages of a chase in which Koevoet constables will themselves have been shot at, wounded, even killed. Guerrillas have died, some have escaped, but one of them, who is wounded, tries to hide or comes out with his hands up. With no prospect of an autopsy, much less of an inquest, there will be no pathologist to raise questions about precise holes made from bullets fired from close range into the head or heart of the cadaver.

A Defence Force spokesman considered 'members of SWAPO to be terrorists and not soldiers, as we do members of the Angolan Army.' British churchmen visiting Namibia met a teacher who was surprised to hear that they had seen captured guerrillas in a camp in Ovamboland. 'Local people . . . up to that time had believed that the South Africans took no SWAPO prisoners.' (*Observer*, 7.3.82.)

When the Red Cross opened an office in Windhoek in August 1982, the Swiss official in charge, Peter Lutolf, complained that he did not know what was happening to SWAPO prisoners and wounded. 'We are not even informed by the authorities if there are any. It simply does not happen in any conflict or battle that you have a clash with 200 people and 45 are killed and no prisoners or wounded are taken.' (*Observer*, 7.3.82.) Red Cross officers must make known their opinions only to their superiors in Geneva. So Lutolf was forced out by the Pretoria government. But his words hit a raw nerve, for in no time the police minister announced that 23 SWAPO prisoners had been taken in the course of some 50 clashes inside Namibia.

South Africa refuses to grant prisoner-of-war status to guerrillas in the face of a convincing body of international law which indicates it should do so. The government did ratify the 1949 Geneva Convention relating to the treatment of prisoners and civilians in times of war, but this did not cover soldiers of a liberation army. As the voice of the former colonies began to be heard in the United Nations and the International Court of Justice, international lawyers turned their attention to wars against colonial subjection. The Protocols to the Geneva Convention were adopted at a conference in Switzerland in 1977. Protocol 1 extends the ambit of the Convention to 'armed conflicts in which peoples are fighting against colonial domination and alien occupation and against racist regimes in the exercise of their right to self-determination.'

Pretoria, to no one's surprise, has refused to sign. But by the beginning of 1988, 71 states had done so.

Given the special international status of Namibia, with *de jure* authority in the hands of the United Nations, which in turn recognizes SWAPO as 'the sole and authentic representative of the Namibian people', a PLAN soldier wearing a military uniform may have been excused for seeing himself in a just war and so deserving of humane treatment if captured. Indeed, in a 1983 case in the Windhoek Supreme court when three members of SWAPO were gaoled under the Terrorism Act, Judge Kenneth Bethune took these developments in humanitarian law into account in mitigation of sentence (Murray 1983, p. 100). On the other hand, a South African judge, David Curlewis, made clear his opinion of the notion of granting ANC guerrillas special status by imposing the death sentence. Much depends on the facts of each case and the perspectives of the judge. The ANC's case for recognition under Protocol 1 is not as strong as SWAPO's. On the other hand, the ANC has deposited a formal declaration under the Protocol, thus binding itself to the treaties. SWAPO did not do so, though it made a declaration of intent in terms of the Protocol, undertaking to treat South African prisoners in accordance with the Geneva Convention. One of its rare white prisoners, Johan van der Mescht, was well looked after and frequently visited by the Red Cross in a camp in Angola.

The Pretoria government likes to project itself as a humane, respected member of the comity of nations, striving to preserve 'Western Christian Civilization'. But granting legitimacy to freedom fighters was anathema to it. However, if they were not granted POW status, due process required they be tried in open court as common law criminals. But political trials, the more so when held in the shadow of the gallows, were a recurring reminder to ordinary people of the martyrs in their midst. So Pretoria ignored these humanitarian advances in international law, and often simply executed its prisoners. The corpses were first searched for relevant papers, items of identification, valuables. Their AK-47s, hand grenades, missile launchers and mortars became South African. Once dead, their bodies were covered with bushes or dug into a shallow hole, sand strewn over or left as carrion for jackals, hyenas and vultures.

In April 1985, pupils returning from their holidays to the Roman Catholic mission school at Oshikuku complained of a stench drifting in from close by. Seven bodies in an advanced state of decomposition were uncovered. The sisters reported the matter, but the police refused to investigate. Brigadier Dreyer, forced into comment by the gruesome find, admitted responsibility. They were, he explained, SWAPO insurgents killed in a 'contact' with Koevoet, and taken to Oshikuku, where there had once been a military camp, for identification. They had to be buried quickly, as the Koevoet team were in a hurry to get back to the contact. Nothing sinister about the affair, Dreyer insisted. His version conflicted with that of the locals, who claimed that Koevoet had taken several prisoners to Oshikuku and killed them there. Relatives of people detained or abducted by the police in the preceding months flocked to the burial site hoping, fearing, to learn something of their loved ones. The bodies were too far gone. Identification was impossible.

Silas Ndapuka testified at the International Commission of Inquiry into the Crimes of South Africa in Luanda in 1981. He had been tortured, first at the Uutapi military base, then at the Oshakati prison, before being transferred to a large detention camp 'and ordered to do various kinds of work, including removing the clothing from the corpses of alleged guerrillas killed by South African troops. The faces of the bodies,' he said, 'were always smashed beyond recognition and they were subsequently believed to be buried in a mass grave.' (*Focus*, April 1981.)

Occasionally relatives would be called in to view corpses at the Oshakati mortuary. *The Resister*, bulletin of the London-based Committee on South African War Resistance (COSAWR), quoted a former member of the SADF on a scene at the interrogtion centre in Oshakati: 'The heads of killed guerrillas are kept in the police morgue at the civilian hospital. . . . Sometimes prisoners are taken to the morgue to view these heads during interrogation.' (No. 23, 1983.)

Another former detainee, Rauna Nambinga, provided an example of the use of the dead for interrogation when giving evidence at the Luanda inquiry.

At Ongongo the day I remember as the most terrible one was when I was taken to a small room and in that room there were many pictures of dead people on the wall. They (the police) told me one of those people was my brother, Usko Nambinga, so I must show them which one was likely to be his. I said I did not know, then they told me that they were a hundred per cent sure that among those corpses one was my brother's. Then I was beaten almost after every question until the whole of my body was in extreme pain and my body was swollen so that even with a soft touch I could always feel pain. [*Resister*, No. 23, 1983.]

Information Gathering

The saga of the rotting bodies uncovered by the Catholic sisters at Oshikuku was not the villagers' first experience of mass murder. The Namibia Communications Centre (16.4.85, p. 2) told of how in 1983, in the early hours of a June morning, black men in camouflage uniforms, carrying automatic rifles with fixed bayonets and 'crooked magazines',

classic description of an AK-47, burst into a kraal at nearby Oshipanda.
They ransacked the huts, stole clothes, a radio and R4,000 in R20 notes
stowed away in a wardrobe, then fired a volley into the windscreen of the
family's van. The family, dressed in their night clothes, were lined up
against a wooden fence and mown down. The oldest was a 61-year-old
man, the youngest a girl of nine. A hundred or so spent cartridges were
afterwards found at the place of execution.

The radio blamed 'SWAPO terrorists' armed with 'Russian-made AK
47 rifles'. Eight people were dead, but one unharmed survivor, who had
feigned death during the fusillade, had run to the nearby security force
camp to report the massacre. A patrol was sent out, but the terrorists
had disappeared. The report was picked up by local newspapers and by
the BBC World Service. Later, the Ondangwa inquest magistrate, J. G.
Retief, found 'terrorists' to be liable for the deaths.

The survivor told another story, The moon was bright and the
attackers were identified unmistakably. The leader, Nakale, was an
infamous commander based at Okalongo Koevoet camp. The kraal
head, Hubertus Mateus Neporo, was a prosperous man by Ovambo
standards, the owner of a *cuca* shop. He may have been a donor of funds
to SWAPO. Either way, he kept his cash from the business at home,
being disinclined to leave money in the bank. By chance, Neporo was
away that night with his brother in Oshakati. Reporting the death of his
mother, wife, children, brother and friends to the Oshakati police
station the next morning, he got the impression that the police had
'foreknowlege of the incident, and made excuses as to why they would
not investigate.' There the matter rested, with the security forces no
doubt chalking it up as a disinformation success, each element having
played its part — Koevoet posing as guerrillas to discredit SWAPO; the
knee-jerk reportage of the state broadcasting station; cowed civilian
police; a magistrate's penchant for not staring the facts in the face;
finally, eight deaths to be added to the propaganda file of innocent
citizens killed by the 'terrs'. Within months, Koevoet constables were
boasting of their part in the Oshikuku murders.

Oshikuku was by no means unique. From immediately after its
formation, starting with a massacre at a wedding where guerrillas were
thought to be among the guests, Koevoet were blamed for mass killings
of ordinary people. The deaths of hundreds, probably thousands, will
not have been reported or recorded. The Windhoek Bar Council put the
matter in perspective in a 1983 memorandum. When the SWA police
claimed that malpractices were investigated and culprits duly brought
before the court, the advocates suggested that the true test was the
number and extent of people killed, raped, robbed, assaulted, who never
came before the courts.

This question cannot be answered without investigation into the number of people who disappear without trace; the number murdered by unknown persons; the number who do not complain because of fear and lack of trust in the institutions of justice; the cases where people are killed and buried without investigation or inquest; the cases where people are not prosecuted because of the shield of protection provided by the Defence Act. [p. 48.]

Koevoet spread its terror in a multitude of ways. Perhaps most traumatic of all was its lightning Casspir-raids on villages. A schoolteacher described one such:

Usually it is one truck, a Casspir, with a white South African as the leader, and a dozen black Ovambo-speaking men, Angolans and Namibians. They just drive across the crops, and don't use the gate. They run to all the people in the kraal, slapping them, shouting 'where's the terri?', and 'identi', and swear words, such as 'cunt, cunt, cunt!' or *atuka panya nenna* ['we'll make you shit', an adaptation of Afrikaans phraseology much loved of white policemen]. If you don't produce your ID card immediately, you are beaten — children, the elderly, pregnant women, it makes no real difference who you are or the state you are in . . . you know anything can happen. People can be shot, beaten to death, things will be destroyed or just taken. . . . [Interview with authors, 1987.]

Once Koevoet arrived and questioned a teenage girl about the whereabouts of SWAPO fighters. She was not sure what they were getting at, and when she asked them to repeat the question, they beat her. Now, said the parent witness (a teacher), when someone mentions *mukakunya*, his two-year-old daughter, reminded of the incident, bursts into tears. The teacher was paid a visit as he was preparing to leave Ovamboland for study abroad. No doubt to 'remind' him of the need for silence, they made his 15 year-old son lie on the ground and fired sub-machine guns around his prone body.

On other occasions Koevoet constables held the face of a boy to the mouth of the exhaust pipe of an accelerating Casspir, ostensibly to find out if guerrillas were in the neighbourhood. Solicitor David Smuts was told by the security police, 'But at least we didn't kill him, did we?' (Quoted in the film *Namibia – No Easy Road to Freedom*, 1988). They also roasted a 13-year-old boy over a fire. Titus Paulus had been sent by his mother on an errand to a neighbouring kraal. A Koevoet patrol arrived in his absence and took the boy's footprint to be those of a 'terrorist'. Shown on television, his burnt-out back, by then healing slowly, was a rare outside glimpse of the war.

That the security forces displayed such brutality towards the Ovambos was not surprising. Here were a people, half a million strong, holding the mightiest army in Africa up to ridicule, spurning the blandishments of self-government, tolerating the assassination of its traditional rulers, misrepresenting South Africa's good intentions to the outside world. 'Every Wambo is a SWAPO,' was a commonly heard refrain. The official version of Koevoet's role was the 'elimination of terrorists'. To achieve this the local population was required to offer up intelligence. But the northerners were resolutely unwilling to 'shop' their brothers and sisters. So the north was sealed off and Koevoet let loose to bludgeon the information out of the 'offenders', and to stop them giving aid and comfort to the guerrillas. South Africa's unstated agenda was to turn the north into a punchbag.

For the terror to work it was essential to cultivate the most devilish aspects of individual personalities. Sergeant Dirk Daniel Johannes Calitz provided the perfect specimen. He was described by a subordinate as 'a true leader, a man not given to fear, a man one can follow irrespective of the circumstances . . . a man who does not recognize death. He would become deeply despondent, and even aggressive, if after a week he had not killed a guerrilla.' Calitz joined Koevoet in 1980 and was one of its longest serving officers. He seldom took holidays. Over the years, he had been in many contacts, in which many of his men had been wounded or killed. Calitz himself had once stepped on an anti-personnel mine and spent four months in hospital.

By two in the afternoon in Ovamboland the accumulated heat of the sun beats down mercilessly. On patrol, you kept off the roads for fear of mines. If you sat on top of the Casspir, arms and face were scratched by the thorn trees, but below, the cab was an inferno. On this particular August day Calitz was worried about the safety of his girlfriend in Oshakati after a guerrilla bombardment the previous night.

Zulu Sierra roared into the hamlet of Ehoma. Calitz instructed his drivers to hive off and see what they could make of the local farmers. Calitz drove over a field, straight through the growing crops, before ramming into a hedge next to the house of Wilhelm Haindongo. The farmer was angry. He remonstrated fearlessly. There was a heated exchange in Oshivambo with one of the 'span'. The farmer was not going to talk to anyone who broke his fence, but 'no', he had never seen SWAPO.

When the conversation was translated into Afrikaans, Calitz jumped down, wrenched a heavy stake out of the fence and clubbed Haindongo to death. The weapon was said by Judge Johan Strydom at his trial to be 'formidable'. When a psychiatrist described the farmer's 'provocation' as 'the match to the gunpowder which led to a total loss of control of his [Calitz's] emotions,' the judge disagreed. The provocation was not all that serious. Calitz should have been able to distinguish between right and wrong as he rained blows over head and body, pursuing his prey across the yard. Having lost the first stake, he grabbed another, though by now Haindongo was 'seriously wounded'.

Sensing he might have some explaining to do, Calitz told his unit to conceal the crime. He concocted a story. Haindongo had pointed a gun at him and he had struck out in self-defence. He ordered his second-in-command, Jacques Fobian, to hide SWAPO weapons and uniforms in a wheat field. (Fobian explained at the trial that while on missions in the war zone they usually took with them arms and ammunition of the type used by the guerrillas for the purpose, he hastened to assure the court, of showing them to civilians to find out if they had seen such weapons before.) The armoury was then uncovered, and two sons of the dead man were ordered to pick them up. They refused, and so left no tell-tale fingerprints. In the meantime, the black 'span'-members buried the father's body. It was dug up when the CID opened an inquiry. The investigating detective went to Calitz's base and managed to page through the Koevoet record book. Wilhelm Haindongo, it noted, had been killed 'in an action against the enemy.' (*Windhoek Observer*, 21.11.87.) Calitz was convicted of murder and sentenced to 10 years imprisonment. He appealed, was granted bail, and was promoted by Koevoet. The appeal has not yet been heard.

There was no suggestion in the trial that Haindongo was suspected of running a PLAN aid-and-comfort station. No informers were produced to state as much. Informers undoubtedly existed, and they could do damage, though often for personal rather than political reasons. A Koevoet policeman would persuade his mother or brother to pass on small talk circulating on the village grapevine. One eyewitness described Koevoet sending 'three or four men into a village with lots of money in their pockets and softening up the children with sweets and presents.' In 1985 one man supplied details of an operation and three guerrillas were killed as a result. Afterwards, Koevoet came to the man's *cuca* and in front of the customers said, 'Here's your watch.' On another occasion, a woman was publicly rewarded for her information. She quit her village in a hurry, no doubt because she knew SWAPO considered informers as much a part of the war machine as any soldier. Once a finger could be justifiably pointed at the culprit, the guerrillas were contacted. There was said to be a scale of warnings from a firm reminder to desist, to execution or an attack on the house of the alleged spy if he or she was protected by tribal guards.

Jonas Paulus

The bespectacled young man in the dock had the air of a first-time traffic offender about to lose his licence. The impression was misleading. It was the Windhoek Supreme Court, and the judge was pronouncing sentence: that Jonas Paulus, Koevoet special constable, 'be taken from here to a place of safety where you will be hanged by the neck until you are dead.' His crimes — the murder of an elderly farmer, attempted rape, attempted murder, robbery with aggravating circumstances. The trial in 1983 was the first time a member of Koevoet had faced capital charges in a court of law. The short violent life of this mission-educated Angolan provides an inside view of how an uncomplicated boy was turned into a machine of death for the apartheid army.

Jonas Paulus was an Ovambo whose father farmed 20 miles north of the Namibian border. At nine he was sent to a Catholic boarding school, where he had no trouble with his work, learnt Portuguese, studied the Bible, attended church regularly. Until the age of 14 life was unruffled and easy-going. Then five centuries of colonialism in Angola came to an abrupt end. The settlers went home or to South Africa, Rhodesia and Zaire. Men with beards drifted out of the forest — UNITA's political commissars — to lecture the boys on the meaning of independence and the dangers of communism.

> Defence counsel Roux: 'What is communism?' — Paulus: 'It is whites and blacks, they have a group and they live together.'
>
> Roux: 'Why is communism bad?' — 'They have a bad government. Communists are the sort of people who, if you have a lorry it doesn't belong to you. If you have a shop, it doesn't belong to you. That is why they are bad people.' [Court transcript, p. 335.]

At the outbreak of the civil war, Jonas' school was closed and he and his friends enrolled in Savimibi's army, by then in league with South Africa. They were given six months training before going into combat with the Angolan army. Kraals were burnt, civilians massacred, the Cubans brought tanks and artillery, the SADF armed and fed the young Jonas and his comrades, and dropped bombs which burnt the land and set people on fire. Asked in court how many people he had killed, Jonas replied, 'I didn't count the number, but I know it was a lot of people.' (Court transcript, p. 334.)

By 1979 South Africa and its UNITA surrogates were losing their grip in southern Angola. Jonas and some friends, chased by 'Cubans' (an omnibus description UNITA used even in reference to MPLA soldiers and PLAN guerrillas) fled across the border and enlisted with the so-called Border Guard (*Grenswag*), undergoing a three-month training course in Ondangwa, SADF headquarters.

In early 1980, Paulus moved to Koevoet, and became an exemplary special constable, a fearless programmed killer. On patrol he liked to sit on top of the armoured vehicle and when a 'conflict situation' arose, would jump down and advance directly to where the guerrillas had taken refuge or laid their ambush. Warrant Officer George Norval testified that 'he ran directly into the line of fire . . . a man who could be described as scoffing at death . . . a fighter storming the enemy.' For Norval, he was 'one of the best soldiers he had yet encountered.' He 'could not say that Paulus attached much value to human life, particularly in a conflict situation.' Norval admitted that black special constables were trained to show no mercy. They were trained with only one idea in mind — extermination. A Koevoet fighter could be described as a 'machine of death'. Twice Paulus had driven over a mine. A rocket had ripped into his Casspir killing a crewman. Paulus had also been wounded several times.

Basic pay was between R300 and R350 a month, but the major incentive was the *kopgeld* or bounty money of R100 to R300 for guerrillas taken dead or alive. Once, after what must have been an orgy of killing, Paulus received R450 in 'head money'. It is hardly surprising that Koevoet policemen, having sated themselves for a week, or been frustrated at not achieving a lucrative contact, were hyped-up when they came off duty. Here they faced other hazards and were obliged to live in Oneshila, the Oshakati location, along with other armed men from the home guard and the army. Wherever they went while off duty they had to be on their guard. A gun would invariably lie on the table as they tried to relax over a beer.

Jonas Paulus lived in Oneshila in a house attached to a *cuca*. On 2 January 1983, he and a fellow Angolan Koevoet, Paulus Mattheus, aged 23, drank a bottle of cheap South African wine, followed it with a half jack of whisky, and at midnight went on a robbery-and-rape spree in the surrounding kraals. They were 'slightly drunk'. Paulus carried an AK-47 and posed as a guerrilla. They entered the kraal of headman Robert Amunwe at Oshandubala, fired three shots into his body and ran off.

There followed a trail of abducting young girls, numerous assaults and robberies. 'We are SWAPO guerrillas', the victims were warned, 'and you will be shot if you do not go along with us'. The Amunwe family complained to the Oshakati civil police, which sent an experienced adjutant officer, Simeon Nghosi, to arrest the two men. He had once made an official complaint to his superiors about armed Koevoet men coming into the location and robbing and wounding, but nothing had been done about it. 'It doesn't matter whether it is a black constable or a white one, they don't care a damn,' he said. In the courtroom, Officer Nghosi was unwilling to reveal all he knew about Koevoet. 'Where I move around they will say I spoke badly of

Koevoet . . . they will curse me, or kill me.' Paulus was eventually arrested after throwing a hand-grenade at his pursuers. It did not explode. His behaviour towards his fellow policemen made his actions difficult to overlook, however valuable a member of his *span* he might be. Besides, he was Angolan and black to boot.

On the opening day of the trial Paulus, who had been bailed on his own recognizances, appeared 'casually dressed with the sleeves of his corduroy windcheater rolled up to his thin wrists . . .' (*Windhoek Advertiser*, 21.9.83). He hardly looked like a man who had spent half his 28 years fighting wars.

After conviction, an experienced neurologist and psychiatrist, Dr. Charles Shubitz, gave testimony in mitigation. He had found Paulus so thoroughly indoctrinated by both UNITA and Koevoet that, although he had been a perfectly normal little boy, his 'sense of moral responsibility had been removed.' The motivation of and concept behind Koevoet was, he argued, 'barbaric'. It was clear that Paulus had been brainwashed into becoming an efficient killer. 'I am certain . . . that his mind was turned despite the fact that he claims to go to church twice a month.' He was not, however, a psychopath,

> a person who, for no apparent reason from a very early age . . . commits anti-social behaviour which is not acceptable to the community. I don't see that picture here . . . he was acting in accordance with instructions given to him . . . he was instructed to behave in a certain way, he did his job, in fact he was a very good soldier. [All Shubitz's quotes from the court transcript, pp. 424–5.]

Paulus was hanged in Windhoek just before noon on 4 June 1985.

After the trial, a police spokesman assured the public that the force would not condone any atrocities by any unit. But there would be no inquiry into the events unveiled in court. 'The accused was off duty at the time of the offence,' he explained. 'He therefore did not act on command for his unit, Koevoet. On the contrary, he was arrested by members of Koevoet, as a result of which justice could take its course.' He added that 'from time to time you get a member who goes out of line. If the police see to it that these people are caught and brought to justice then there is little more they can do.' (*Cape Times*, 7.12.83.)

Death in Kavango

When, in 1982, SWAPO made deep inroads into western Kavango, the response was particularly ill-tempered. The government had, after all, characterized SWAPO as exclusively Ovambo. The shortish life and sudden death of Jona Hamukwaya illustrates the hazards of being an educated black under South African rule.

The Okavangos live along the river from the point where it emerges from Angola to where it leaves for the final charge into the swamps of Botswana. Fish are plentiful and there is irrigation for virtually any crop they choose to plant. One day it could be Namibia's breadbasket. Isolated, self-sufficient, the people were not welcoming to outsiders. But war blasted the rural idyll asunder. Its capital, Rundu, lay at the crossroads of several conflicts. Here was a large army base and Koevoet's regional headquarters. Here too South Africa trained Savimbi's UNITA's rebels, while the Angolan Buffalos came for 'rest and recreation'. The town's commercial prosperity was a product of war — high-spending soldiers and civil servants, the ivory and timber Savimbi sold to finance his operations, oil and arms going east to make his resistance possible. This was not the place for SWAPO to rear its troublesome head. When it did, the region was subjected to a reign of terror, untold deaths, and widespread depopulation as thousands of peasants fled the areas of most intense conflict.

Sergeant Norman Keith Abrahams was unusual in the police force in being English-speaking. Stationed first in Caprivi, he was then transferred to Kavango as section leader of a Koevoet span. His personal knowledge of his black subordinates was restricted to nicknames. When it came to surnames, he said, his mind went blank. In mid-November 1982, Abrahams' four Casspirs were ordered to the Nkurenkuru area of western Kavango, so extensively infiltrated it had been designated a 'red area'. They linked up with another Koevoet group, under Constable Phillip Kriel, to converge on the hamlet of Namatatu. Abrahams had with him a local informer who told him that insurgents were 'coming in the evening and are being fed and helped.' Accompanied by the informer, Abrahams entered the kraal of a 30-year-old teacher, Jona Hamukwaya, and his wife, Katriena. The couple denied harbouring terrorists, and were butted in the back and chest by the visitors.

The team returned to Namatatu primary school the next morning. The teachers were standing in the sun waiting for classes to begin. The informer pointed out Hamukwaya. The previous evening, he said, seven insurgents had visited his kraal. Abrahams later claimed that he arrested the teacher under AG 9 to be taken back to Rundu for questioning. But first he wanted 'to find out in which direction the insertions [infiltrators] had gone, so that I could act on the spot.' Abrahams drove to the river, stopping 100 yards from the bank. He sent his black constables away to search for the spoor of guerrillas. The radio black man, nicknamed Mugabe, was left in the Casspir. Abrahams and Constable Kriel walked their prisoner to the river.

What happened next is not entirely clear, because at the inquest

Abrahams refused to answer fully for fear that he might incriminate himself. But Mrs. Hamukwaya, who had gone to the river with other women to draw water, was horrified to hear the screams of her husband. She ran to see what was going on, but three black Koevoet constables headed her off. It is not known for certain what injuries Hamukwaya had sustained during his 30 minutes alone with Abrahams, but the whole village believed he had been beaten to death with a stick.

In court, Abrahams gave a version of how the injuries were sustained. After the interrogation, Hamukwaya's vest was removed and tied tightly over his eyes. As the blindfolded prisoner climbed into the Casspir, he had tripped over the sharp edge of a box of mortars and hit his head. Later, at Nkurenkuru police station, Abrahams had ordered his two white subordinates, Sergeant Alberto Sciotatti and Constable 'Spook' (Ghost) Gouws, to take Hamukwaya to an underground canteen. Suddenly, the prisoner, still blindfolded and allegedly firmly clasped by his captors, slipped feet-first down the eleven wooden steps, once again hitting his head. Over the previous decades, an uncommonly large number of political prisoners held by the South African Special Branch had had similar 'accidents'.

Abrahams said the prisoner 'was busy getting up by himself, but he was still blindfolded. When I got to him, I removed the blindfold and asked him whether he was hurt . . . He said in the negative that he was alright . . . I then helped him to sit . . . and told him to sit against the wall.' He had then asked Hamukwaya if he wanted something to eat. He said, 'no', but asked for water. Then Sergeant Abrahams started on his lunch.

Abrahams continued his story:

> He lay down and I finished eating . . . then I heard the deceased making gurgling sounds . . . I took his tie off and opened his shirt and I saw something there is not right, so I tried to give him chest massage. I was under the impression that he was having a heart attack . . . Then I found that he had already expired.

Abrahams had then gone upstairs and said to Gouws and Sciocatti, 'It seems as though this guy, the deceased, had expired.' Mr Farlam (the Hamukwaya family lawyer) asked: 'Then they came and looked?' — 'Only Sergeant Gouws, they didn't believe me.' Farlam: 'Sergeant Sciocatti?' — 'He stayed at the top. He was busy making tea.'

Pathologists from Cape Town's Groote Schuur Hospital told a different story. The 'injuries indicated that he had been dragged and subjected to massive trauma on his back, probably inflicted by a blunt object. He was dead by 10.30 am, well before the fall.' Their evidence suggested what the villagers believed to have occurred — Jona was beaten to death at the river. The inquest magistrate found that death was caused by 'an unlawful act or omission by certain members of Koevoet who could not be identified.' Abrahams, though warned of the possibility of a murder charge six months before the inquest, was not prosecuted. The government paid out R58,000 to the Hamukwaya family, as much as the dead man would have earned in a life-time's teaching.

But Koevoet constables did appear in the Rundu magistrate's court after the killing of a farmer, Kudimu Katanga. He and a friend had crossed the Kavango river to cut poles for their hut and were intercepted by Koevoet on their return. Katanga was forced to run 10 kilometres in front of the Casspir, allegedly to find a gun. Exhausted from the run and beaten repeatedly with sticks, he collapsed, was hit with an ox yoke, and died soon after. Two black constables were convicted of common assault and fined R30 [£12] or 10 days and R60 [£24] or 20 days respectively. The white officer in charge was, said the magistrate, 'highly irresponsible' for failing to intervene, but that did not constitute an offence (*Star*, 14.11.83.).

The 200 mourners who crowded into the small church at Nkurenkuru to bury Hamukwaya and mourn Katanga were not cowed. Rudolf Ngondo, though a former member of the Kavango Ministers' Council, vowed to establish a new graveyard next to the main road where people who died at the hands of the Security Forces would be buried for future generations to see when they passed. A year later, Koevoet section commander 'Jumbo' De Villiers complained that 'the entire western Kavango is rotten and we get no cooperation from the local population.' (*Windhoek Advertiser*, 29.10.83.) Small wonder, given that it was the self-same De Villiers who had taken another Kavango teacher out of his classroom and encouraged him to talk about guerrillas by attaching wires from a field radio to his ear lobes and turning the current on.

The publicity surrounding the Paulus and Hamukwaya cases forced the government onto the defensive in parliament and outside. White MPs and journalists were briefed in the operational area. An Atrocities Liaison Committee, comprising members of the Ovambo government and security force personnel, was said to sit on Wednesdays to hear cases. 'We do not have any serious problems with atrocities in Owambo,' Commandant A. A. Kleynhans told them, 'but that is not to say we have no atrocities.' (*Star*, 7.5.84.) Namibia's police chief, Lieut-Gen. Verster, explained that allegations against Koevoet were investigated 'from an entirely neutral point of view', in other words, by the 'SWA police and their CID'. (*Windhoek Advertiser*, 21.2.86.)

Colonel Gerrit Badenhorst of the Security Police gave the assurance that 'clear instructions were given to all policemen to see to the bodily and spiritual welfare of any detainees.' 'Sterk' Hans Dreyer resorted to the 'honest copper' version. 'They are merely ordinary policemen engaged in what is essentially police work, protecting the law-abiding bulk of the population against the depredations of those who seek to electioneer with guns and mines'. (Both quotes *Windhoek Advertiser*, 30.11.83.) As if to prove the point that Koevoet were just a squad of plodding flatfoots, Andreas Shipanga, the 'turned' cabinet chairman of the interim government, inspected a Koevoet guard of honour in Oshakati, and praised them for their performance (*Namibian*, 1.5.87). Government propaganda sought to situate Koevoet in a Western mould. A pamphlet described Koevoet tactics as 'reminiscent of the Hearts and Minds campaign used so successfully by the British in the Borneo campaign against the Communists between 1964–72'. (*On Record*, 16.11.84.)

What Did Koevoet Achieve?

If Koevoet's achievements were measured purely on a brutality scale, then it must be said to have been a brilliant success. Sometimes a critic pierced the egocentric armour. *Cape Times* political columnist, Gerald Shaw, was moved to write that 'the Koevoet strong-arm squads are outdoing General Kitchener's farm-burning bully-boys of 1900 and 1901 and creating frightful legends of oppression.' (7.4.84.) The comparison with the worst excesses of the British general who, almost a century after the Boer War, retains a prime place in Afrikaner demonology, will have struck a raw nerve. Most Afrikaners would not be happy to see their own anti-colonial struggle cited as a precedent for that of the Namibian people.

It must be remembered that what is known of Koevoet's activities is the one-ninth of the iceberg. Only rarely was the public able to follow the proceedings of a trial or inquest, though the advent of the *Namibian* newspaper (1985) and the Namibia Communications Centre in London (1984) provided more regular exposure. But the day-to-day details of its terror remain locked in the collective memories of the people of the north. Only true liberation from South Africa will provide a fuller picture.

For individual members of Koevoet, the unit's ten-year reign of terror brought social and economic rewards. The crowbar killers became a new elite, with money in their pockets and the ability to enjoy it. The prospect of being able to buy a *cuca* shop was incentive enough on its own to enlist. The *cuca* is the centre of Ovambo social life, a general dealer's store doubling as a pub. (The name is derived from an Angolan beer once brewed in Lubango.) Owning a *cuca* gave status and an income considerably in excess of what could be earned in the abattoir, hospital, petrol station or market. While it may have been unsafe to return to their home villages, among their friends the constables had the protective muscle to run successful businesses.

But the social cost was high, and not only in an increased incidence of alcoholism. The high-spending, heavy-drinking men of Koevoet turned Oshakati into a Wild West town, with guns loosed off at random by off-duty revellers, an epidemic of rapes, and cinemas and discos frequented at one's peril. On weekday mornings the radio phone-in programme, *Eyakulo loshiwana* (literally, 'serving the nation'), broadcast messages from parents searching for missing daughters, condolences for loved ones killed in accidents or assault, apologies to girl-friends injured in brawls.

With the civil police terrified of Koevoet, many murders remained unsolved. A resident explained:

> When an off-duty Koevoet kills someone, the police will be called and the man is arrested. But I can guarantee that he will be free as a bird within a month . . . Within a week, his combat unit goes to the police station, makes up a story that they are going into the bush and the person being held is their best man, so either you give him to us or we are not going out. Everybody knows the obligation to fight SWAPO, and the police are frightened, so they let him go. And then he is free for good.

Sometimes, however, a prosecution was unavoidable, as when a Koevoet warrant officer shot a woman outside an Oshakati *cuca* shop when she tugged at his coat and asked for ten cents. He was gaoled for four years for culpable homicide (manslaughter). In command of ten men, the officer had had no formal education and was unable to read or write. Sometimes the killing habit was turned on comrades. Filipus Shetikela returned to his home in Oshakati to find another constable in bed with his girl-friend. He emptied his sub-machine gun into the couple. He pleaded drunkenness, but was convicted of murder with extenuating circumstances. Killings of this sort were happening too often, the judge said, and he had to impose a salutary sentence. Shetikela was gaoled for six years, two suspended (*Windhoek Advertiser*, 14.6.84).

It is probable that Koevoet killed more people, person for person, than any unit in African military history. Yet in crude monetary terms, was its 'terr-hunting' cost-effective? Provisional figures in 1984 indicated that each SWAPO 'kill' cost R1.7m (*Star*, 28.1.85). By this measure, more than R1 billion was spent on 584 corpses. If purely military costs, estimated at R547 million, are factored in, then the guerrillas came more cheaply at R937,000 a head. On the other hand, if the unknown number of bogus PLAN kills claimed by Koevoet are factored out, the operation becomes more expensive once again. With a monthly average of 21 contacts, the Treasury was being drained for a low return.

That so much was invested in counter-insurgency reveals the seriousness with which South Africa took the SWAPO threat. Koevoet was developed as part of the strategy of exporting the war to Angola, while neutralizing the Ovambos and Okavangos. For a few years after 1984, guerrilla activity did appear to decelerate, but it did not cease and South Africa could never reverse the tide. All the while, Koevoet's terror had the powerfully negative effect of hardening more and more people against the occupation. In the widest diplomatic sense, Koevoet's role was an abysmal failure. Defeating SWAPO depended in the end on winning over the north, as much as on overcoming the guerrillas. The decision to go ever deeper into Angola in order, first, to destroy PLAN, and then to deliver a decisive blow against the Angolan and Cuban armies, had its roots in the resistance of the Namibian people. A direct thread from this unwavering northern support for SWAPO (backed by a substantial southern following) runs to the enormous Russian and Cuban commitment of arms and men and P. W. Botha's 'Stalingrad' at Cuito Cuanavale. In retrospect, all Koevoet achieved was to delay slightly the inevitable, which it did with the bludgeoning effectiveness of a crowbar.

The depressing fact of South African politics, however, is that the terrifying decade of Koevoet will be turned to good use by Pretoria. Those who, over the years, have done their stint on the border, have returned more brutalized, but also with some mean ideas for containing the next great battle for African liberation. Like a cancer, the Flecha–Selous–Koevoet brand of state counter-terror has spread its tentacles across the sub-continent. Angolan Portuguese were fighting for South Africa's Buffalo unit against the MPLA government; former black Rhodesian Scouts were enrolled with the remnants of the Muzorewa contingent trained by South Africa in the north-eastern Transvaal to destabilize Zimbabwe; Ron Reid Daly was commander-in-chief of Chief Kaiser Matanzima's Transkei bantustan defence force until he was sacked for overplaying his hand; black and white Flechas have formed the backbone of the South African-backed Renamo bandits which threaten the very existence of the Mozambican government. One-time Selous Scouts and Rhodesian mercenaries joined the ranks of Koevoet. An unholy diaspora of South African surrogates, black and white, African and western, are in the field fighting to keep the white man in power a while longer in his last Southern African redoubt.

4.

Life in the War Zone

It is early 1988 in Ovamboland, year 22 of a seemingly endless war. The curfew starts promptly at six p.m. In January, the sun is still high above the western horizon, but the women hurry back from the fields, baskets balanced on their heads, calling out to family and neighbours that the dangerous hour has come. Children, cattle, dogs, ducks, bicycles, all that moves must be within the reed walls of the kraal in good time. Trigger-happy soldiers once fired on a boy herding cattle only minutes after the curfew had begun, though he was within hailing distance of his home. If the north of Namibia is under military occupation by day, at night it is a dark prison, its 600,000 inhabitants locked into their cells like dangerous criminals.

Inside, in their kraal near the Angolan border, the Ehandu family (names are fictitious for security reasons) settles down for the evening. While Mrs. Ehandu prepares the meal in the kitchen, her eldest daughter, Miriam, a student nurse, pounds millet next door. In the boys' hut, Theo, a standard 7 pupil in the local high school, works on his arithmetic homework. It is getting darker, and though the hut has only one small window, he will continue with the natural light until he can no longer avoid turning on the spirit lamp. Outside, his two younger sisters try to tempt him into a game of hide-and-seek.

In his private hut, Pastor Hidipo Ehandu sits at the table preparing his sermon for the coming Sunday. He has managed to cycle home in time, having visited the family of a parishioner, a member of which has been arrested on suspicion of aiding a group of SWAPO guerrillas reported to be travelling south towards the white farmlands. He half hears the comforting household noises: the crickets, a hectoring cock, the kid separated from the nanny goat. A thunder crack rolls across the sky. The blessed rain is hours away still. He ponders a suitable text . . . his flock expects firm words, couched in biblical orthodoxy, to buoy their spirits against the endless occupation. He picks up his fountain pen, but is interrupted by the call to supper.

The pastor waits for his family to settle down, says grace; then they lean forward and dip their fingers into the clay pot. The *oshifima* (thick millet porridge) is hot, but they scoop it into their mouths before any damage is done. Tonight, as well, they dine on onions and cabbage from the vegetable patch alongside the kraal wall. They drink *oshikundu*, a thirst-quenching light beer Mrs. Ehandu brews from millet. The family discusses the expected return of Mrs. Ehandu's brother from his job on the uranium mine. The pastor reads from the Bible, and then, once again, recounts the story of how he was overcharged by a taxi driver while on a church mission to London . . . gradually the family retires to their huts and soon all is dark and silent.

A mile away across the dusty plain an armoured personnel carrier stops in a cluster of thorn trees. A cloud scurries by and the moon reveals a group of uniformed men, all black, dropping noiselessly to the ground. The vehicle lumbers off and they gather round their leader for a final briefing, then set off at a trot. Scouts split off to the right and the left.

At 2 a.m. the household is woken by a loud rapping on the main gate of the kraal. The dogs bark excitedly. Mrs Ehandu calls out to her husband. The pastor asks who is there. A voice answers in Kwanyama, the local language: 'We are comrades', implying they are from SWAPO. The pastor: 'Which comrades? There is a curfew, we cannot go out.' The voice: 'No, come out, we are your brothers, fighting for the freedom of this country. We are lost and want to find out the way.'

He opens the gate. They warn him to watch out for South African soldiers. But when he steps out, he finds at least 20 men dressed in green camouflage uniform, with SWAPO badges and forage caps, standing around seemingly unconcerned about detection. Each carries the guerrilla's favourite weapon, an AK47 sub-machine gun, and bazookas, even a mortar, are on open display. The pastor asks himself how they can be so numerous in the midst of 'enemy' territory.

The men say they have just arrived from Angola. They are not locals and the pastor cannot be expected to know them. But they have been told he can be helpful to them. 'You must wake your wife so she can prepare food for us.' No, says the pastor, it is too late, and a fire would be noticed.

He plays for time. They say they want to kill 'puppets'. The usual term for informers is *omalandwambongo* (people who are bought with money), but they use the word *eepappeta*, from the English. The pastor protests. 'They are our brothers. You are fighting in the bush for their freedom as well. By killing them you are doing what the South Africans want.'

He asks their names. The leader says he is Dengambulu, meaning 'hit the Boer'. Another is Ndilimani, for 'Dynamite', a third is Kapanya, the 'Bully'. All are *noms-de-guerre* commonly used by SWAPO combatants.

Then the leader says: 'Look, you are evidently not sure of us. We will come back tomorrow night and will give you a chance to think about it.' They leave, going directly to the home, five miles away, of a prosperous *cuca* owner, Meme Maria. Her husband is away in Windhoek. They knock on the door. 'Ah, Meme Maria, we are your children in the bush. We come from Pastor Ehandu, who told us you collaborate with him in helping us, your children, from SWAPO. Please cook us some food.'

Meme Maria says, 'OK, my children, Pastor Ehandu is my pastor, I know him well. Welcome.' She makes *oshifima*, kills a chicken and cooks it. They eat and drink. 'Thanks very much, Meme. Perhaps we shall return in two weeks time.' They leave.

At seven a.m. the next morning, before there is time even to sweep away the tell-tale footprints, three Casspirs carrying white soldiers and black men surround her house. 'Meme, tell us what happened last night. We hear SWAPO was here . . .'

'Yes', she replies, 'it is true, they were here. I cooked for them because I had no choice. They were heavily armed and the young men threatened me. And they told me they had come from my pastor.' The white officer: 'You must choose. Either we burn down your house or you go to prison.' Meme Maria: 'The house does not belong to me. It is my husband's. He did not give food to SWAPO.'

Meme Maria spent three months in Oshakati prison, where she was beaten up by her interrogators. The night of her arrest, a woman had come to tell Pastor Ehandu that Meme Maria was in prison. There were rumours that he had sent soldiers to her house. But everyone knew that the uniformed men going round impersonating SWAPO belonged to the police extermination squad with the emblem of the green mamba and whose name was Koevoet.

Behind the White Wire

A South African attorney-general in Windhoek once suggested that 'the public haven't the foggiest idea what's going on in the operational area'. Whites in the south, he said, 'continue to have parties and even the blacks are able to live relatively comfortably.' (*Pretoria News* 12.12.83.) Used to turning a blind eye to rebellion in black suburbs five miles from their homes, it was small wonder the whites of the region, let alone Namibia, mindlessly ignored the havoc in Ovamboland.

The most charitable thing one could say of the whites living within the war zone is that they were not overly interested in the methods used to enforce their occupation. They remained emotionally, if not always physically, behind the fence in Oshakati East '*wit dorp*' ('white town'), sealed off from real life. On seeing the rolled wire fortifications of South Africa's most northerly group area, Archbishop Desmond Tutu remarked how strange it was that 'those who claim to be protecting the people are safely living behind fences in Oshakati, while those who are supposed to be protected are walking freely around.' (*Namibian*, 15.4.88.) Blacks had to show their identity card at the entrance-gate, where a board once proclaimed 'SWAPO's struggle is futile'. They entered only for labour — once the parcel was delivered or the lawn mown, they departed.

Here was a graphic example of the white South African raj in operation, with South Africans of no particular distinction, other than a pale pigment, enjoying subsidized housing, some with swimming pool thrown in, sports grounds, free education for the children, regular flights home, salaries in excess of what was available in the Republic. A petty bureaucrat from the Orange Free State lived the life of a prince.

In comfortable *wit* suburbia, civil servant and businessman, soldier and Koevoet officer, gathered at one anothers' homes to *braai* (barbecue) Namibian beef or game shot in the veld, sipping Windhoek Export lager and eyeing a Charles Bronson or Steve McQueen video, or, for the true patriot, an Afrikaans war feature like *Boetie gaan Border toe* (My brother goes to the Border). 'The Border', a group of visiting white women pointed out, 'is where our sons become men'. (*Paratus*, August 1988.) Saturday afternoons were for the national sport, rugby, or you stayed at home with the soldiers' radio request programme, Forces Favourites. On Sunday morning you made your appearance at the Dutch Reformed Church.

Oshakati was not entirely a white bed of roses. The Koevoet base lay close to the white ghetto, and there were also army installations in the neighbourhood. Every house had a sand-bagged bomb shelter in the back garden and every so often the guerrillas drew near and lobbed rockets into the homes lining the tidy streets. In an effort to deter them, at regular intervals during the night, tower-mounted machine guns fired into no-go areas which were lit up by flares. A resident, writing under the cloak of anonymity, complained to the press that the army were 'hiding among the locals' and, being the intended target, should build their bases far away.

One bombardment in July 1985 caused extensive damage, including a direct hit on the house of a Koevoet warrant officer. The shells were aimed at the nearby Koevoet base. A defence force statement gave an idea of the resulting damage. There were hits on a swimming pool and a car at house number 162; damage to a caravan and a mobile house parked in the north-western section of the town; a mortar bomb landed on a football field; three mortars struck the tarred surface of the Oshakati civilian airfield, causing no damage; mortars landed on the houses of Mr. Piet Moller of ENOK (the state development corporation), Mr. Niewoudt, an employee of the Water Board, Staff

Sergeant 'Spanners' van Heerden, Commandant Rinus van Heerden of the Armed Forces, Warrant Officer Coen Coumms, and Warrant Officer Nick Smit of the police security branch. The assault group were chased by an army unit, but were reported to have got clean away across the border. The suburb's racial exclusivity did ensure that if anyone was going to get hurt, they were white — or 'honorary white' — Laban Hamata, head of Radio Wambo, was permitted to live inside the town. His car was destroyed by a SWAPO shell.

To venture beyond Oshakati was considerably more chancy. On a Sunday outing with his family, Warrant Officer Frederick Petrus Johannes Cornelius, stationed at Ondangwa, drove over a mine, and died later. Oshakati was by no means the only apartheid fortress in the north. Communities of colonial administrators, traders, teachers, magistrates, soldiers, policemen, their wives and children, were scattered across the country, surviving in an alien environment through the exercise of terror, real or threatened.

How 'The Other Half' Lived

In another world, distanced by the thickness of a Casspir's armour plating, lived the people of the north. In the face of occupation and war, of 12,000 deaths and tens of thousands in exile, they struggled to preserve normality. This, to be sure, was not always possible, for long before the outbreak of hostilities their world had been disrupted by outside forces. Yet, for the many living away, on the mines and farms, in camps and colleges abroad, in the squalid shanty towns of Oshakati, the homestead, fringed by *makalani* palms and hut-high anthills, was a nostalgic focus of family life. Here, more than in Windhoek or Angola or the UN Security Council, was waged the essential struggle for liberation. The resistance of ordinary people, often illiterate, unversed in political dogma, without a consciousness of similar struggles elsewhere, was the knot South Africa could not unravel. Their bodies were not broken by Koevoet, nor their spirit by a campaign for their 'hearts and minds'. If one were to ask a northerner about this heroic resistance in the face of all odds, the questioner would be looked at quizzically, and then told: 'But the South Africans had no right to be here.'

The Ovambos crossed into Namibia in the 16th century, the south-western vanguard of the Bantu migrations sweeping towards the Indian Ocean. They were cattle-raisers and, finding the grazing in the floodplain of the Cuvelai to their liking, trekked no further. Indeed, the name Kwanyama, the largest Ovambo clan, is derived from *onyama* ('meat'). They are inveterate meat-eaters. The soil's crust, though fragile, provided food for a varied diet. The land is table-flat and by the time the summer rains have ceased in February, water will have flowed from the hills of southern Angola to fill a vast flood plain, the *efundja*, enveloping great stretches of northern Ovamboland. The small fresh-water fish, the bream and pink-bellied barbel of this inland sea, are a delicacy of the local cuisine. Silt washed down by the river enriches the soil, and the water refreshes the baobab and the wild maroela tree, whose overripe fruit 'makes the monkeys dance'. Here, half the population of Namibia could survive on a mere six per cent of its land surface, provided the rains were abundant. These days *mahangu* (millet) is the staple, eaten as porridge and drunk as *oshikundu* (light beer). 'Millet rules our lives,' they say, and the proud family cattle graze the harvest stubble, fertilizing the soil. In 1853, an early British explorer, Francis Galton, came across a prosperous land of honey and porridge and sleek, fat cattle. Later, the Swede, Charles Andersson, described the homestead encircled by a hedge of thorns where girls pounded millet for storage in giant baskets, out of reach of vermin. The grain in the baskets was said to provide enough food for five years of drought.

The German missionaries came, but the soldiers kept to the south, and the Ovambo escaped the fate of the Herero and Nama. But cyclical drought and disease brought death on an epidemic scale. A quarter of the Ovambos, some 40,000, may have perished between 1915 and 1918 from famine and influenza. (Moorsom 1982, p. 17). Then came the worst curse of all. Having driven the German army out of the territory, South Africa turned its attention to Ovamboland. It was anxious to fix the precise border with the Portuguese, which entailed cutting the Ovambo-speaking people in two. The Kwanyama were the largest Ovambo clan, and their chief, Mandume, aged only 21, was determined to retain its integrity. He fought the Portuguese, losing some 5,000 men before fleeing south. When the South African commander demanded his surrender, Mandume refused. 'If the English [for South Africa was considered a British colony] want me, I am here and they can come and fetch me. I will fight till my last bullet is spent.' (First 1963, p. 99.)

Mandume's head was taken to Windhoek and displayed as a trophy, then buried near the present-day Windhoek railway station. The administrator could then report:

The country is now tranquil. Our representatives will continue to watch the situation closely and do all in their power to induce the able-bodied men of the different tribes to go south to engage themselves as labourers on the railways, mines and farms. . . . The supply from the Ukwanyama tribe has been much interrupted of late owing to Mandume's action, but I am hopeful that it will soon be restored.' [First 1963, p. 100.]

If the mines and farms had not needed an assured supply of cheap labour, Ovamboland might have been left to the rough-hewn mercies of the missionaries. But the end of the Second World War triggered a boom that only the sweat of the Ovambo could fuel. The cash brought back by the migrant workers was the nest egg for times of drought or illness, though without changing the subsistence nature of the farm economy. It bought clothes, plates, a bicycle, more recently a second-hand car, out of savings from Oranjemund or Tsumeb. To the children at home these were the 'sweetsmen', their rare appearance remembered — and looked forward to — from the gifts unpacked from tin suitcases. There came a time when the southern money was essential for the higher standard of living. Hence, the new material prosperity was constructed on the foundation of permanently fissioned family lives.

The homestead continued to function much as it had for centuries: the women planted, weeded and harvested, kept the house clean, stamped the grain and cooked the meals, bore babies and brought them up; the young boys herded cattle; the daughters bent their backs in the fields; the men steered the ox plough and built the mud or clay-brick huts. The father still slept in his individual hut, with its floor of cattle dung and roof of reeds. There was a hut for his wife (one only, since the missionaries had foreclosed on polygamy), one each for the young boys and the young girls, and for those who had reached puberty, and a spare room for guests. Elderly parents or relatives would have a hut to themselves, there being no need for the senior citizens retirement homes prevalent in the West with the break-up of the nuclear family. A row of sticks separated the sleeping quarters from the conversational and cooking sections; a larder, a place for storing pots and pans, an area for stamping the millet, the cookhouse. Meals were eaten in the open, often the men sitting separately on benches dipping fingers into the communal pot of *oshifima*, meat and dried cabbage, washed down by *oshikundu*.

The truth of the maxim, 'millet rules our lives', was proved, sometimes every three years, when the whole kraal was uprooted and moved to a pristine site so that the earth did not lose its fertility for planting the precious *mahangu*. Houses of bricks were broken up and relaid. The headman was paid two head of cattle, one of which he kept, with the other given to the chief, in whom the 'ownership' of the land resided.

In the late 1950s, Ovambo society began the sea change which has continued unabated ever since. The furnace of war and revolution has turned the soul of rural Ovamboland. Traditional values of obedience to the chief have been eroded by the new responsibilities thrust on women, the assertiveness of youth and the political consciousness of their fathers. Subservient attitudes to the white man have become a thing of the past, even if individuals still appear to treat officials with deference.

Oswald Shivute of the Ovambo administration has written of the days when 'the black man laughed when he should have got angry . . . said yes when he should have said no . . . went to places where he shouldn't have gone . . . was made to do things which he shouldn't have done . . .' (*Namibian*, 1.4.88.)

The break-up of Ovambo society accelerated in the mid-1970s, with the exodus of young men and women into exile. The war altered the balance between town and countryside, when as many as 250,000 people were driven out of the border area and dumped along the Ondangwa to Oshakati road. The urban population of Ovamboland is now said to be anything between 80,000 and 250,000. In 1981 the official figure was 4,700. At first, those in the north with money in their pockets were the teachers and nurses, or shopkeepers who had set up business with the savings from migrant labour or connections in the tribal hierarchy. But with the growth of a consumer society oiled by the easy money of the war, the region's socio-economic profile changed dramatically. Black soldiers and Koevoet became a new economic elite. The money came home in the form of 'ghetto-blasters', bicycles, or the blue-chip investments of the *cuca* or the panel-beating and motor spares shops lining the main roads, a testimony also to the driving habits of the military and Ovambos alike. *The Guardian* (30.11.87) quoted, without comment, an army colonel who claimed that the 6,000 small shops in Ovamboland once built of corrugated iron, because the canny Ovambo traders wanted to have mobility in unsettled times, were now of brick because these 'Jews of Africa' had come to recognize that the army had stabilized the area!

The wars in the region have, if anything, been more demoralizing for the San hunter–gatherers (so-called Bushmen) catapulted from the Stone Age into the most acquisitive of societies. When the San fled Angola into Caprivi in the 1975 war, the SADF settled them and their families at the remote Omega base. One visitor described the camp as having 'all the classic characteristics of a total institution: all the menfolk are in the army; the children go to a military school where they are taught Afrikaans . . . while the wives of the [white] officers arrange activities to keep the Bushmen women occupied. In addition, all widows and pensioners receive R25 a month plus food, rations and housing.' (Gordon 1984, p. 19) A later visitor said the men were paid R700 a month for hunting guerrillas. The base was a 'consumer society gone mad, with more bicycles per head than in Holland. It had got to the stage where, if a bicycle had a flat tyre, the owner might simply discard it and buy another.' (*Natal Daily News*, 16.1.87.)

The future of the San is uncertain, though SWAPO is likely to take a generous view of their collaboration. Theo-Ben Gurirab, when representative at the United Nations, talked of the tragedy of South

Africa stooping 'so low as to use these people who are not conscious of what they are doing.' As trackers, he said, they walked in front of patrolling soldiers, and in most cases 'they receive the punishment meant for the racist soldiers. Their population is small, [and] our concern is that it may be eliminated.' (Gordon 1984, p. 19.)

At least the countryside and the teeming animal life that once lived on it have a good chance of recovering from the off-duty plundering expeditions of South African officials, army officers, even P. W. Botha himself. When, in the late 1970s, SWAPO moved in to the Kaokoveld, between Ovamboland and the Atlantic Ocean, the army set the Himba tribesmen up in a home guard, arming 3,000 bow-and-arrow hunters with .303 rifles. An observer reported that, coupled with a decade of drought 'which has severely affected the delicate desert and semi-desert ecology, the effects have been devastating.' Where once were large herds of elephant and antelope, now 'long distances have to be travelled before even small pockets of wildlife are found.' (Weaver in Tötemeyer et al. 1987, p. 247.)

The Women's Lot

The dual exodus from the countryside left parishes inhabited by women, the old and the young. Trapped in the reserves, rarely recruited for work in the south, the *mater familias* was often the sole fully active adult in the homestead. In 1970, women in Ovamboland aged between 15 and 59 outnumbered men by almost two to one. The disparity can only have widened over the years. The partial relaxation of the pass laws in 1977 made it theoretically easier for a mother and her children to join a working husband, but family housing was rarely available and who would have looked after the children in her absence?

So the mother stayed at home, cultivated the fields, held the household together and bore the brunt of Koevoet. Moorsom described the typical lot of a northern woman interviewed in 1977:

> . . . apart from something like a one hour break at about 10 am to go for breakfast and to feed children, women in these areas work from 5 am to 1 pm from Monday to Saturday, every week. This is true whether you are talking about cultivation, weeding or harvesting seasons of the years. . . . After seven hours of backbreaking labour in the fields, women in the rural areas do not retire to rest for the day. They must also fetch water, grind grain into flour, prepare meals, not to mention washing the babies . . . [Moorsom 1982, p. 60.]

The woman's predicament was rendered more vulnerable by the long hours of the curfew. Koevoet knew when a woman was alone and unprotected. At best she was the object of unrestrained verbal abuse, especially when denying knowledge of guerrillas. 'This woman is talking shit, let me beat her up,' was a repeated refrain. She provided added incitement to men hyped by drink, their self-respect impaired by the knowledge that they were despised by the local population. A witness described a fairly uncommon incident:

> When they come to an area with beautiful ladies the first thing they do is to capture the women and take them in their trucks or just do the thing there in the open. It is not often reported, because of fear, and is much more prevalent than you think. If a Koevoet man is a good fighter, he can do what he likes. As for the white officer, he sits up in the driver's seat smoking a cigarette and pretends not to know what his men are doing. [Authors' interview, London, 1987.]

The ravaging of women by an occupying force is the concomitant to slaughtering their men on the field of battle. When Koevoet moved into Ovamboland, all Ovambo males came to be seen as 'SWAPOs', and it did not much matter whether the absent husband was guerrilla or migrant worker. Mrs. Maria Kamutukwata, aged 30 and pregnant with her fourth child, was sleeping in her hut near Ondangwa with her smallest child and an old lady. One morning in September 1986, before the curfew had ended, she heard knocking and after a little while the door was forced open. She identified three black soldiers (Koevoet). 'They pulled me outside and raped me. The old woman ran to the nearby houses seeking help but nobody dared come.' Mrs. Kamutukwata had been raped by Koevoet once before. On both occasions her husband was working in the south.

The number of rapes and sexual assaults reported to the authorities is thought to have been a fraction of the actual incidents. The civil rights lawyer in Windhoek, David Smuts, told a London conference (1988) that every month Oshakati hospital alone treated 10 cases of rape by members of the armed forces. Hospital staff reported an increase in the number of new-born babies abandoned on the doorstep — often fathered by members of the armed forces and with their mothers living in squatter camps; the extended family back-up was no longer available.

These exacting emotional and material presures have produced women of enhanced authority. Women had an inferior legal position in traditional Ovambo society — they did not own status property like cattle, nor become chiefs, nor participate in decision-making, though their opinions could hold weight in tribal politics. War and the absent menfolk have brought changes — women now make household decisions about cattle and crop planting, about children's schooling, about church, social and political organizations. Women hid and fed passing guerrillas, and sometimes suffered the consequences. One was 'blindfolded, subjected to electrical shock torture and repeatedly raped by South African soldiers for denying knowledge of SWAPO combatants in 1981.' (A. Murray-Hudson in Wood 1984, p. 618.) In the exile camps, female illiteracy was tackled head on. Namibian women acquired education and status abroad that would have been a social impossibility at home. They also became PLAN soldiers, drivers and mechanics, apart from the more usual nurses and doctors. Outside, mothers developed new ambitions both for themselves and their children. For their children they sought more than jobs as the teachers, nurses, and petty civil servants of colonial Namibia; and for themselves, nothing less than an equal seat round the foodbowl.

Dusk to Dawn

Beneath the cloak of the curfew, Koevoet and the army had the 'PB' (*plaaslike bevolking* or local population) at its mercy. The curfew killed, no doubt about that. Curfew-breakers died regularly, shot usually without warning — a woman with a baby on her back; a 64-year-old teacher leaving home to visit a neighbour before dusk; a woman gunned down on the outskirts of the Ondangwa air base in the dawn light of a Christmas morning. Two pregnant women getting up from their beds on a veranda to relieve themselves in the bush inside hospital grounds were shot as curfew-breakers by members of the Ovambo battalion. One died (*Weekly Mail*, 27.11.87).

But the curfew did more than kill. It outlawed the ordinary habits of daily life, the conviviality out-of-doors, the courting couple, the social visit, lads kicking a rubber ball at tree stump goalposts, the extra hour in the fields. Indeed, the summer sowing and the autumn harvest, when the whole family worked feverishly till after dark, were now occasions fraught with danger. No longer could young girls from neighbouring villages meet in the forest clearing to do traditional dances in the moonlight. These were before the war their 'night clubs', but without musical instruments, entrance fees, wine or flashing lights. No longer could the young boys, with a torch of dried palm leaves to light their way, stalk bird or rabbit with bow and arrow.

The curfew was more a punishment for being on SWAPO's side than a measure for winning the war, a resort to an old South African device for keeping the black person in their place. When a maid or garden 'boy' in South Africa wished to visit a friend or attend some function, even a church meeting, which might go on beyond the benighted hour, 'madame' would write a *laissez-passer* which had the authority of a passport in the eyes of the constabulary. In the war zone, there were no white madames.

By 1978 the war was going badly enough for Pretoria to prohibit driving in Ovamboland at any time during the night without the SADF's permission. The road curfew allowed the army to move large convoys without attracting attention. There was an understanding that night driving was allowed in the built-up area connecting Oshakati with Ongwediva but, then again, much depended on who was behind the wheel. A star of the Oshakati City football team, Ismael Mwandingi, was shot by soldiers manning an observation tower as he drove through Ongwediva one evening in July 1987. The car belonged to a prosperous businessman considered a friend of SWAPO. Ismael's girl-friend, sitting next to him, was killed, and he himself is now confined to a wheelchair.

The full curfew came into operation in 1979 with a dusk-to-dawn prohibition on movement outside the home in Ovamboland and much of Kavango. Those whose 'freedom' was being protected from the 'terrorist onslaught' were banned from being 'outside the boundary of a stand, lot or site or other place intended or normally used for human habitation, at any time during the night without the permission of a police officer. . . .' The two measures were intended to have a drastic effect on the lives of half a million people, and they did just that.

To begin with, there was a delicate problem of interpretation in the definition of the Ovambo farmer's area of human habitation. Was it restricted to the fenced-off area where people ate, slept and socialized? or did it include the outlying fields of grain and cattle? An *egumbo* (homestead) may have been unfenced, so that a family could not be certain of the limits of safe passage. By the 1980s the homestead might include a *cuca* shop, adjacent to but technically not part of the living quarters. The owner might have to check during the night that no one was breaking in thirsting for beer. A special constable found in *flagrante delicto* by the *cuca* owner could open fire and justify his action as a breach of the curfew.

As Nathaniel Petrus, a 54-year-old farmer of Oshushe discovered, the soldiers made the rules. In the January twilight he walked with a neighbour across the 200 metres of *mahangu* fields separating their homesteads. He helped herd his neighbour's cattle into the kraal, then walked through the gate separating the two homesteads. As he bid farewell, a voice shouted from the gathering dusk: he waited. The voice called again. He stayed where he was. A shot rang out and Petrus was hit in the leg. The man who fired was black, but Petrus could see that the white officer in charge was the man who had detained him at his home earlier that day. (Sworn affidavit, 15.10.86). He had not been held, but the curfew was a legalized 'catch-all' for dealing with someone known to be out of sympathy with the regime.

The imprecise language of the regulation meant that even inside the home one minded what was said and done. Villagers were told by

Koevoet that lighting fires or turning on the radio might be viewed as a way of communicating with guerrillas. The SADF even removed the bells from St. Mary's Anglican church at Odibo, accusing the ringers of relaying messages in code. The most innocent household matters had to be discussed in whispers. The melodious Kwanyama singing was stilled. Tuning in to SWAPO broadcasts from Luanda was as perilous as listening to the BBC in occupied France in World War Two. The homely sounds of the tropical night, the chirruping cricket, the restless cows and barking dogs, were drowned out by the rattle of bullets, the boom of shells, the convoys rumbling back and forth. If guerrillas were about, a light aircraft would fly over, 'sky-shouting' a warning not to shelter them. The head of the family ended the evening meal with an earnest request to the Almighty to let them wake up safe and sound, and, please, send the *makakunya* somewhere else.

The curfew was especially irksome in the matter of toilet facilities. There is no water-borne sewerage in the rural areas. For reasons of health and modesty, buckets inside the living area are a rarity, and latrines may be sited 80 metres outside the *egumbo*. Responding to a call of nature, therefore, could have fatal consequences. The Anglican bishop, James Kauluma, complained that it was 'unlawful to go to the toilet during the curfew hours for thousands of residents, including myself.' (NCC, 6.11.86.)

The curfew achieved a Kafkaesque absurdity when permission had to be sought for exemption from it. With no telephones in rural Ovamboland, permission had to be obtained in writing, in practice from a member of the security forces. A lawyer described the procedure:

> Either such member happens by the most arbitrary or capricious happenstance to be immediately accessible to the aspirant applicant, or the latter must travel — by definition, often in the night . . . to a security force member of whose presence he is aware, to get permission. The system provides no guidelines or criteria whatever according to which an ordinary security force member — who may be the rawest and most unsophisticated conscript — is to grant permission. One member may consider toothache, or an unpersuasive (or ill-understood) account of cardiac arrest, or compassionate grounds (the desire to visit a dying child, or parent) to be a basis for exemption, and another, not.

When the request was refused, he was left stranded, often at night, without permission either to go on or to return.

> He is in fact liable to arrest, imprisonment, interrogation, trial and conviction (or being shot at if he decides to return without

permission) because . . . having unsuccessfully applied for permission to be out after dark, he is now inevitably out after dark without such permission. (Court transcript, p. 41.)

In a crisis at night, one balanced the odds of getting shot against those of saving the life of a dying parent or a pregnant mother who had developed complications. Dr. Salamo Amadhila, consultant pediatrician at Oshakati hospital, noticed the 'very prejudicial consequences for the provision of medical services in the area, especially among children.' The real and potential harm stemmed from the speed with which a child's condition could worsen. 'I have seen many emergency cases where a child has suffered, and when asked why it was not brought in time to the hospital, the mother frequently said it was because of the curfew.' (NCC, 11.6.88.)

The way in which sinister forces, always presumed to be Koevoet, exploited the curfew was tragically illustrated by the case of the Ithete family, husband, wife and seven children who lived 15 kilometres outside Oshakati. They were woken at 11 p.m. one evening in May 1986 by an intruder 'on an apparent vendetta against my husband while we were sitting on my bed with our two youngest children, there was a sudden explosion in our room and we fell on the floor.' A second blast destroyed the family car. Though bleeding profusely from a leg injury, Mrs. Ithete dragged her seriously wounded husband out of the room, fearing it would catch fire. He was in severe pain and his voice became weaker and weaker. 'My mother-in-law and I were unable to seek help of neighbours to convey my husband to hospital, as we feared that if we broke the curfew we would be shot at and killed.' Six hours later, he died [Affidavit, 11.10.86].

In November 1986 the three northern bishops brought an action in the Windhoek Supreme Court to have the curfew regulations declared null and void. They claimed that the regulations contravened the government's own Bill of Rights, in particular the right to life itself. With church services, night prayers and Midnight Mass completely disrupted, freedom of religion was also under attack. Lawyers submitted 200 affidavits detailing the unhappy effects of the curfew. Peter Kalangula, the Ovambo Chief Minister, not a reliable friend of the established churches, was moved to call a special sitting of his legislative assembly, which authorized a hard-hitting supporting affidavit.

Responding to the action, the government and the military were of the opinion that, even if the curfew did cause some minor inconvenience, the measure was necessary for the security of the state. The five white judges, none of whom were ever likely to have been restricted to an *egumbo* overnight, dismissed the application on a technicality.

In time the curfew came to be synonymous with the 'bearded and scar-faced' men of Koevoet, those of the 'loud, irreverent voices'. (Hooper 1988, p. 194.) Since the unit had the task of softening up the north, much of their work was after hours. South Africa chose to make them the hated epicentre, the lightning conductor, of the occupation. Local recruits, home from a tour of duty could, if restless and ready to be amused, to drink and womanize, put their hand to some 'free-lance' work. They knew who was 'SWAPO-friendly' or had money stashed under a mattress. Sometimes it went horribly wrong. The following event took place at the kraal of a schoolteacher at Onheleiwa, five kilometres from the border. The knock on the front door came at one a.m. They were from SWAPO, said the visitors, and wanted advice from this 'well-known teacher'. Sorry, he shouted through the door, there was a curfew and he was not allowed to go outside. He secured the doors and windows as best he could —fortunately it was a brick house. Then he took down his bow and arrow and waited. The men outside were determined to get in. One of them forced the top of a window and started climbing through head first. The teacher took aim and shot an arrow into the intruder's chest. At dawn the family found the body of the unwanted visitor lying where it had fallen. The teacher went to the Koevoet base at Omungwelume to report that he had shot an *omukwaita* (guerrilla). From the house, the police followed the footsteps of the second man and found him hiding in the hut of an old woman. They identified him as a Koevoet constable. Yes, he said, they had intended stealing money from the teacher. He was arrested and, the teacher subsequently told, would be sacked. There is no way of checking if he was.

The curfew was also an admission that South Africa's policies had failed. The war zone had been isolated from the outside world, even from the rest of Namibia; it was overflowing with soldiers and paramilitary police, yet the inhabitants still needed to be kept indoors for half their lives. The clear conclusion is that all these measures simply increased the Ovambo people's awareness of their plight. Ovamboland became an intensely political society. Many knew the details of resolution 435, and understood the small print of international developments affecting Namibia. Western visitors would be subjected to a volley of critical questions, as with one British party, who were asked, 'Why does Mrs. Thatcher support South Africa?'

'Ombili, ihena shili, otai twala, kombila'
('Peace without truth leads to the grave' — Kwanyama saying)

In 1976, army headquarters in Pretoria issued two manuals which became the basis for the conduct of a war to win the hearts and minds

(WHAM) of the people of Namibia by weaning them away from SWAPO. The security forces were advised that any attempt to influence the locals should be based on the truth, 'insofar as the population can appreciate the truth.' After which they were recommended to use the 'planned rumour', spread by undercover agents. 'Even if its authenticity is sometimes doubted by the target, and its origin is impossible to fix, the rumour will rapidly spread if it is well chosen and put out at the right time.'

Each white conscript received an instruction manual on psychological methods of counter-insurgency. The manual attempted to justify the war to the soldiers themselves, at the same time cautioning against communist 'softening up' techniques. But its main thrust was a series of tips to the young soldier on befriending black people. Thus they were advised not to run down cattle or shoot at them, nor, for that matter, bayonet them to death. Good relations could be ruined by kicking over beer pots when searching a kraal, the more so when the beer is for 'ceremonial purposes'. Nor should they assault someone who might turn out to be the son of a headman. Moreover, 'a black man expects his superior [i.e., white man] to greet him first.' At the same time, senior officers were issued with a restricted 90-page document entitled 'Guide to Psychological Action', or 'Psy-Acs'. They were advised to 'retain or regain' black support by protecting 'spirit mediums' and providing sporting facilities. 'Ceremonies and martial music in the operational area . . . raise the morale of the population and demonstrate continuing presence,' they were told. There was also official approval of the practice of displaying 'deceased insurgent leaders' bodies to the population, among whom they had built up a reputation for invincibility'. They should, on the other hand, take care 'not to create martyrs.' There is a hint that the army psychologists who drew up the document understood the pitfalls. . . . Soldiers, they said, should be prepared for tricky questions, as in 'Who are the terrorists, SWAPO or the whites?', or 'Why do they (the whites) assault us?' (*Sunday Times*, London, 3.4.77.)

A Civic Action Programme was introduced in Namibia in 1974, four years earlier than in the Republic, an example, perhaps, of the colony as laboratory. Its architect was Major General Phil Pretorius, a reputed expert in psychological warfare and former commander of the Transkei bantustan defence force. Thus, from the mid-1970s, national servicemen served as teachers, doctors, engineers and agronomists in Ovamboland. Teachers were the most numerous and had the closest contacts with the locals. But, with revolvers in their holsters or guns leaning up in the corner of the classroom, they were not well received. Kalangula, the Ovambo chief minister, expelled them in August 1985 amidst allegations that they were organizing unauthorized extra-mural activities.

With the creation of the National Management System, the Namibian regional Joint Management Centre inherited the running of the counter-revolutionary war. The guiding light in the formulation of this national strategy throughout South Africa and Namibia was the JMC's Communications Committee, shortened in its Afrikaans version to 'Komkom'. The committee had three main goals: to justify through lectures, the media, pamphlets and the publication of local newspapers, action taken against opposition organizations; welfare work and the implementation of reforms; and 'the coordination of disinformation via a variety of media forms, pamphlets and township graffiti.' (Swilling and Phillips 1988, p. 17.) The overall WHAM aim was described by the former Namibian warmaker-turned-secretary of the SSC, General Charles Lloyd. 'We are not here just to make war. Through the whole history of the National Management System the military was concentrating not so much on making war, but on making love.' (*Weekly Mail*, 23.6.89.)

In Kavango, black soldiers from 202 Battalion built schools and drilled boreholes; medical teams were sent into kraals; meetings were held and, in the words of Colonel Dion Ferreira, leader of 32 Battalion, 'We . . . generally managed to discredit SWAPO by openly inviting them to participate in these projects.' (Hooper 1988, p. 41.) The purpose was to 'prove to the rural Kavangos that we had more to offer them than SWAPO' — an unwitting admission that the liberation movement could improve the quality of life. But when the soldiers built roads in Kavango, they were perceived as having a military as well as an economic purpose. Nor did the repeal of inter-racial marriage and sex laws and urban residential restrictions have much relevance in the north. The same applied to smear pamphlets depicting Sam Nujoma as a 'puppet of the USSR', especially when Namibians were attacked daily by black collaborators in the pay of Pretoria. Likewise, anonymous leaflets vilifying SWAPO's best-known white member, lawyer and labour leader, Anton Lubowski, were simply confirmation that the government was racist. No amount of speechifying could dissuade Namibians from what they saw and heard every day of their lives. When Colonel P. M. Muller explained at a medal parade in Rundu that the war was not between white and black, 'but between communism and democracy' (*Paratus*, Jan. 86, p. 49) the army portrayed a shallowness of understanding of those who were supposed to buy these ideas. In the last resort, as one observer has pointed out, in the minds of Namibians, 'the non-coercive activities of the SADF and SWATF cannot be separated from the notoriously violent and cruel acts of COIN (Koevoet and 101 Bn) units.' (Grundy 1988, p. 62.) Indeed, from 1979, it is hard to believe how anyone in authority could have been serious about the success of WHAM.

In the late 1970s, Pretoria also created Namibianized instruments of propaganda in the form of black cultural vigilante groups — Etango (in Ovamboland) and Ezuva (in Kavango). Both terms meant 'rising suns' in the vernacular. The military origins of Etango were revealed in its constitution. It spoke of the need 'for better communications between the Owambo members of the security forces and the Owambo public. A course which aimed to inform members about their role in the community and also to enhance their knowledge about the true enemy' was thus developed. The actual motive for the formation of Etango is probably best explained by the state of mind of the young Ovambo 'turncoat' members of Koevoet. Isolated by their betrayal from fellow villagers, often from their own family, they desperately needed to 'belong', to have a set of values, however flawed, as an intellectual justification for their actions. Thus runs the document, Etango aimed to motivate the 'Owambo people to resist SWAPO and any form of communist infiltration.' Key phrases abounded: 'God-given country', 'conservation and love of their heritage', 'eternal truths of the Bible'. It claimed Etango to be 'independent of any political party, and practices no politics.' Its slogan, however, was, 'We fight for true freedom'.

The organization may have had 5,000 members. Its links with white South Africa were everywhere apparent. Etango's chief coordinator, based next to military headquarters in Oshakati, was a teacher from the Transvaal, Andre van der Kolff. Though denying Etango was party political, he admitted that 'most of its community activators are ardent supporters of the National Democractic Party', a small Ovambo grouping in the DTA orbit (*Windhoek Advertiser*, 21.11.86). The Caprivian counterpart of Etango, the Namvi Foundation, ran courses for local blacks on an island in the Okavango River used by the army and police as a 'recreational camp'. Namvi's standard, incidentally, featured two elephants, one black, one white, staring benignly at each other. It had purloined the SWAPO colours, suggesting unexpected political canniness.

Behind the sloganizing, these bogus cultural organizations attempted to achieve their political aims through culture, religion, sport. Their constitutions talked of 'supporting the youth in the discovery and optimal utilization of their talents.' Though singularly unsuccessful in Ovamboland, and in western Kavango, where the chiefs and headmen banned the wearing of their T-shirts, Ezuva did make inroads in eastern Kavango. There were reports of a recruitment centre in Jamba, Savimbi's UNITA headquarters across the border in Angola. Courses were compulsory for administration and local authority officials, and the organizers were on the look-out for recruits to the army or Koevoet. The east Kavango youth flew in by helicopter for lectures ranging from the Bible and communism to physical exercises. They would be shown an innocent movie, followed by a video of the Ethiopian famine. The message was plain — this is what happens when the 'communists' (i.e. SWAPO) take over. The CCN reported that teenage girls were also given contraceptive pills as part of the sex education programme, or, to be more precise, population control.

Documents prepared for these exercises revealed the Ezuva fixations: free enterprise; 'leadership' in the person of headmen; and democracy, which had the 'advantage that every five years the government could change'. The document on politics declared that 'South West Africa wants to become independent', and this should happen in a democratic manner.

> Father is the authority and leader of the family. A few families form a tribe. Each tribe has a captain with the authority. He makes the laws. A few tribes form the group. Government is head of the group. Legislative assembly makes the laws. Executive committee consists of a member or several members of various tribes.

At the end of a course, participants swore an oath of secrecy to Ezuva (or Etango) and went home with a diploma.

This counter-revolutionary freemasonry was allied to a separatist Christianity preaching a conservative message aimed at taking the faithful's mind off the events of the day. An Evangelical Reformed Church was formed under Revd. N. Paulus of Etango and member of the black section of the Dutch Reformed Church. It built a large church, placed between two military bases, hoping to wean northerners from the opposition. Followers would use services to distribute Bibles with the SADF insignia. Activators moved from house to house talking of 'God's word' and offering free religious literature. They handed out medicines in hospitals and clinics.

Large amounts of money were required to spread this gospel. Van der Kolff claimed that 'West Germans' donated R30,000 in 1986, and 'not a cent' came from the government. This still left the way open for a variety of pro-government worthies ready to dip into their pockets. In addition, South Africa's defence budget contains a myriad secret funds for special operations. Etango/Ezuva were as much weapons of war as the G-5 gun and the Casspir.

What is clear is that these 'rising suns' were at the forefront of Pretoria's struggle to delay independence, and thereafter to assure a neo-colonial dispensation. A key aim of the strategy was to get Peter Kalangula's Christian Democratic Action for Social Justice Party (CDA) to join the interim government in Windhoek in the years after 1985. Kalangula at first flirted with Etango, then claimed to have seen the light, after which he became one of its sternest critics. Though he controlled a minority party in Ovamboland, he could have brought a hint of respectability to the tribal-based interim government which had no real representation from the majority Ovambo people. Bogus SWAPO pamphlets insulting to Kalangula did the rounds. His assistant, Oswald Shivute, who attended Etango courses 'before my eyes were opened', said its goals were to 'take our thoughts away from the true struggle, to forget about independence in terms of UN Resolution 435, to forget apartheid and discrimination and oppression; and instead to regard SWAPO, Communism and the Cubans as our big enemies.' (*Namibian*, 8.4.88.)

If Etango–Ezuva was the oblique weapon, the radio services of the South West Africa Broadcasting Corporation (SWABC) were the unashamed mouthpiece of the occupying forces. (Television was of little utility as most northern homes are without power). As in South Africa, SWABC programmes were rigorously controlled. Deviation from the Afrikaner nationalist world view was not tolerated. Some listeners tuned in on short wave to the BBC World Service or SWAPO's Voice of Namibia from Luanda, though the latter was often effectively jammed. Blacks, relentless radio devotees, were encouraged to buy cheap, low transistorized F.M.-only portables, making them a captive audience of the white man's message on local Radio Wambo and Radio Kavango.

The radio's saints were the army, SWATF, Koevoet, Etango and Ezuva, tame chiefs and headmen, the Windhoek government, the Zulu chief Gatsha Buthelezi, UNITA, Renamo in Mozambique, Thatcher, Reagan and Bush, anyone with a kind word to say about South Africa. The sinners, SWAPO apart, were the churches, trade unions and students, the United Nations, the sanctions-friendly US Congress, Cubans and Angolans, Archbishop Desmond Tutu, the ANC. Civil war elsewhere in Africa, in Ethiopia or Chad, a natural disaster in Mexico, bad news from anywhere other than home, was likely to be the lead item on the main evening news, ignoring terrible events on their own doorstep. But listeners were canny. Once, when the radio quoted a report that 76 per cent of security forces' successes in the fight against terrorism and communism were due to the help of the people of the north, people were not taken in. Even Kalangula complained that they were referring to 'spies and informers rather than talking about the people of Owambo.' (*Namibian*, 19.2.88.)

Outright politics was a minor part of SWABC output. Broadcasts offered an air of normality . . . pop music, education, health, cultural programmes (supplied by Etango), church services, Sunday hymn-singing, phone-in quizzes. The most popular programme was the daily *Eyakulo loshiwana* (literally, 'serving the nation'), when listeners phoned in to air their feelings, announce a wedding, appeal for a missing girl, condole with a family in mourning. Sometimes there was a slip-up, such as, 'Get well Festus in hospital at Oshakati after being beaten up by the *makakunyas* . . .'

As with radio, so the press. The vernacular church newspapers *Omukwetu* and *Omukuni*, as well as *The Namibian*, and to a limited extent *The Windhoek Observer*, were perceived as being against the government. A single copy of the *The Namibian* was read by perhaps 25 people. As a result, those supermarkets, *cucas* and garages which sold the paper were seen by friend and foe as SWAPO shops. Not surprisingly, for it was *The Namibian* which was most likely to run pictures of Koevoet flaunting dead guerrillas, depict SWAPO matter-of-factly as the next government, its combatants as freedom fighters and human beings. The most compulsive propaganda of all was to reflect what the reader already knew.

The vast fortune spent in the propaganda war was quite literally money down the drain. This was brought home to Pretoria by a voice from its heartland — that of Professor J. S. Malan of the University of the North, a black ethnic college in the Transvaal. In 1986, he published his findings on political allegiances in Ovamboland. He found that 60% of the people supported SWAPO, another 20% were neutral, some 17% were for Kalangula's CDA, with the remaining three per cent favouring the splinter groups in the Windhoek interim government. 'The image of SWAPO as the liberator of the black man is in a great measure imprinted in the hearts of the population,' said Malan, who admitted that black government politicians acknowledged openly that the success in the scrapping of apartheid could be ascribed to concerted pressure by SWAPO. Though SWAPO stood 'no chance' of winning the armed struggle, he thought it did possess the capability to decide the psychological and political struggle in its favour. If anything, Marais probably underestimated the extent of SWAPO's support. After 20 years of war, there must have been some reluctance on the part of Ovambos to admit to support for SWAPO to a white Afrikaner from an apartheid university. This probably explains the high percentage of neutrals.

Junior Revolutionaries

In the cauldron of the north, the schoolchildren were closest to the fire. 'You are all SWAPOs and communists,' they were told by Koevoet, and while the second connection was absurd, most teenage Ovambos proclaimed unashamed allegiance to the liberation movement. Having known nothing but war and military occupation all their lives, they have been unsurprisingly the most radical element in Namibian society. South Africa waged a war-within-a-war against them. In mid-1987, at least 14 primary schools close to the Angolan border were blown up by unknown assailants. An unconvincing attempt was made to blame

SWAPO — in one case the assailants' footprints were followed to the Omungwelumwe army base.

Army and Koevoet bases were positioned within shelling range of secondary schools. When attacked by the guerrillas, they would vent their fury on their neighbours, lobbing shells indiscriminately into classrooms and hostels. Or Koevoet might put on a 'body display', as they did for pupils in the playground of Outapi secondary school, driving by with the corpses of guerrillas strapped to the Casspirs. Drunken soldiers and Koevoet frequently broke into school dormitories to rape schoolgirls. Once, disguised as guerrillas, they kidnapped boarders, released them the following day in Angola, then arrested teachers and the Namibia National Student Organization (NANSO) leaders for not reporting the incident! (NCC 29.4.88.)

Matters came to a head in April 1988 when pupils at Ponhofi Secondary School launched a class boycott in protest at the location and activities of the Ohangwena Koevoet base next door. Nine of their pupils had recently been wounded in 'crossfire', and two had subsequently died from a mortar shell launched from the base. (CCN 28.4.88). The children called a meeting and voted unanimously to boycott classes. Their parents got together and backed them up. The sole audible voices in favour of retaining the bases were two local headmen, fearful of guerrilla wrath once the protective shield had gone — an example of the lack of support for the occupation forces.

As in South Africa in the early 1980s, the school strike spread like wild fire to Tsumeb, then to Windhoek, Gibeon, Walvis Bay, Swakopmund, and the Rio-Tinto Zinc uranium village, Arandis. By June 40,000 students from dozens of primary and secondary schools were out in solidarity with Ponhofi and two other schools. Matti Amadhila, the Lutheran vice-bishop, explained that the children valued education very highly, but were determined not to go back until the bases were removed. 'The problem now is that these children are roaming round and have been beaten up by the army and Koevoet, who ask them why they have left school.' (House of Commons, press conference, 4.5.88.) Kalangula pleaded directly with the visiting P. W. Botha to get rid of the bases, to be told by the Administrator-General, Louis Pienaar, that they were there to protect the children against abduction by SWAPO. Why not, he suggested, build bomb shelters instead? In the course of the strike, several thousand children fled to Angola.

Trade unions went on strike for two days in a show of solidarity. Then, in July 1988, NANSO ordered the pupils back from their three-month stay-away, excepting the three Ovambo high schools and the Rundu college where white teachers had collaborated with the special branch to have strike leaders expelled. The interim government panicked and passed a Protection of Fundamental Rights Act which authorized fines of R10,000 or imprisonment for 10 years for attempting to persuade someone else to go on strike. The bases remained, for the time being, but the schoolchildren had demonstrated enormous cohesion in the teeth of the intimidation. The stay-away underlined SWAPO's huge following beyond the confines of Ovamboland. At a time when the army was no longer getting its way in Angola, the strike may well have contributed to South Africa's decision to quit Namibia.

Even without these interruptions, South Africa leaves black education in Namibia in an appalling state. Statistics tell part of the story. In 1986, children of the white six per cent of the population accounted for 30% of those in the final school-leaving year. In the national end-of-year exams, 797 white children were successful, a pass rate of 85% (including 323 university entrances), compared with a mere 35% of the 788 blacks. Of these, only 112 were eligible for university. At lower levels, the most remarkable feature is the drop-out rate. In Ovamboland in 1986, there were 409 pupils in the top grade. Ten years before, 28,544 Ovambo children had started out in sub A. The great majority, having left in the next four years, were therefore functionally illiterate, constituting a ruinous waste of state resources and pupil effort.

Black Namibians, as with other children in the developing world, suffer social disadvantage even before entering the classroom. They work long hours herding cattle or helping in the house. They often have to walk many miles to school, possibly leaving home without breakfast and not eating till supper time. Very few homes have electricity, making homework difficult. Their parents may be illiterate, unable to listen to their reading or correct their arithmetic. Being taught in Afrikaans, a language both alien and despised, exacerbated their problems.

From the earliest days of the Mandate, there was little doubt as to what black Namibians could expect from their education. When, in 1930, the League of Nations Permanent Mandates Commission, which watched over the treatment of the indigenous inhabitants, voiced mild criticism, at the slow pace of educating 'native children', the South African government hastened to defend its policy on 'primitive people'. It was probable, it pointed out, that:

> Any attempt to increase the present rate of progress will do more harm than good. . . . The aim is definitely not to Europeanise the natives. They must retain their language and customs as far as the latter do not clash with the great general principles on which civilization rests. Hereros must develop into better Hereros, the Hottentots into better Hottentots. . . . [South African government report to Permanent Mandate Commission, 1930.]

After World War II, Namibia was subjected to the ideological strictures of Christian National Education, a spiritual bulwark of apartheid. With the emphasis on tribal pride and Christian nationalism CNE was a means of preparing the black child for its predestined place in society. Dr. Hendrik Verwoerd, who as minister of native affairs and later prime minister was an inexhaustible racist innovator, explained the basis of Bantu Education in the 1950s. 'There is no place for the native in the European community above the level of certain forms of labour. . . . Until now he has been subjected to a school system which drew him away from his own community and misled him by showing him the green pastures of European society in which he was not allowed to graze.' Today the mixed-blood Basters will not allow Damaras into 'their' schools, while whites have fought a successful rearguard action against classroom integration. The fragmentation goes even deeper — in Rundu, Kavangos go to junior secondary schools according to their sub-group, Sambyu or Kwangali.

Several ethnic education departments, the Ovambo among them, have given up bantu education and opted for the syllabus used in the Cape Province. But the old habits — and textbooks — die hard. The Cape Syllabus still offers a white view of the world. Greater opportunities for pupils have been made available, as befitting the neo-colonial strategy of building a buffer middle class. Consequently, more Coloured and Basters have matriculated, though other black Namibians have also benefited. The mining houses, looking to the time when skilled and semi-skilled whites will be hard to find, have exerted pressure. A number of independent schools have been established with church backing; but they face official intimidation. The 300 parents and children celebrating the opening of their school in Beerseba in July 1987 were attacked by troops wielding sjamboks, teargas and rubber bullets. Those injured included a Catholic priest and a Lutheran pastor.

For blatant budgetary–political reasons, education has been an ethnic and not a central government matter. The central government paid a flat rate to the ethnic administrations for each of its pupils, which these governments could then top up from tax revenues. Generally speaking, income tax revenue raised by a particular group stayed with that group. By raising an amount from tax far greater than the rest of the country combined, whites were able to provide for 80% of their educational requirements. In 1982, with the central government allowance at R225 for each Namibian pupil, whites spent R1,762 on each child. In Ovamboland the figure was R240, Kavango R314, and Caprivi R370. (A similar system applies to medical provision. In 1988, the white second tier authority, representing about 6 per cent of the total population, had a budget of about US$22m, while the health budget of the Ovambo authority, respresenting half the population, was about US$330,000). Nor do the figures tell the whole story, for they do not take into account the large number of black children on white-owned farms who have never been to school at all.

The paltry funding is reflected in the poor quality of the instruction. Twice as many white schools as black offered mathematics as a subject. 'Mathematics, science and English are officially on the curriculum,' an observer noted, 'but in practice, in the classroom, there are often no teachers for the subject or no funds to buy the materials needed. . . . In March 1986, students at Uis secondary school stated there were no teachers for mathematics, although it appears on the syllabus, nor was there money for textbooks.' (WUS-UK 1987, p. 6.)

The result is that most schools were the bare bones of a real place of learning. Primary school pupils counted themselves lucky if they had a desk to sit at, even to share. Many did not even have a classroom, sitting under a tree hoping the rains would be late in coming. Textbooks, laboratory equipment, writing materials, blackboards were in short supply. The pupil–teacher ratio in white schools was 14. In Ovamboland it was 41. Again, this tells only part of the story. Staff in white schools were fully qualified, usually with degrees or teacher training certificates. In the north, a principal would be lucky to have one teacher in 20 with suitable qualifications. Teachers with a standard 8 certificate may have had to teach matric (standard 9 and 10) classes. Unsure of themselves,they inevitably resorted to rote learning. They feared for their jobs, worried about who in the class might be the police informer.

The solution to the teacher problem was not simply money. Many of the best teachers, especially at primary level, were in SWAPO settlements in Angola. The interim government, which staked much of its reputation on 'opening-up' schools, failed even to open the whites-only Windhoek teachers' training college to all races. Here 200 white students availed themselves of facilities intended for 1,500, while hundreds of blacks could not gain entrance to black training colleges. At the beginning of the 1988 academic year, there was an enrolment of 38 new white students. This racist-inspired blocking of the pipeline that should have been churning out desperately needed teachers makes a mockery of any claim to South Africa being a civilizing influence in the colony.

South Africa's battle for hearts and minds could only succeed if it won over the young. The clumsy nature of this mind-twisting campaign was well illustrated by the textbooks. Black Standard 5 pupils (the last year of primary school) studied *A History of South West Africa* by P. S. and C. F. Malan. Published in the Republic, it offered a strictly Afrikaner-nationalist version of history. For example, it ignored entirely the existence of a 'sacred trust', the ethical basis on which South Africa was to govern the territory. According to the authors, 'the Union Government realized that peace could only be maintained in the country by allowing each indigenous tribe to have its own tribal area.' Or, in

1946, when South Africa sought UN sanction to incorporate 'Southwest' as a fifth province, 'the communist countries and the Afro-Asian states were not in favour' — no mention that the United States, Canada and Belgium were also against, or that few African and Asian countries were yet independent. No pupil depending exclusively on this textbook for an understanding of his country would know that in 1966 the United Nations revoked the Mandate. SWAPO was dealt with in ten lines, as in, for example — 'originally founded by a group of Wambos [sic] supported by certain white communists in Cape Town.'

Though from 1985 white soldiers were not allowed to teach in black schools in Ovamboland, they remained in Kavango, Caprivi and Damaraland. Pity the child who mouthed, or wrote on the blackboard, the words 'Namibia', 'freedom', 'Security Council', or 'SWAPO'. The white teacher might have been tempted to reach for a gun rather than the duster. In these circumstances, geography, social studies, even religious instruction were minefields for the questing mind. White civilians, often the wives of army officers or colonial officials, taught in black schools. In the north, their salaries were topped up by an 'inconvenience allowance' (*ongeriefstoelaag*), code words for 'danger money'.

The gun leaning in the classroom corner, bases looming over the playground, moronic syllabuses, money flung away on a divided and corrupt educational system, were certain proof that apartheid civilization offered the youth of Namibia nothing but servitude. Its only merit was that it quickened the will to resist.

A Healthy Body

The South Africans, having failed to make the children of the north conform, have, however, kept them in a state of chronic ill-health. It is worth repeating that Namibia is a wealthy country by African standards, yet its riches are reserved for others. Urban slums and rural poverty imply contaminated drinking water, poor food, ill-fed babies, in turn encouraging the spread of tuberculosis, gastro-enteritis, marasmus, malaria, pneumonia, meningitis, whooping cough, measles, bubonic plague. Some of these diseases were unknown before the arrival of the white man.

In 1983, the territory's per capita health expenditure was about US$30, but with whites receiving ten times that of blacks. UN figures show black infant mortality to be well above the African average, with a black Namibian having seven times more chance of dying in infancy than a white (Smith, 1986, p. 53). Black infants were also 40 times more at risk from meningitis, gastro-enteritis or TB than white infants. In the case of coloured (also Nama and Baster) the ratio is 26 times — an example of the racial pecking order in operation.

One outcome of the war and the unhygienic shanty towns has been the spread of bubonic plague. Infected rats, starved by years of drought, infested the refugee settlements along the Ondangwa–Oshakati road to such effect that in 1983 there were 450 cases of 'Black Death'. Though fatalities have not been at Middle Ages' epidemic levels, the authorities have been unable to stamp out the disease. Houses without water-borne sewerage leave little alternative but to urinate and defecate in the street. With the rains, stagnant pools become laboratories for the spread of disease.

Hard liquor has been one of the more destructive of the white man's contributions to rural societies, often more so than the rifle. The *cuca*s may have made fortunes for some but they have been destructive of health and family life. Alcohol abuse has become rampant among the San (Bushman) since their induction into formal army life. Yet in 'white' Namibia the sale of 'strong' is controlled by licensing laws.

Health in Namibia is geared to a white, Westernized constituency. It cures illness, and as most whites are reasonably healthy, their requirements are easily satisfied. Whatever provision is made for blacks is incidental. Patients inhabit different worlds. When a white child has diarrhoea, the family GP makes a house call and in no time it is being treated. A child in a remote Ovambo village enjoys no such luxury. The doctor or, more likely, the nurse, must be seen at the nearest clinic or hospital, which may be a day's donkey-ride away. The overburdened church and state hospitals of the north would collapse if every case of gastro-enteritis were admitted or even treated as an out-patient. State hospitals in white Namibia, which have the money and the advanced technology, are run on a strictly racial basis.

But the war also killed more directly. Dr. Amadhila listed 41 cases of children under the age of 12 at Oshakati hospital alone who had been killed or wounded in the less than two years to October 1988 (NCC, 12.12.88). Eleven were from shootings, 26 from grenade or other explosive devices, with the remainder from beatings, rape or crushed by army vehicles. On occasions, children picked up Coke or Fanta bottles which then exploded in their hands, prompting one doctor to suggest that they seemed specially designed for the purpose. Any child in the barren landscape of a battlefield wants to handle an attractive 'toy'. Unborn children were not spared, as pregnant mothers were shot, blown up or run down by military trucks. After one expectant mother was raped at gunpoint, both she and her child were found to be infected with syphilis.

The war led to the closure of many clinics — at the very time when more should have been opening. The Lutheran Church's mobile health service in Ovamboland collapsed in 1982 after the mining of two ambulances — the drivers killed, patients and nurses injured. Foreign doctors, Finnish and German men and women, augment the few Namibian graduates in the Lutheran and Catholic mission hospitals. They are well respected, considered free of race prejudice, and are preferred to white medical staff at the South African-run state hospitals. Blacks feel intimidated in the presence of a uniformed SADF doctor. The violence of a colleague in Koevoet or the army may have been the cause of their hospital visit in the first place. Patients complain that many South African doctors show no respect for the elderly. Some 'do not like to touch black people, diagnosing from a distance.' (Authors' interview with Vice-Bishop Kameeta.)

Health, community and social workers, especially when working for the churches, were regularly detained under security laws, often tortured, but rarely, if ever, tried in court — a further disruption to the treatment of the sick. In 1978 a notice on the board at Oshakati hospital advised staff that they could treat PLAN fighters, provided their presence was reported to the police within 24 hours (Amadhila interview, October 88). Once, a Koevoet captain, Frantz Ballach, barged into a hospital where a badly injured guerrilla was being treated, tore a drip off his arm and flogged him with a hosepipe (Testimony in Heita trial, 1977).

The SADF's limited or secondary concern for the health of black people was illustrated by the events of February 1986 when the military demanded to take over the hospitals. Kalangula, responsible for health and welfare in the bantustan, refused. Within 24 hours, a dozen army doctors were pulled out of Oshakati and Onandjokwe hospitals, and from several clinics. Oshakati, the largest hospital in the north with 750 beds, was reduced to 15 non-military medical officers, and Onandjokwe to one. A party of Filipino doctors were drafted in to fill the gap, but most departed following complaints, by black and white staff, that their qualifications were insufficient.

Access to clean water is a primary aim of governments throughout the Third World, but in the Namibian countryside it remains a luxury. Few ordinary people benefit from the pipeline running south-east from the Ruacana dam. One either walks long distances to fetch water or digs a well. Those with the means purchase pipes to run water nearer their homes, but even then soldiers have been known to dig up and destroy the pipes. Water affairs staff have shot holes in buckets as water was tapped from the pipeline. Churches and overseas aid agencies have tried to assist with wells and pipelines. An Oxfam report cites the case of a well it wished to line with concrete in a small northern village. The only drinking water came from dirty holes frequented by animals. But the local authority refused to help, claiming that the villagers would only quench the thirst of passing guerrillas.

The stability that will hopefully accompany independence will allow for a country-wide primary health care network. It is possible, by comparing improved health provision in other southern African countries since their independence, to assess the number of lives that might have been saved had the war ended a decade earlier. A UNICEF report (April 1989, p. 58) estimates that in 1988 alone 10,000 black infants and young children died who would have lived had Namibia achieved independence in 1978.

Namibian doctors are determined to make up for lost time. Prevention, rather than cure, will become the basis of treatment. In each village a health worker will watch out for illness, weigh babies and immunize them, dress wounds and send serious cases to the clinic. This revolutionary concept, as Dr. Amadhila says, 'means empowering the people to decide on their own health affairs, instead of a small group of so-called professionals sitting in air-conditioned rooms in Windhoek.' (NCC, 12/12/88.)

An offering. A Namibian suggests an alternative to war to an uninvited guest at a rally in Katutura. 1987.

The traditional Ovambo homestead.

The Lord's Word. A church worker surveys the ruins of the Lutheran printing press at Oniipa (Ondangwa) blown up by 'unknown' bombers in 1980.

Ovabimba boy holds South African army flare. Ruacana, northern Namibia, June 88.

Church procession through the streets of Katutura. June 88.

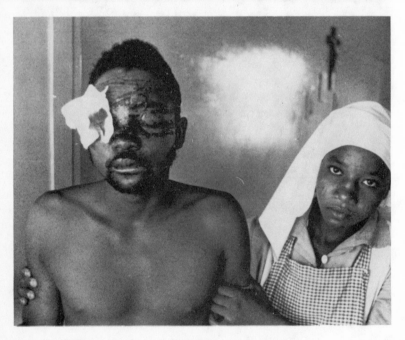

A victim of Koevoet 'interrogation' is cared for by a young nurse.

Female fighter. A SWAPO combatant at Chibemba, southern Angola, May 89.
Women guerrillas did not go on missions but worked as mechanics, drivers and in
similar critical back-up jobs.

A Koevoet Casspir on patrol in the war zone.

Lessening grip. The war goes wrong in Angola, but security police still harass unarmed civilians at home. This woman had earlier been assaulted. A police video records the event. Windhoek, September 88.

SWAPO supporters at a rally commemorating the massacre of Cassinga eleven years before. May 89.

A Centurion tank is loaded on to a South African Transporter, Ombalantu, northern Namibia, October 88.

Guerrillas exhumed as South African soldiers go swimming near their base at Omblantu. 8 April 89.

Throwing bodies of freedom fighters into a mass grave near Oshakati, April 89.

Tomorrow's world. Children in a Katatura community centre show whose side they are on. May 89.

The torture ends. Jason Angula (left), church official and SWAPO labour secretary, embraced by the movement's internal chairman, Dan Tjongarero, at the end of 14 months' detention in Osiri.

5.
Namibia Inc.

Albion Commercial

In the last 100 years Namibia has been, successively, a German Protectorate, a land conquered in the name of George V of England, a mandate ruled by South Africa, and finally an occupied country in which the shell of legal title was vested in the United Nations, but with *de facto* control residing firmly in Pretoria. The people of Namibia were reined in by missionaries and soldiers; then put to work digging mineral riches from the earth; latterly, enrolled in the security forces to defend the white man's ill-gotten gains. One thread has run through this entire process — commercial opportunism. It began with bird droppings.

Demand for fertilizer was growing apace in the 1840s. The discovery of large deposits of guano droppings on Ichaboe Island, up coast from Luderitz, precipitated a British stampede. On one day in 1845 some 451 ships were clustered around the islet, as 6,000 labourers worked an area barely a mile in circumference. 'Within three years, deposits 70 metres thick, the accumulation of centuries, had been stripped off and over 200,000 tons exported, fetching R4 million.' (Moorsom 1984, p. 16.)

The British had shown a passing interest in the duned coastline of what is now Namibia after acquiring the Cape Colony in 1795. They sent a warship as far as the Angolan border, turning over the regulation clod of earth at landing-stages along the way, hoisting the Union Jack and firing three salvoes. This was a time when Britain faced the prospect of a Napoleonic invasion, but, once it subsided, Namibia was forgotten. The first permanent white settler is reported to have been a Gideon Visagie, a Dutchman on the run from the Cape police, who was seen by explorers in present-day Keetmanshoop in 1791.

It was German missionaries who undertook the main burden of reaching the Namibian soul. By 1864, the Prussian flag flew over the small religious and trading settlement at Otjimbingwe. As Namas and Hereros warred around them, the Germans turned to Britain for protection. With the request backed by the Herero Supreme Chief,

125

Samuel Maharero, now in a brief truce with the Namas, the British appointed the explorer, William Palgrave, Commissioner Extraordinary for Namaland and Damaraland, a Major Manning became adviser to Maharero, and a justice of the peace was sent to Otjimbingwe. In 1878, in a move the consequences of which reverberate to this day, Commander R. C. Dyer sailed in a British ship to annex Walvis Bay and the guano islands in the name of Queen Victoria. Six years later they were incorporated into the Cape Colony.

Britain seemed to be gearing up to colonize, the more so as the Prussian Chancellor Bismarck appeared to display a lack of interest in colonial expansion. Then, with the resumption of Nama–Herero fighting, Britain withdrew its officials from the interior. In 1883, Germany informed the British government that a Bremen merchant, Adolf Luderitz, proposed building a factory on the coast at Angra Pequena, and would London provide protection. When Britain declined, the German government said it would do so 'without the least desire to establish a footing in Africa.' Luderitz first 'purchased' Angra Pequena and surrounding land from the Nama chieftain of Bethanie, Josef Frederiks, then the coastal strip 20 miles wide down to the Orange River mouth, planting the German flag along the way. The price for the two lots was £600 and 260 ancient rifles, the latter supplied by a Rhenish missionary named Bam.

A generation earlier, the Whig prime minister, Lord John Russell, and his colonial secretary, Earl Grey, were wont to 'throw British protection over any chief who needed it.' But times had changed. The Zulu humiliation of the British army at Isandhlwana in 1879 had contributed to the electoral defeat of Disraeli, though his successor, William Gladstone, was soon embroiled in the future of Bechuanaland, which faced occupation by the Transvaal Boer republic. The combination of the Cape government, Cecil John Rhodes and the missionaries persuaded London to proclaim a protectorate over the Batswanas.

At this point the Cape government, granted 'responsible' status in 1872, became anxious about the sale of arms to the Namas. There had been a government crisis in Cape Town so that when, in 1884, the legislature eventually approved the annexation of the whole Namibian coastline, it was too late. Bismarck had proclaimed his protectorate and a gunboat patrolled off shore.

None the less, very soon the Namibian economy came to be dominated by British capital, in particular by that past-master of territorial accumulation, Cecil Rhodes. As early as April 1885, with no visible signs of exploitable gold or diamonds, Luderitz was forced to sell out to the German SWA Company, a syndicate of his country's wealthiest financiers. Still there were no mineral finds, but the company refused to inject more capital. For four years the colony stagnated, then Rhodes stepped in and acquired a controlling interest. With concessions in Barotseland (modern Zambia) and southern Angola, he had contrived to box in the Germans in their own *Sudwest-Afrika*. Reports of a diamond find near Gibeon gave the Germans hope that Rhodes's power would be broken. It was not to be. Rhodes made sure that he would control both the new mines and the amount of stones unearthed. The German *Colonial Journal* lamented — as might Namibians with greater justification today — that 'the De Beers Company [the new name] will . . . only permit a limited number of mines to be opened for fear of overproduction, so that, perhaps the richest mines in the world may be in our Colony which, without the consent of De Beers, will be of no use to us.' (PRO, CO 879/51 item 546/66 & 155.)

So Britain's apparent vacillation over whether to colonize stood her in good stead. Without having to ladle out millions in making the country safe for developers and, more especially, without the opprobrium of neutralizing Nama and Herero resistance, British capital was presented with a secure bolt-hole. The Rhodes company, in an agreement made in Berlin, was granted 13,000 sq. km. of so-called no-man's-land; in reality, it was a huge chunk of the Herero domain. (Drechsler 1980, p. 112).

Still, despite growing rivalries, Britain and Germany co-operated well enough. They considered themselves a cut above the other colonizers, particularly the Belgians and Portuguese. In 1898 they secretly agreed on the desirability of partitioning Portugal's colonies among themselves. In the field of battle, Britain was also ready with a helping hand. In 1897, the Afrikaaners, a Nama clan on the Orange River, rejected rigorous cattle culling measures to counteract rinderpest. After inflicting an initial defeat on the Germans, they were then hemmed in by a larger force and fled into the Cape. The British handed back their leader, Kivdoe, his three sons, and other tribesmen. They were duly executed.

From Walvis Bay, Britain had a grandstand view of the Nama–Herero war of liberation. General von Trotha's extermination order was made early on in the fighting (October 1904). Yet Britain either turned a blind eye or helped behind the scenes to have the rising put down. Early in 1905, the German ambassador in London complained to the colonial secretary, the Marquess of Lansdowne, when the Cape government refused to allow supplies to be landed at Port Nolloth, just south of the Orange mouth. The Marquess explained that the Cape authority was trying to 'avoid doing anything calculated to create in the minds of the tribes subject to us the impression that we were actively helping the German government against other black tribes with whom ours (in the Walvis Bay area) had a certain amount of affinity.' The ambassador pointed out that the operations were not directed against Hereros, but against a 'rebel faction under Morenga, who was not a chief, but a mere robber.' The Marquess noted that 'it seemed to the Germans a new departure that a civilized power should be denied facilities for putting down a mere raider.' (PRO, CO 879/86, item 766, p. 25.)

Some months later the Cape governor received a Colonial Office note to the effect that the government would

> deprecate a sudden restriction of the source of supply which until now has been available to Germany, and should afford to them every facility which it is possible to give without exciting the natives on the British side. The latter consideration must, however, be paramount. Your government will no doubt act accordingly. [PRO, CO 879/86, item 766, p. 204.]

Jacob Morenga, a great guerrilla fighter, was eventually forced to retreat into the Cape, where the British sent a large force to track him down. He was killed in September 1907.

Eight years later during World War I, Britain sent the South African army to capture the colony. The invasion did not result from 'a unilateral decision by South Africa to rid itself of a hostile neighbour.' (Cooper 1985). The real purpose was to destroy German wireless installations transmitting intelligence to Admiral von Spee's fleet in the South Atlantic — a real threat to British naval power. Once the Namibian Germans were defeated, the British government hastened to publish a 'Blue Book' cataloguing the atrocities of their predecessors. The motive was to ensure that Germany would not have the moral standing to seek the return of the colony after the war. There were limits to this embryonic manifestation of a human rights policy — the 204 defeated German officers and 3,166 other ranks were 'allowed to keep their arms for defence against the natives and to return to their farms.' (Williams 1945, p. 99.)

In the anti-German climate, blacks who had lost their land had high expectations, encouraged by Britain's governor-general in South Africa, Lord Buxton, who toured the territory promising the Hereros 'the old freedoms along with great possessions of land and unlimited herds of cattle.' (Katjavivi 1988, p. 16.) They were to be disappointed. South West Africa was to be Pretoria's perk for fighting the war against the Kaiser.

The British were understandably grateful for the manner in which the South Africans, including many Afrikaners (though Namibian blacks too), fought in *Sudwest*, and later in German East Africa (Tanganyika). In a eulogy in the House of Commons in 1915, Liberal Prime Minister Herbert Asquith praised General Louis Botha, the warrior-premier who had led the campaign. He had 'broadened the bounds of human liberty'. Botha's deputy, Jan Smuts, a member of the British war cabinet, was revered by his former Boer War antagonists. At the peace conference in

Paris, while US President Woodrow Wilson preached the gospel of no territorial aggrandisement, Asquith's successor, David Lloyd George, engineered the presentation of South West Africa as a League of Nations mandate to South Africa.

The British government had no illusions about the future of the territory. In the Commons debate on the peace treaty, Lloyd George explained that:

> South West Africa, running as it does side by side with Cape Colony, was felt to be so much a part, geographically, of that area that it would be quite impossible to treat it in the same way as you would a colony 2,000 miles or 3,000 miles away from the centre of administration. There is no doubt at all that South West Africa will become an integral part of the Federation [sic] of South Africa.

There was another reason for handing the German colonies over to the care of countries which themselves were still technically colonies. Heavily in debt after the war, Britain was only too happy to offload the expense of administration.

Yet, by 1919, Britain should have known that white South Africans were thoroughly unsuited to promote, as the mandate required, 'the material and moral well-being and the social progress of the inhabitants of the territory.' Though not yet called 'apartheid', the regime of the Boer generals had set about segregating South Africa with a vengeance. In the House of Commons a back-bencher, Lord Henry Cavendish-Bentinck, spoke of the natives of the Union being 'most shamefully misgoverned . . . whereas five million natives are given only 13 per cent of the land, 87 per cent of the land is given to the whites, who are only one and a half million . . . these natives are working under a system which is more or less veiled slavery. They are subject to the law of passes.' He was ignored.

Smuts's attitude to blacks was revealed a few years later when he bombed the Bondelswarts clan into submission, ostensibly for resisting the arbitrary increase of a dog tax, though the dispute was over land stolen from them. A Labour MP, Colonel Wedgewood, drew the attention of the Commons to the bombing of 'Hottentot' women and children by South African airforce planes. Was the government proposing to put a stop to these proceedings, he inquired. Would it take up the matter at the League of Nations? The reply, from the Conservative colonial secretary, Winston Churchill, was worthy of a Pontius Pilate. 'It is surely not a matter in which I am concerned. The Government of the Union of South Africa hold the mandate, and they are responsible to the League of Nations. There is no locus either for me or for the honourable and gallant Member to interfere in the matter.' Pressed again by the colonel, Churchill said, 'I hope we shall find something better to do in the League of Nations than attack our own Dominions.'

So Britain washed its hands of Namibia, as it had of South Africa in 1909 when an ANC delegation had travelled to London to plead for a role for blacks in the new Union. The annual reports on what it was doing to advance the moral and spiritual well-being of Namibians, which Pretoria was obliged to furnish to the League, occasionally set alarm bells ringing among non-colonial delegates. But effectively, the world forgot about Namibia for the next 25 years.

Clement Attlee's Labour government took power in 1945 and launched an impressive social revolution at home. But for the people of Namibia there was no change. Smuts, once again in the British cabinet's inner war circle, remained an admired figure to the outside world. He now sought the permission of the UN to incorporate Namibia as a province of South Africa, and was backed by Britain. Kenneth Morgan, a Labour historian, wrote, 'Its faith in Smuts led the British government . . . to take the grave step of accepting his demand for the absorption of South West Africa into the Union of South Africa and the winding up of the old mandate system.' (1984, p. 198) A British representative at the UN, Arthur Bottomley (later commonwealth secretary at the time of the Rhodesian UDI), argued that the figures submitted by South Africa purporting to prove black approval for the incorporation should be believed. But the attempt failed miserably, although many blacks voted 'yes' believing they were being restored to British rule under George VI.

The Afrikaner nationalist government which ousted Smuts in 1948 refused to submit annual reports on the condition of black Namibians. Those who could report to the UN on events at home — Revd. Michael Scott, as well as the black Namibians Mburumba Kerina Getzen, Jariretundu Kozonguizi, Hans Beukes — were hindered by a coterie of imperial powers sheltering behind the argument that 'the Charter does not allow it'.

While the British Conservative Party, with long-standing business connections in southern Africa, has understandably resisted radical action against Pretoria, the behaviour of the Labour Party has not been noticeably different. In opposition, it has been condemnatory. Hugh Gaitskell, Attlee's successor as Labour leader, once asked Macmillan's Tory government 'to make it plain that they will support the decisions and recommendations of the World Court on the matter [of SWA], whatever they be.' Gaitskell promised much, but died without taking office. James Callaghan, a later Labour premier, in a debate in 1960, spoke of 'increasing oppression and slavery' in Namibia. Elwyn Jones, a later Labour lord chancellor, argued powerfully that Britain had 'a direct and legal responsibility' for the territory.

So the let-down was the more profound when Labour took office under Harold Wilson in 1964. In the historic General Assembly vote revoking the mandate in October 1966, Britain abstained. When the Tories returned to power in 1970, Labour called on them to abandon their 'negative stand on a doubtful legal interpretation of the UN Charter and to take action not to protect the position and interests of the South African government but to help the Namibians in their endeavour to achieve their freedom.' The Tories felt free to ignore the advice.

Much of the political jousting in the years after 1945 centred on the legal point as to whether the UN had inherited the League's responsibilities over the former mandates. If not, Pretoria was free to do as it chose. At the Hague International Court of Justice, Western jurists, led by the positivist-minded British judge Sir Gerald Fitzmaurice, looked kindly on South Africa's case. Earlier in his career, as a foreign office legal adviser, Fitzmaurice's conservative views were indelibly stamped on British behaviour at the United Nations. By 1971, however, the court had a 'human rights' majority and in a historic advisory Opinion it confirmed that the UN had been competent to terminate the mandate five years earlier. But old British habits died hard. Sir Gerald issued a 100-page dissenting opinion, which began: 'Although I respect the humanitarian sentiments and the avowed concern for the welfare of the people of SW Africa which so clearly underlie the Opinion of the Court, in this case, I cannot as a jurist accept the reasoning on which it is based . . .'

In the 1970s, following the Portuguese withdrawal from Angola, Washington took over as the activist Western power in the sub-continent. However, it was a British company, Rio-Tinto Zinc, which launched at Rossing on the edge of the Namib Desert what was to become the world's largest open-cast uranium mine. The operation contravened Decree 1, a UN measure calculated to prevent foreign interests from exploiting Namibia's natural resources. The fact that the mine came on stream in 1976, two years after the passing of the decree, made it different from other, well-established enterprises in the colony. Very soon Rossing had become, with De Beers' CDM diamond mine, Namibia's largest money earner. In the late 1960s, Tony Benn, the technology minister, not yet a radical voice, signed a deal to buy uranium from Rossing. Decree 1 was several years away, but he must have been aware of the controversial nature of the contract. Benn's diaries record that in 1968 the British Atomic Energy Authority had 'particularly asked officials at the ministry [of Technology] not to tell ministers that the uranium came from SW Africa.' (*The Independent*, 29.9.88.) Again with the Tory victory in 1970, opposition Labour MPs called for the contract to be rescinded.

But with Labour back in power in 1974, principle again went by the board. James Callaghan became foreign secretary. Forgotten were his allegations of 'slavery' and pleas to respect the decisions of the Hague Court; rejected was the request to cancel the uranium contract. Labour's dual-policy stance — humanitarian in opposition, perceived national interest when in power — prevailed once again (*New Statesman* 31.10.86).

So for a century Britain has exploited the riches of Namibia while exhibiting considerable indifference to the aspirations of its people. Its colonial attitudes, though more refined and less forthright than those of the Boers, were hardly less racist. Indeed, a 19th century British governor of Natal, Theophilus Shepstone, enacted the formal segregation laws which set the pattern for 20th century apartheid. A better solution would have been for the Namibia mandate to prohibit outsiders from acquiring land, along the lines of British Basutoland. But that would have impeded the exploitation of the fertile earth. As it had done in South Africa, Britain ensured that the Afrikaners undertook the dirty work of government while its own businessmen concentrated on getting rich. Their hands stayed clean; the Afrikaner became the world's favourite pariah.

South Africa's Vassal

Though a colony of settlement, Namibia was also very much a colony of exploitation. The unexpected bounty of this land had to be quickly consolidated by a backbone of reliable white farmers and civil servants. Only two decades after the Boers' own war against the British, they now had an empire to themselves. The farmers from the Transvaal, Orange Free State and Angola who settled the 'empty' land were loaded with subsidies, agricultural extension services, a transport and marketing network, the black helotry. Even then they struggled to make ends meet. The boom began after World War II, as karakul and beef ranching became profitable, and South Africans moved heavily into fish processing in Walvis Bay. Farming and fisheries were geared to the metropolis. In 1977, a UN Institute for Namibia study described the colony as a 'classic case of an economy which, in respect of goods, produces what it does not consume, and consumes what it does not produce.' (Cooper in Wood 1988, pp. 294/5.) Thus, Namibia's entire supply of canned meat had to be imported because its own production was all exported, and it re-imported from South Africa the very same canned pilchards which its factories produced for export, shipped out and railed back on South African-owned boats or rolling stock, setting their own tariffs to a captive market.

But the 'big money' was in mining. Initially the sector was dominated by American and South African multinationals, but after World War II many small and medium-sized operations were developed, often by South African para-statals. The Industrial Development Corporation acquired shares in Rossing, while ISCOR (Iron and Steel Corporation) bought the Rosh Pinah lead mine, and large Afrikaner public companies, Federale Volksbeleggings and Federale Mynbou, acquired holdings in copper, tin, wolfram, vanadium and other base metals. The Tsumeb Corporation, through Goldfields South Africa, is now to all intents and purposes South African, and Consolidated Diamond Mines is a wholly-owned subsidiary of De Beers.

Profits from mining have been enormous, but not for black Namibians. In 1980, Moorsom estimated that 90 per cent of foreign company profits were expatriated, accounting for half of Namibia's gross domestic profit. He described how the distribution of national income exposed the

> devastating impact of foreign exploitation most clearly. If business taxation is added to net profits, about 70 per cent of gross domestic profit is swallowed up by gross profits — 40 per cent by companies, 9 per cent by small businesses, 20 per cent by taxation. Another 18 per cent goes on the wages of white employees, whose functions are mainly to administer, supervise and control the black workers who actually produce the goods. [1982, p. 31.]

This, he calculated, left a mere R145 million, or 12 per cent of GDP, to one and a quarter million people. About two thirds of this was wages, another tenth the cash earnings of small traders and transporters, and the remaining R25 million the subsistence production of the peasantry. The incomes ratio of white to black, calculated as 25 to one, was more disproportionate even than in the Republic.

Still not satisfied, in the mid-1970s Consolidated Diamond Mines began to overmine in order to extract as much as possible as a hedge against the uncertainties of independence. Matters got so out of hand in the 'Wild West' of Namibian mining that the South African government ordered a judicial inquiry under an assiduous judge, P. W. Thirion. His revelations embarrassed the mineral exploiters, but, in the meantime, the life of the world's largest deposit of alluvial gemstones had been contemptuously depleted. The decade of respite provided by P. W. Botha and the Contact Group reaped a tidy profit for South African and Western transnational corporations.

Arms and Trade

South Africa has been able to turn this greed to its advantage in waging war in south-western Africa. Embargoes have not excluded the acquisition of arms, oil and technology, either by open or secret purchases. The 1977 UN mandatory arms embargo made the creation of a domestic arms industry an urgent priority. An Armaments Productions Board already existed by 1977, and out of it an Armaments Corporation (Armscor) was established as the sole procuring authority for the Defence Force. It organized a tightly-controlled network of state-owned and private contractors to acquire the means with which to defend the *laager* against a hostile world. And, up to a point, it has been brilliantly successful, enabling South Africa in large part both to fight its regional wars as well as to contain the internal township uprisings of the mid-1980s. It has also become a major source of revenue. Within ten years Armscor became the country's largest single exporter of manufactured goods, claiming outlets in 23 countries, some in Africa (*Citizen*, 21.1.88).

Armscor advertises its wares in military magazines at home and in friendly countries abroad — conventional and mine-protected vehicles; grenades, mines, mortars, 'pyrotechnics and demolition equipment'; and a range of naval, airforce and army weaponry. But the 'polecat' status ruled out the ordinary business decencies. The corporation's chief executive, Johan van Vuuren, explained that sometimes at arms shows 'we take hotel rooms to talk to potential customers privately, but we can't come officially.' (*Jane's Defence Weekly*, 2.4.88, p. 619.)

South Africa has also had the priceless advantage of being able to test its products in real combat laboratories; conventional battles in Angola, anti-guerrilla warfare in northern Namibia, civil uprisings in Katutura, Soweto and New Brighton. At a 'birds-of-a-feather' arms show in Chile, Armscor offered a portable barbed-wire barrier with razor-sharp spikes for controlling hostile crowds — a weapon devised for use in the black townships. The bouncing cluster bomb delivered from aircraft was another innovation. The inventor was a 'Rhodesian' who had 'taken the gap' from black rule. (*Jane's Defence Weekly*, 2.4.88 p. 623.)

However important a factor the export trade has been in offloading development costs, the priority has been to acquire weapons for self-defence. South Africa likes to foster the myth of self-sufficiency, yet most of its major weapons systems developments have been crucially dependent upon imports. Once acquired, the weapons have been assembled under licence or manufactured on the basis of imported technology. *Defence and Armament* magazine (January 1986) reported that 'in essence, South Africans say, "what we can't buy, we will make; and what we can't make, we will steal. From our enemies or from our friends."' Just as the Japanese before them copied and modified foreign inventions and marketed them as their own, so South African technicians have built on outside expertise to create the country's own home arms industry. Technicians have been sought through the British scientific press to work in South Africa's arms industry. In the mid-1960s, the Kentron Company (today a major Armscor subsidiary) commissioned French companies to adapt the Crotale, a low-level surface-to-air missile, to bushveld specifications. The end-product was the Cactus missile. In the same way, South Africa's Kukri dogfight missile is suspiciously like a replica of the American Sidewinder, the Israeli Shafir, and French Matra's Magic R550. Kentron still depends heavily on the transfer of technology in both the design and operational fields. Another example of equipment engineered from foreign models is the Ratel armoured personnel carrier, born out of the Belgian Sibmas. *Jane's Defence Weekly* (25.2.84., pp. 290–6) reported that Pretoria put up the finance for Belgium to develop the Ratel, as well as the German Magirus Deutz civilian truck which was adapted for military use.

Armscor's main export earner, the mobile G6 gun with a range of 35 kilometres, is a modification of a 155mm system based on designs illegally imported from the American Space Research Corporation's plant on the Canadian border. Without American R & D, the G6 was beyond South Africa's technical grasp. The machinery used in the manufacture of the weapon was imported from West Germany and other countries. The gun was a direct response to the long-range Russian 'Stalin's Organ' which wrought physical and emotional havoc among South African national servicemen in Angola (Cawthra 1986, p. 10).

The South Africa Air Force (SAAF) has traditionally depended on Britain, the United States, Italy and France, for aircraft. Its Impala, despite the African resonance of the name, is actually the Italian Aeromacchi MB-32 jet trainer, built under licence by another Armscor subsidiary, Atlas Aircraft Corporation. The French helicopters, Alouette, Puma and Super Frelon, designed for logistical purposes, have been converted in South Africa to gunships by Atlas. The old French Mirage 3s and F-1s were, by the 1960s, obsolescent, if not obsolete. The delta-winged Mirage 3, first delivered in the early 1960s, was transformed into the Cheetah. The *Financial Times* reported (1.9.88) that, with major modifications to the engine and airframe, new avionics and missiles, 'the end result bears a close resemblance to the Israeli Kfir fighter.'

But it was not enough. With the intensification of the air war following the appearance of advanced Russian Mig-23 fighters in the skies of Angola, the yawning gap in South Africa's defences was an armoured combat aircraft to match improved Angolan and Cuban hardware and pilots. Van Vuuren of Armscor admitted as late as April 1988 that 'it doesn't take a genius to see that our biggest problem is going to be engines. . . . Unless the political situation changes, this is going to be a priority, despite the cost of development.' (*Jane's Defence Weekly*, 2.4.88.) The military situation had already changed dramatically, and the absence of a state-of-the-art fighter plane left South Africa and its allies fatally exposed.

The arms embargo has also been extensively circumvented through the import of dual-purpose products. In 1985 Messerschmidt helicopters, supplied to the police for use in traffic control, were seen on television deployed against black youths demonstrating in a Cape Town suburb. South Africa has also boasted of buying water cannon abroad, presumably in the category of 'general crime prevention'. They were probably made at the Israeli Kibbutz Beth-Alfa, which subsequently decided to stop supplying them to South Africa. The bantustans have also been used to get round the embargo. Ciskei Aircraft Industries is an Austrian company building spotter planes. These have a clear military potential. The sale of civil aircraft may seem innocent enough. Yet when, in 1986, SAA bought wide-bodied Boeing 747 airliners for inter-continental (boycott-beating) routes, the displaced Boeing 707s were sold to Safair, a subsidiary of the state shipping company, Safmarine. Soon they were ferrying war cargo from Waterkloof airfield in Pretoria to the Grootfontein base in Namibia (*Windhoek Observer*, 27.9.86).

The embargo was circumvented in other ways. In his biography, P. W. Botha revealed how South African agents had bought 90 Centurion tanks in India, put them on a boat bound for Maputo, which actually sailed to Durban, after which the carcasses were rebuilt into Olifants (D. and J. de Villiers, 1984.) More comprehensively, the British Anti-Apartheid Movement (July 1987), alleged that Britain was the centre of a multi-million pound operation, involving front companies, false end-user certificates, third countries, shady arms dealers, the reclassification of equipment — machinery, tools or computers not regarded as having a military application. The allegations were given dramatic currency in an arms trial in Birmingham in June 1986. Four Britons and four South Africans, undercover agents for Kentron, faced charges of sending to the Republic by circuitous routes sophisticated components for radar and heat-seeking missiles, and parts for detonators and precision gunsights. West Germany was said to be a link in the chain. Electronic devices for jamming radar were exported under the guise of mining equipment. The four South Africans were granted bail, and a South African diplomat at the London embassy guaranteed they would not leave Britain. They did, and the four Britons took the rap for them. The South African government forfeited £400,000 in bail and sureties. The Foreign Office appeared more annoyed at this cavalier treatment of the British legal system than by the crimes themselves. The diplomat, André Pelser, despite a solemn undertaking that the men would stand trial, was not expelled by the Thatcher government. He later became an aide to the administrator-general in Windhoek (*Namibian*, 13.12.85).

A large loophole in the embargo has been the export of spares and components by the West. A French newspaper reported in 1985 that for four years Aerospatiale had been sending parts via Israel and Algeria for the upgrading and maintenance of South Africa's Puma aircraft. If a left-of-centre French administration was prepared to flaunt the arms boycott, then the chequered record of apartheid's three closest friends in the West, conservative-ruled for much of the decade, is no surprise. In 1983, the British Department of Trade issued a licence for the export of a Marconi radar system which enabled South Africa for a few years to maintain air superiority in southern Angola. The home secretary Douglas Hurd, then a foreign office minister, justified the contract as being 'for use in air traffic control . . . for a civil organization predominantly for civil purposes.' 'Predominantly' was the give-away, the ultimate purchaser being Air Space Control Authority, a state body described in a 1982 South African Defence white paper as 'co-ordinating air traffic, air defence and air defence artillery.' (*World Campaign*, April 1983.) Earlier, the British government had sanctioned the export of the Plessey advanced mobile military radar system for use on SAAF planes and SADF personnel came to Plessey in England for instruction. The radar shield gave South Africa the confidence to launch a series of destructive raids on the Frontline States. Small wonder that Plessey South Africa sponsors a nationwide Permanent Force Golf Tournament 'to foster good relations between its members.' (*Paratus*, August 1988.)

In terms of the UN's voluntary 1963 arms embargo, the United States was committed to a ban on arms sales, though the State Department continued to licence some items on a munitions list. By the end of the Carter presidency, however, the flow had dried up. The first Reagan term ushered in a 'constructive engagement' contratrend, so that licences for commercial military commodities rose dramatically, indeed accounted for more than the entire sales of the previous 30 years. Items included electric shock batons, advanced computers and nuclear technology. South African police and military contacts into America were facilitated. At a time when Common Market countries were terminating military attaché exchanges with Pretoria, *Paratus* regularly featured photographs of US military personnel and their Chilean, Paraguayan and Taiwanese counterparts, enjoying official South African hospitality (eg., January 1988, p. 34).

All of this sometime cloak-and-dagger activity would have been irrelevant had the Republic, without natural deposits of petroleum, been deprived of the means of lubricating its machines of war. Cabinet minister Chris Heunis once admitted that oil was more difficult to acquire than arms. None the less and despite an OPEC embargo since 1973, oil has reached South Africa through a conspiracy of producers — the United Arab Emirates, Oman, Saudi Arabia, Brunei, Iran and Iraq (the latter two in barter deals for arms). However, there were also shipments from the British side of the North Sea. The nerve centre of these operations was London, where South Africa's state oil company, SASOL, had its sole overseas office.

The Shipping Research Bureau in Amsterdam (bulletin, 13.9.88) has estimated that between 1973 and 1984 South Africa paid R22 billion over the odds for smuggled oil. Most of it went to international dealers (Mark Rich, a Swiss-based American, and the German firm Marimpex), and the carriers, Norwegians predominating. On arrival, the oil was refined by the European transnationals, Shell and British Petroleum, and the American Caltex and Mobil. Neither companies nor government publish details of the amount of oil and associated products used by the military. But five years ago, the estimate was 30,000 barrels a day, which is why Heunis warned that an oil embargo 'could have destroyed this country'. (*Observer*, 3.6.84.) Yet the United States, Britain and France vetoed a Security Council call for mandatory oil sanctions.

To this solid clandestine backing must be added the more open collaboration of the pariah states, regimes with an outlook on the world or colonial policies akin to South Africa's — Chile, Paraguay, Taiwan, Israel. In 1981, SADF General Jack Dutton was appointed ambassador to Santiago, followed in 1984 by the retiring air force head (Lt. Gen. Muller). Dutton then became marketing director of Sandock Austral, a South African firm with a share of the Punta Arenas shipyard, which builds and repairs the warships of both navies (*Resister*, April–May 1987). After a visit to four Chilean ports by the new fleet replenishment vessel, SAS Drakensberg, a rating commented: 'At all times you felt as if you were among friends, amongst people like us.' (*Paratus*, May 88, p. 27.)

Much the same can be said of the links between two unlikely allies, the Afrikaners and the Jews. During World War II, many Afrikaners joined the terrorist *Ossewabrandwag* (OB) and daubed swastikas on synagogues, or sometimes burnt them down. One OB general, Johannes Vorster, was interned for his pro-Nazi activities. In 1976, by then prime minister, he visited Israel to launch a fruitful commercial and military collaboration. Pretoria, according to Armscor chairman, Commandant Piet Marais, had helped develop an Israeli version of the G5 gun (*Citizen*, 31.3.76). In the other direction, Israel's defence minister, General Ariel Sharon, visited troops in northern Namibia and southern Angola in 1981. Since then, there have been persistent reports of Israeli technicians stationed in the Angolan border area. When South Africa launched a damaging raid on PLAN headquarters in Lubango, southern Angola, in February 1988, Israelis were said to. have helped jam Angolan radar (*Africa Analysis*, London, March 1988).

Most worrying for the Frontline States in this 'unnatural alliance' was

Pretoria's reputed nuclear capability. When Pik Botha boasted that South Africa could make a nuclear bomb if it so wished, few doubted the role of Israeli know-how. As early as 1977, a Soviet satellite had espied what looked like a test site in the Kalahari desert. It could have been preparing for a nuclear test. The Soviets persuaded the Americans to put pressure on South Africa to get it dismantled. Two years later an American spy satellite detected an unexplained double flash in the south Atlantic — an indicator of a nuclear explosion.

It is not known whether South Africa's or Namibia's uranium is used in the military nuclear programme, or in the French-built nuclear power station at Koeberg, north of Cape Town. Both fall within the ambit of South Africa's official secrets laws, which blocks disclosure of any information, however innocent. What is important is the intermeshing of countries and governments which have used the Namibian product in defiance of the rule of law. The Rossing company is controlled by the majority shareholder, Rio-Tinto Zinc, and its Canadian subsidiary, Rio Algom, with a 55.5 per cent stake; other shareholders are the partly state-owned German Urangesellschaft, the French petrol giant, Total, the South African mining house, Gencor, and Pretoria's Industrial Development Corporation, with the remaining 3 per cent going to the Windhoek client government.

Since Rossing came on stream in 1976, details of its customers have been kept secret, but journalists uncovered the 'yellow cake' trail by which the uranium oxide was first shipped to conversion plants belonging to British Nuclear Fuels and its French counterpart, Comurhex. France is Rossing's biggest European customer, taking one-third of its output. Since the mid-eighties, the British no longer purchase the converted uranium hexafluoride for civil domestic use —though there is believed to be a separate ministry of defence contract for 'hex' to power Trident nuclear submarines. British 'hex' is sent to Japan (more than half of its uranium requirements come from Namibia), Belgium, Spain, West Germany and Taiwan. After the 'hex' stage, uranium may be enriched by Urenco, the Anglo-Dutch–German plant in Almelo, Holland, or in France, by Eurodif, jointly owned by France, Spain, Italy and Belgium. The 'hex' bound for Japan is enriched in the United States. The complicated web of intrigue is essential in order to disguise the illegal origin of the Rossing uranium. It is one good reason why Western governments are against mandatory economic sanctions.

In 1987, after many years of preparation, the United Nations Council for Namibia brought a test case in a Hague civil court against Urenco for breach of UN Decree 1. Lawyers and officials noted that the Soviet Union, a member of the Council, did not appear enthusiastic and had vacillated over preparations for the case. Then in October 1988, the

Campaign Against Uranium Contracts, part of the Namibia Support Committee, a SWAPO solidarity group in London, disclosed that Russia itself was receiving uranium hexafluoride produced by British Nuclear Fuels. BNFL were pleased to point out that between 50 and 65 per cent of a typical shipment would have originated in Namibia and South Africa (*Financial Times*, 2.11.88).

After a six-year tax holiday, Rossing made its first contribution to the Namibian treasury in 1983. Today it accounts for almost 20 per cent of the country's GDP and 40 per cent of exports, while producing one-tenth of the world's uranium. It has become a state-within-a-state, maintaining a private army in case of 'any attack', according to a leaked memorandum (*Guardian*, 27.5.82). The company had experienced a SWAPO-led strike in 1979. Skilful public relations were called for. Unlike the South African diamond magnates, RTZ directors had to answer disconcerting questions at their annual meetings in London. The company has tried to cover for all eventualities — at various times Lord Carrington (a former Tory defence and foreign secretary, and head of NATO) and Lord Shackleton (Labour Party leader in the House of Lords) and Lord Byers (Liberal Party chairman) were on the board. Training schemes and overseas scholarships, a glossy magazine and visits for British mining journalists, were necessary to mitigate its illegal presence. RTZ claimed a good safety record, but in the absence of independent monitoring, no one knows the long-term impact of radiation on the workers and their families.

Pinning down responsibility for the illegal presence of a British company is like a paper chase in a high wind. RTZ said it was up to the British government to damn the operation. Foreign office ministers, for their part, regarded it as a commercial decision. In the absence of the vertical integration of all the uranium-related processes in any one country, Western multinationals tried to exculpate themselves from a direct association with the Namibian product. The Japanese did not import uranium from Namibia — technically true, as it went via Britain. And British power stations claimed not to use it, so that BNFL, while presumably making vast sums from processing and enrichment, could throw clean hands in the air. All the same, the Rossing product ended up in civil and military reactors around the world.

Japan, the world's second-ranking economic power, has been more adept than the West at deflecting criticism of its dealings with Pretoria. In the 1960s, with the wave of the apartheid wand, their businessmen in the Republic were transformed into 'honorary whites'. Since then, through the import of coal, uranium, iron, chrome, copper, and other metals, Japan has become apartheid's largest trading partner. The Tokyo government prohibits direct investment in South Africa and restricts diplomatic relations to the consular level, but it is their biggest post in Africa. Their own officials readily admit that 'our businessmen are skilful at getting round bans'. (Interview with Herbstein, August 1986.) Their motor companies in South Africa like to place former cabinet ministers on their boards. In 1985, 40 per cent of all cars sold in South Africa were Japanese, while Toyota's largest foreign plant was in the Transvaal. Official figures indicate that imports far outstrip exports, but then much of the machinery and computers are shipped through third countries. When America banned the sale of computers destined for military, police and government use, the Japanese were quick to fill the gap.

Apartheid and Namibian independence are not burning issues in Japan. Official declarations that 'we are a non-white people' need to be counter-balanced by former Prime Minister Nakasone's statement attributing American 'backwardness' to the presence of Afro-Americans, or blacks. The small but active Japan Anti-Apartheid Committee reported in July 1986 on the 'government's hypocrisy in pretending to comply with UN resolutions while importing uranium from Namibia.' Their fishermen hauled $16 million of lobsters out of Namibia's sea in 1985. Their firms have provided technology for the offshore oil drilling rigs operating illegally in Namibian waters (*West Africa* 6.3.89, p. 354).

The ransacking of fish from Namibia's ocean is a scandal on a par with that of mining. Though a renewable resource, biologists say it will take years of careful husbanding to restore marine life to its former abundance. The delay in achieving independence has led to a free-for-all from which friend and foe have profited. The termination of the mandate deprived South Africa of its right in international law to act on behalf of the colony. Its proclamation extending Namibia's fishery zone to 200 nautical miles has therefore been ignored, so that effectively Namibia's international waters extend a mere 13.6 nautical miles. Beyond that, fishing quotas are determined by the International Commission for the South East Atlantic Fisheries, whose membership spans a wide political spectrum. South Africa, the Soviet Union, Poland, Spain, Cuba and Angola clean up. Claiming that Namibia benefits from less than one per cent of the catch, South Africa cites an estimate that in one year (1982) a potential R800m in fishing profits was lost. With its small population and lengthy coastline, Namibia should reasonably expect to provide a cheap protein-rich diet for all its people and still have a substantial surplus to export.

Karakul pelts are at the luxury end of the export trade, controlled by an elaborate intermeshing of foreign companies. The Persian lamb, raised by white farmers in the centre south, must be slaughtered within 24 hours of birth or they lose their lustre for the lady of fashion. Karakul farmers belong to the Agra Coop, one of Namibia's largest trading enterprises. Swakara (for SWA Karakul) pelts are sold by the Hudson's Bay and Annings company at quarterly auctions in London. British registered, it is owned by auction companies in Finland, Norway and Denmark, though the latter claims to have ended all trade with apartheid. In Namibia, Agra Coop owns a third of the British registered company, Eastwood and Holt, which has close associations with Hudson's Bay and Annings. In 1987, one-third of the 900,000 Swakara pelts sold abroad went to West Germany, and the rest to Italy, Spain, Switzerland and Austria, earning R20 million. The lambs are bred on land once belonging to indigenous cattle-raisers. The future of these pastures — as a source of foreign earnings or a means of feeding the hungry — will be decided after independence. By then the disincentive of the South Africa connection might be replaced by the objections of the animal rights movement.

Europe's and Japan's connections with Namibia have been strangely unaffected by the war and the association with a regime condemned as illegal by their own governments. Only the Americans, their arms twisted by public opinion and congressional sanctions, have disinvested in determined fashion. Newmont Mining, in financial difficulties at home, sold its minority stake in the Tsumeb Corporation. American sanctions' legislation makes no distinction between South Africa and Namibia, unlike the Common Market measures aimed exclusively at the Republic.

European connections still abound; the naïve, the sentimental, the ideological blood brother, the business opportunist. A party of Dutch schoolboys visited an army unit in Bushmanland to be 'taught the secrets of living off the field during a two-day survival course.' (*Citizen*, 24.1.87.) The Frankfurt mining house, Dresdner Bank, launched a Namibian subsidiary (SWAbank) in 1973. J. G. van der Wath, a Namibian once in the South African cabinet, sits on the board. German tourists in South Africa invariably include a nostalgic visit to the 'old colony'. The shrinking rand has encouraged many of them to buy 'white' farms, managed in their absence by Namibians. Perhaps the most suggestive symbol of the pervasive European business connection is the presence in Windhoek of eight of the city of London's leading firms of accountants, companies like Peat Marwick McLintock and Price Waterhouse.

One lethal European contribution to the Namibian war has only recently become apparent. Since October 1984, under the Citizenship Act, foreign citizens between 15 and a half and 25 years with permanent residence in South Africa are liable for conscription. Older foreigners could also be enrolled in the Citizen Force or commandos. As a result, many dual nationals serve in the armed services. There may also be as many as one million British settlers who have become South African by choice or birth, but who are entitled to regain their first citizenship at any time. It could be that one in three members of the SADF have a claim to the citizenship of a European Community country. It is estimated that 600,000 South Africans could claim Portuguese nationality; 100,000 German, 50,000 Italian, 40,000 Dutch, 25,000 Belgian and 2,400 Irish, though some 75,000 other whites may be eligible for Irish passports. Here lies the kith and kin connection, so skilfully exploited by Ian Smith in the name of Rhodesia (*Resister* 58/59, Oct/Dec 88).

Empty Notebook, Silent Camera

The connections were a comfort as Namibia's whites understood that, whatever the harsh words the West reserved in public for Namibia, under the counter it was business as usual. The world saw, heard, and read very little about this faraway place, and, when it did make the news, it was likely to bear the stamp 'SADF approved'. Pretoria's first line of defence in protecting its story has been to keep it as boring as possible. It was not difficult. With no foreign staffers based in Windhoek, the media relied on stringers, who had to queue for the southern Africa slot behind the full-time correspondent in Johannesburg. The story was little known, its coverage episodic, obliging the reporter to begin with an explanatory, 'Namibia, formerly South West Africa, the one-time League of Nations territory whose mandate was revoked by the United Nations in 1966 but is still illegally occupied by a 100,000-strong South African force, pitted against the South West Africa People's Organization of Namibia (SWAPO) liberation movement etc. etc. . . .' The reader's concentration span is under strain. A foreign editor, picking up the despatch from his copy taster's tray, might well prefer something from a better understood hot-spot.

Here was another obstacle to the reporting of Namibia. The rebellion in South Africa's black townships was a 'sexier' story. The nightly exchanges between police and black youth witnessed on American and European television led the world to believe that the country was on the brink of revolution, until the tough media restrictions cleared South Africa off the screens. In the case of Namibia, free-ranging television cameras had never been there in the first place. There was no official state of emergency in Namibia, but martial law across much of the colony effectively kept snoopers out. British television occasionally showed documentaries shot secretly by reporters travelling as tourists. Staffers from the *Washington Post* or *The Independent* and *The Guardian* in London did travel north to interview atrocity victims. The veteran American Walter Cronkite made his acclaimed 'Children of Apartheid' programme posing as a tourist, but he did not get as far as Namibia. Usually, however, the foreign correspondent went into the war zone courtesy of the SADF.

The all-expenses-paid press flights into the Ondangwa base would include a briefing on the latest 'terrorist' body count, the Namibian-ization of the war, and the progress of WHAM. There were on-flights to Ruacana, Caprivi or Rundu, or into an occupied town in Angola. The evening would be spent in the mess chatting up a senior white officer, often English-speaking to provide a sense of camaraderie with the Anglo-Saxon visitor. A hiccough might ruffle the operation; two black South African reporters were refused service at a white-owned Ondangwa supermarket. For the most part, however, the visiting fireman or correspondent was impressed by the certainty of South Africa's position. No matter that five minutes walk from the base black Namibians could recount a different story.

These reporters, it will be remembered, were already subject to clearance by Pretoria, and could be expelled for reports deemed not objective. Radicals, friends of SWAPO and ANC, representatives of outspokenly critical organs of information, had been weeded out. South African embassies cut out and record all despatches about the country and consult bulging folders to remind them who is tolerable and who not. South Africa enjoyed a further propaganda advantage in its war with Angola. The MPLA was for long deeply suspicious of foreign, and particularly, 'imperialist' journalists. It may have stemmed from the world's unwillingness to credit reports in October 1975 that South Africa had invaded their country. The security risk is certainly a factor too — in 1982 a convoy of pressmen, which included reporters from the BBC and *The Financial Times*, was strafed by South African jets (*New Statesman*, 9.9.83). Recent signs of openness in Luanda seemed to coincide with growing confidence on the battlefield. In the months-long bombardment of Cuito Cuanavale, the Western media carried regular reports from the Angolan side. Yet the BBC prefaces the MPLA with 'Marxist' and SWAPO is sometimes referred to as 'Moscow-backed', but only rarely is Pretoria characterized as 'racist' or even 'white minority' — though UNITA may be labelled 'South African-backed and American-armed'.

An unspoken prejudice underlies the Western coverage of Namibia's war. It could explain why a small country struggling to free itself from 'illegal', and not simply 'colonial', rule was still denied the benefit of doubt over a government which was the step-child of Nazi Germany. A useful comparison is Poland, where, as in Namibia, a hated rump ruled over the unaccepting mass of citizens. Both are religious, law-abiding peoples. The Solidarity trade union movement, which embodies resistance to Soviet domination, is the darling of the West. Human rights became an acceptable international rallying cry when Lech Walesa and other union leaders were imprisoned, and President Reagan imposed sanctions and suspended Poland's favoured trading nation status. Western reporting of the murder of the Polish priest, Father Jerzy Popieluszko, was raised by Archbishop Tutu in his Nobel Prize acceptance speech in December 1984:

> I am glad that the death of one person can cause so much concern. But in the self-same week the South African police kill 24 blacks who had been taking part in protests. . . . Are we being told something that I do not want to believe; that we blacks are expendable and that blood is thicker than water; that when it comes to the crunch you cannot trust whites, that they will club together against us? [*Star*, 17.12.84.]

Tutu was clearly hinting at the role of racial prejudice, or the introspection bred of skin colour, in the attitudes of the Western media. A black guerrilla army attempting to overthrow a white-run state by force of arms means that whites will get killed. It is hard to win over Western readers, who may number white South Africans among their friends, but have few black acquaintances. In the same way, the visiting reporter finds that interviewing white Namibians will ease the story into the newspaper. When the German-speaking Namibian, Hans Rohr, called a press conference to expose brutalities in Kavango, it received detailed coverage the next day in London and New York. Anton Lubowski's 'coming out' as a member of SWAPO merited interviews in the London *Times* and the *Dominion* in Wellington, New Zealand. When a free-lance reporter likened Sam Nujoma to George Washington in an article for the *International Herald Tribune* (1.11.84), the editor deleted the sentence. The unspoken inference — it is not done to compare the patrician white general with the black peasant.

The American discovery of apartheid was sparked by black identification with people of their own colour. Black American journalists have worked in South Africa, something on which the British media lags behind. Les Payne wrote a revealing series on Soweto for *Newsday* in 1976, and the paper has been barred ever since. With blacks playing a minority but influential role in City Hall, Congress, the presidential primaries — even Reagan's last ambassador to Pretoria, Edward Perkins, was black — what they feel about South Africa is made to matter. Blacks in Britain are proportionately fewer and, having lived there less time, lack political clout. Their views on South Africa are not reflected in the nationwide organs of communications.

In general, the British media may not take a less liberal line, but they are more inclined to do what they are told. With the expulsion of the correspondents of the two major news stations, including the BBC's respected Michael Buerk, the shock was so great that the Corporation and ITN appeared to buckle under. (When Indira Gandhi expelled the BBC's best-known radio correspondent, Mark Tulley, for running foul of the state of emergency, the corporation pointedly refused to replace him.) The specific language of the US constitution relating to freedom of speech makes Americans feel strongly about interference with reporting. In March 1988, the House of Representatives African Affairs Sub-Committee conducted hearings on the difficulties of South African coverage. They heard testimony from Charles Freeman, a senior state department official, that 186 foreign journalists had been refused South African visas in the previous year. 'It goes without saying,' said Freeman, 'that these restrictions are abhorrent to us . . .' (*AWFile*, 21.3.88). A black journalist, Kenneth Walker, at one time the ABC correspondent in Johannesburg, criticized the networks for failing to utilize the 'one bold idea' they had come up with to get round the restrictions. 'The US networks have distributed video cameras into private hands in the black townships. But they resolutely refuse to use the tapes. What are they saving them for?' By maintaining bureaux in South Africa which were forced to operate under the press restrictions, Walker said the networks were 'perpetrating a fraud on the American public.'

What made the hearings especially sinister was the last-minute withdrawal of five senior American newsmen, including the redoubtable Walter Cronkite. The hearings chairman, Howard Wolpe, commented: 'They suggest that South Africa's manipulation of the US press penetrates well beyond South Africa's borders.' (*West Africa*, 28.3.88.) The episode was a reminder that South Africa's hearts and minds war is fought abroad as well. Its foot-soldiers are everywhere. They are not just government employees, but public relations firms, parliamentarians, students, well-intentioned ideologues, the occasional cleric, 'reds-under-beds' hunters, some well paid, others genuine amateurs. Their opinions range from those who believe South Africa's presence is best for Namibia (and for their business activities) to those who fear a 'communist SWAPO' take-over.

Dirty Tricks

Dirty tricks played a part too in the attempts to hold up Namibia's independence, with West Germany a leader in the field. Take the case of the International Society for Human Rights, founded in Frankfurt by anti-Soviet emigrés of dubious ideological rectitude, who subsequently turned their attention to Namibia, emerging as apologists for South Africa. The society's hand was evident in an attempt to blacken the name of SWAPO president. Sam Nujoma. It brought to Europe two members of the Windhoek-based Parents Committee, a group which campaigned on behalf of SWAPO dissidents imprisoned in Angola. On 13 May 1987, Nujoma came to the European parliament building in Strasbourg to address a meeting. As he walked through the lobby one of the 'parents', Mrs. Talitha Schmidt, pushed towards him, asking the whereabouts of a relative.

Though eyewitnesses agreed there was no physical contact. Mrs. Schmidt was to claim that Nujoma had slapped her in the face. A group of German right-wing Euro MPs, led by Count Otto von Habsburg, promptly called a press conference to describe how the 59-year-old black leader had 'punched' her in the face. The hype journeyed to London where, the following day, Mrs. Schmidt reappeared at a press conference, chaired by Tory MP. David Atkinson, British head of the ISHR. Though 'punch' had by now been reduced to 'slap', the journalists were unable to detect a bruise on her face. Still, a sympathetic *Sunday Telegraph* repeated Mrs. Schmidt's version, as if it were the gospel. In Namibia the story was gratefully received by radio, television and a friendly government press. Meanwhile, in Strasbourg, Mrs. Schmidt had made a formal complaint to the parliament's security officer, assault proceedings against the SWAPO leader being the ultimate prize. In his official report, the security chief said he had examined Mrs. Schmidt's face 'without being able to establish the slightest sign of an attack. My advice to get herself examined by a doctor,' he said, 'was not followed by Mrs. Schmidt.' (NCC, 7.8.87.)

South Africa has devoted much time and money to foreign persuasion. Here is how the *South African Digest*, a Bureau for Information publication distributed through its embassies, described the Namibian war of liberation in an article marking the 75th anniversary of the SADF:

> Limited intervention in Angola became necessary after that country's independence. Initially it was limited to the protection of workers in the south of the country. Later it deflected the effects of the Angolan civil war from the northern border of SWA/Namibia; and endeavoured to stop the terrorist threat against the inhabitants of South Africa and SWA/Namibia. [10.7.87.]

The Trafalgar Square embassy buys full pages in London newspapers to proclaim its reforming zeal. Britain's best-known letter-writer on South Africa. L. Clarke, a reformed (Pretoria) department of information ad-man, has pointed out that claims by foreign governments are exempted from the Advertising Standards Authority's strict code of practice. This means, he wrote, that foreign countries 'can spread as many untruths as they like in paid advertisements in the British press.'

As few people know of this exemption, 'most readers automatically assume that the code applies, and that South Africa's distorted and untenable claims for apartheid are "legal, decent, honest and truthful".' (*Guardian* 17.2.84.)

In 1981, with the Muldergate scandal still smouldering, Pretoria, through its administrator-general, established 'Namibia Information Offices' in Washington, London, Bonn and Paris, four of the five Contact Group capitals. The American lobbyists, Shipley Smoak (Marion Smoak, a former diplomat; Carl Shipley, a Washington Attorney), registered their activities as South West Africa/Namibia Trade and Cultural Council, Inc., with offices in the capital's National Press Building. The cultural side of their activities was reflected in attempts to obtain a place for a Namibian in the Miss Universe competition. They also harassed SWAPO. In 1984, they mounted an unsuccessful court challenge against the tax exemption status of the Africa Fund, which had long provided aid for SWAPO and other southern African refugees. The administrator-general's office in Windhoek denied, to general surprise, that it was behind these actions.

In Britain, where Namibia, and apartheid in particular, were better known, South Africa chose Sir Trevor Lloyd-Hughes, once press officer to Labour prime minister, Harold Wilson, to put its case. Almost simultaneously, a House of Commons all-party Namibia group was set up under the leadership of Nicholas Winterton, right-wing but independently-minded Conservative MP with good friends in Pretoria and the Trafalgar Square embassy. The group specialized in 'fact-finding' trips to Namibia, the bills picked up by Lloyd-Hughes. A typical trip occurred in the autumn of 1983, when five British parliamentarians paid a six-day visit to the territory led by a Tory MP, the late Martin Stevens. Stevens, who doubled as a marketing consultant, had never previously put a foot into Africa south of the Sahara, and was not known to have expressed a public view on Namibia. While there, his contacts were restricted to the military, white officials and anti-SWAPO black politicians. Lord Molloy, one of two Labour peers in the party, admitted that 'we never spoke to more than three or four blacks on the whole tour.' The churches were ignored, and SWAPO refused to have anything to do with the delegation, which is probably why the final report claimed that 'SWAPO is in exile'. Namibia, it recommended, should become a South African protectorate for five years (*Windhoek Advertiser*, 28.11.83).

With the appointment of the interim government in 1985, Pretoria decided on a more concerted public relations operation. Shipley and Smoak were kept on but Lloyd Hughes was sacked, and the London Namibia Office was handed over to two of his former employees in a rancorous episode in which he claimed to be fed up with taking 'apartheid money'. The importance of these offices was underlined by the co-option of Sean Cleary, an experienced South African diplomat who resigned from a senior job in the A-G's office in Windhoek to oversee a new propaganda set-up. In London, his Strategy Network International opened in a suite close to the palace of Westminster — a far cry from SWAPO's run-down headquarters in a poor suburb of north London. There, the Namibia Office, now representing a home rule government, saw itself as a pre-embassy in advance of independence. Press releases sent to MPs and journalists attempted to distance the interim government from the worst aspects of apartheid and Koevoet brutality. The 'freeby' trips continued, as clerics, politicians, retired generals and the press were given the *braaivleis* and game park treatment. Strategy Network International also lobbied for Savimbi and sent Tory MPs on visits to his Jamba camp in Angola.

There were no limits to South Africa's ambitions. One of the English workers in the London office, Steven Govier, sent a karakul coat to the Princess of Wales, compliments of the Karakul Board. On a visit to Namibia, he said, he had found that the people had a great respect for the British Royal Family. A courteous 'thanks awfully but no' reply from the next Queen's secretary was a firm indication that royalty would not be used as a public relations tool for Pretoria, or be seen wearing the pelts of day-old lambs.

The Namibia Office and the Pretoria-friendly MPs may not have impressed the Foreign Office, but they understood Mrs Thatcher's distaste for left-wing liberation movements and her preference for an independent Namibia well disposed to British industry and nuclear defence needs. Their aim has been to bolster an anti-communist internal settlement, while denigrating SWAPO and the churches, sprinkled with a ritual condemnation of apartheid (though the Stevens report saw 'no evidence of apartheid'). MPs who could claim to have visited that faraway country would ask parliamentary questions, mostly about Britain's policy of not providing aid or whether the Foreign Office had met with a visiting delegation of collaborationist politicians. The effect of this activity on the minds of MPs and peers could have been no more than minimal. But when the propaganda emanated from organizations with titles sporting terms like 'human rights', 'trade and cultural council', 'all-party', not to mention 'Namibia', the uninitiated in matters southern African were liable to be misled.

6.
The Deceitful Decade

Human Rights to Cold War

It was a war that should have ended a decade earlier. In January 1981, SWAPO, South Africa's client parties, and the governments involved in the negotiations, attended a UN-sponsored 'pre-implementation meeting' in Geneva. SWAPO was ready to sign a cease-fire so that Resolution 435 could start running. The previous October a UN team under Brian Urquhart and the secretary-general's special representative, Martti Ahtisaari, had been to Pretoria for discussions. Hopes were high that South Africa would honour its oft-repeated commitment to the plan. But it was not to be. Danie Hough, the administrator-general, shattered all hope by declaring that the 'time was not yet ripe'. The white DTA leader, Dirk Mudge, demanded that the United Nations first prove its impartiality by revoking SWAPO's special status and that constitutional guarantees similar to those in the Zimbabwe deal at Lancaster House be agreed. The meeting broke up in disarray.

'There is no question [but] that the failure of the Conference in Geneva . . . was the fault of the South African government,' Sir Ian Gilmour, British Foreign Office number two, told the House of Commons. Despite the forthright words, Pretoria's torpedo was simply an outward sign that it already knew that Reagan and Thatcher would go along with its regional security concerns and its opposition to SWAPO.

Until the 1960s, the US had had only the slenderest of connections with Namibia, but they were governed by a certain high-mindedness shaped by a consciousness of their own anti-colonial origins. Without President Woodrow Wilson's role at the Versailles peace conference, South West Africa might simply have become South Africa's legal trophy of war. With the emergence of the civil rights movement and an anti-segregation Supreme Court in the 1950s, the White House's condemnation of apartheid became axiomatic. With Democratic presidential candidate John Kennedy's words on the 1960 Sharpeville shootings, the US intruded critically into the politics of southern Africa. Kennedy hoped that the 'African people of South Africa will be able to obtain redress for legitimate grievances by peaceful means.' Months before his assassination, Kennedy instituted a voluntary arms embargo of South Africa, which worked effectively until relaxed by the Nixon administration.

The United States also supported a series of pro-Namibia measures at the United Nations and the World Court — the 1946 vote against incorporation, the 1966 revocation vote, the various Hague decisions, including the 1971 Opinion — in contrast to vehement British and French opposition. In 1969, following the Pretoria Terrorism Trial, the US was instrumental in launching the first debate on Namibia in the Security Council. It supported the resulting resolution declaring that South Africa had no legal right to try the SWAPO prisoners. A year later there was support for a Security Council resolution banning commercial dealings with Namibia. But then, later in the 1970s, the US changed its stance on Namibia. Once seen from across the Atlantic as a colony deprived of human rights, it became just another piece in the Cold War.

By the late 1960s, the intransigent southern African governments had serious independence wars on their hands. Richard Nixon's national security adviser, Henry Kissinger, opted for the Tar Baby Option, the outcome of a National Security Council policy review. In effect, it abandoned the long-established principles on southern Africa. It called for the maintenance of 'public opposition to racial repression but relaxing political isolation and economic restrictions on the white states.' Change, it argued, would only come through the white governments, and blacks 'would not gain political rights through violence'. Thus Portugal, a member of NATO, received material and training, the Rhodesians were allowed to sell chrome in the United States despite sanctions, while the Nixon and Ford administrations supplied equipment with a dual military and civil use to South Africa. In April 1974, the Lisbon colonels gave way to the African freedom fighters and turned Tar Baby's two major premises upside down.

Kissinger's global view of politics suggested that the FNLA liberation movements, whose leader, Holden Roberto, was a CIA remittance man, should take power in Angola. Correspondingly, the MPLA was perceived as the threat to an Angola 'safe' for the West. The CIA's intervention in the Angolan civil war was also aimed at protecting the Mobutu regime in Zaire, an African country second only to South Africa in mineral importance. Once the CIA's clandestine role in the war was uncovered, Kissinger set about devising a policy of regional security for the sub-continent. It would reflect his and the general American obsession with Fidel Castro, a personification of that greatest dread of all — spreading Soviet influence. No longer could SWAPO, or any

Namibian liberation movement on the side of the MPLA and the Cubans, be considered worthy of support. The Kissinger global view provided the intellectual seed bed out of which would emerge 'linkage'.

The Carter presidency of 1977–81 proved a brief break to the developing conservative consensus over southern Africa. The ending of apartheid and Namibian colonialism again became first-string priorities, and not adjuncts to the achievements of other foreign policy goals. Carter and his advisers viewed Castro's intentions with some alarm, but argued, correctly as events have shown, that once Pretoria got out of Namibia, the Cubans would have no reason to stay in Angola. Donald McHenry and Andrew Young, the two officials most intimately involved in framing the Western Contact Group's positions, had regular contact with Theo-Ben Gurirab, the SWAPO representative at the United Nations, and other of his colleagues when they were in town. It was the trust that developed out of these contacts that enticed SWAPO into acceptance of the plan. This exercise in conventional diplomacy might have worked had the occupation of the American embassy in Teheran not rung the death-knell for the Carter presidency. The country now entered a more brutal, callous period. Ronald Reagan was indifferent to human rights, especially those of black southern Africans. America, he declared, was no longer going to be pushed around. The people of Namibia would be made to suffer for their allegiances.

In 1979, Dr Chester Crocker, director of African Studies at Georgetown University's Centre for Strategic and International Studies in Washington, voiced serious misgivings about US southern African policies in the journal *Foreign Policy* (his co-author was a former Carter-era state official). The Carter administration, they wrote, 'is not the first to have devised an inadequate Africa policy. But it is the first administration since John. F. Kennedy's to make any pretence at conducting an activist policy on the continent and the only one (so far) to fall short of both its own promises and requirements of the African situation.' A significant criticism of Carter's policy was that it sought to build 'human rights and basic human needs criteria' into US policy and assistance programmes.

A year later, between Reagan's election and inauguration, Crocker published a timely piece in the influential journal *Foreign Affairs*, entitled 'South Africa: Strategy for change'. By then Rhodesia had become Zimbabwe, and the 'Marxist terrorist' Mugabe sat in Ian Smith's office in Harare. The 'fundamental goal [of an African policy] is the emergence in South Africa of a society with which the United States can pursue its varied interests in a full and friendly relationship, without constraint, embarrassment or political damage.' Constructive engagement, he explained, 'is consistent with neither the clandestine embrace nor the polecat treatment.' (p. 346.) Pretoria, he argued, should be treated as a fully paid-up member of the world community, the better to cajole it into decolonizing Namibia.

Crocker's view fitted well into the Reagan scenario. As assistant secretary of state for Africa, he unveiled his 'constructive engagement' plan for the sub-continent, one of the lengthiest exercises in diplomatic engineering ever undertaken by an American official. It was a natural outgrowth of the Kissinger thesis and gave a local dimension to 'linkage'. Years later, Crocker put the argument in blunt terms:

> You can find another apparently intractable problem and, by linking it to the first, open the possibility of trade-offs between an expanded list of parties. We recognized that hard realities linked the problem of Namibian independence with that of Cuban troop withdrawal from Angola. Acceptance of this 'linkage' could promote a broader peace in the southwestern African region. [*AWFile*, 2/5/89.]

Despite his manichean vision of the world, Ronald Reagan had the sense to recognize that 'one man's freedom fighter is another man's terrorist'. His freedom fighters were the Nicaraguan contras, the Afghan mujahedin, UNITA. The sole African movement in a 1989 Pentagon booklet, *Terrorist Group Profiles*, was the ANC, but not Renamo, despite the latter's branding by the State Department as mega-killers. Had he been living in the New England of the 1770s, Reagan would have faced a dilemma — George Washington, terrorist or freedom fighter? What would Reagan have made of Lutheran pastor Peter Muhlenberg, who tore off his clerical garb in the pulpit one Sunday morning in 1776 to reveal the uniform of a rebel officer? The freedom fighter became a brigadier-general in Washington's army. Namibian churchmen and politicians repeatedly referred Reagan to the US War of Independence in their appeals to drop linkage, but to no avail.

Low Diplomacy

From the moment the ink dried on the 1978 Contact Group's peace plan, South Africa had been backtracking and 'small-printing'. As Crocker noted, 'South Africa would . . . invent one reason or another to delay it,' adding, 'although, to be fair, it did have some genuine misgivings about certain aspects of the report (on Resolution 435). So we spent the first year and a half working on some of those, while also developing linkage and trying to get it established.' (*Optima*, June 1989, p. 51.) But even before then, the surrender of Walvis Bay and handing over control of the election timetable to Pretoria under 435 had marked the start of a series of damaging concessions squeezed out of SWAPO.

Throughout 1979/80, the Contact Group attempted to appease South

Africa's quibbles over the deployment and size of the UNTAG (monitoring) force, and the executive powers of the police (at the time there were a mere 350). In January 1979, a United Nations team visited Namibia to prepare for implementation, followed by a call from Waldheim for a cease-fire on March 15. South Africa then objected that the secretary-general had made provision in the plan for SWAPO bases to be monitored by the UN inside Namibia. Though the issue had apparently already been settled, Pretoria used it to stall throughout 1979 and into 1980. In March 1979, at proximity talks in New York arranged by the United Nations and the Contact Group to resolve problems raised by Pretoria, South Africa's delegation was allowed to go through with the charade of not sitting in the same room as SWAPO. A month later, most of SWAPO's internal leadership was imprisoned without any retaliatory action or protest from the major powers. Despite the concessions, Pretoria still characterized the UN plan as pro-SWAPO.

With Thatcher's election as British prime minister in May 1979, South Africa was able sell Britain the idea of a demilitarized zone (DMZ). A senior official, Sir James Murray, came and went for the best part of a year. President Agostinho Neto of Angola was brought in to the negotiations, and General Prem Chand, the Indian head of the UNTAG forces, visited Namibia to investigate the DMZ. In May 1980, Pretoria agreed to terms, while still seeking provisions for 20 bases for itself. Murray's plan of a DMZ of 50 kilometres on each side of the border was eventually agreed, but dropped in 1982 when full-blooded linkage was adopted as the Western line. It had served its purpose as a stalling tactic.

When Thatcher met Reagan in Washington in February 1981, Namibia was on the agenda and Thatcher declared her opposition to sanctions. The president described South Africa as 'a friendly nation'. Thatcher was followed to Washington by a DTA delegation and by General Piet van der Westhuizen, chief of South African military intelligence. His visit was said to be linked to aid to UNITA. In mid-March, South African troops invaded Angola. That same month, Savimbi flew to Washington. (There were two more visits in 1981.) In April, American military advisers visiting Savimbi were told that UNITA needed ground-to-air anti-aircraft missiles. The new administrator-general, Gerrit Viljoen, declared that a peaceful settlement was no longer possible under 435. In April 1981, Crocker sent the president a review which noted that an unrestricted SWAPO government in Namibia would not be in the best interest of the United States, and that 435 was no longer a sufficient basis for agreement because South Africa opposed it. (*Africa News*, 25.5.81.) After Crocker had visited South Africa as part of his sounding-out mission to Africa, the Contact Group announced they were working on changes to the UN plan. Once again, in May 1981, the three permanent Western members vetoed sanctions in the Security Council.

America's new 'whiter-than-white' policy came into sharper focus in May with Crocker declaring that there could be no Namibian settlement without a Cuban withdrawal, and that Savimbi had to be brought in to any arrangements for Angola. In mid-May Pik Botha, a guest at the White House, asked the president for help in establishing constitutional and security guarantees for the white minority in Namibia and South Africa. The election of the socialist president, François Mitterrand, in France seemed for a moment to offer hope for a new push on 435, but it was too late. The Contact Group had become an American tool. The invasion of Cunene province, Operation Protea, the SADF's biggest undertaking since World War II (*Paratus*, May 1989, p. 23), began South Africa's lengthy occupation of southern Angola. Reagan vetoed a Security Council resolution condemning the invasion. Britain abstained — because the resolution described South Africa as 'racist'.

When, in October 1981, the Five thrust their constitutional principles on SWAPO, the goalposts were once more seen to have been moved to the white minority's advantage. The 'principles' featured some Lancaster House-type provisions — restrictions on the expropriation of private property as well as fundamental freedoms in a bill of rights. In addition, the West now proposed that the final constitution should only be accepted by a two-thirds vote of the elected assembly, and no longer a simple majority. This was an indirect acknowledgement by the West and South Africa of SWAPO's dominant support. The SWAPO leadership, under internal Frontline pressure as a result of Pretoria's military actions, conceded these provisions but objected to the dual voting system contained in the same package.

Few episodes illustrate the anti-SWAPO machinations better than those relating to this voting system. The West and South Africa proposed procedures similar to those used in West Germany. Instead of straight proportional representation

> with voters casting ballots for national lists of candidates, the State Department proposed that Namibians should each effectively cast two ballots, one for a national list, with seats in the constituent assembly to be allocated proportionally, and one for individual representatives in specific constituencies. Half of the seats in the assembly would thus be filled by each method. [Rotberg 1983, p. 37.]

SWAPO's leaders objected that this complex method was too open to abuse by South Africa and was clearly unsuitable for a semi-literate country about to experience its first free national election. The Western negotiators had the evidence of extensive South African cheating at successive internal elections in Namibia but were again willing to go along with Pretoria. SWAPO and the Frontline States turned it down. The Contact Group tried again, proposing in April 1982 a revised 'one person, one vote, two counts' system, but the African leaders rejected that too. For them, it was another device to manipulate the vote to get a 'blocking third' of compliant politicians.

By mid-1982 when linkage was formally enunciated, the original 1978 peace plan bore little resemblance to the current state of the document. Substantive negotiations were no longer about the UN plan since, for all practical purposes, agreement had been reached by all parties. The one snag was Crocker's 'Cuban factor' and his insistence, eagerly seized upon by South Africa, on a prior Cuban withdrawal. Echoing this, Prime Minister P. W. Botha said on 21 June 1982: 'We cannot enter the third phase of the agreement [i.e., actual implementation] with the Western Five unless the Cubans are withdrawn from Angola.' (Quoted in Wood 1987, p. 17). Linkage gave the South Africans a seven-year breathing space and condemned countless thousands of innocent persons to needless death.

The US–South African strategy acquired another card by resurrecting the almost defunct UNITA. In the aftermath of the Angolan civil war, ignored by black Africa, UNITA lay low in the far reaches of south-eastern Angola. Then in March 1977, Zairean exiles in Angola invaded the Shaba province of Zaire. President Mobutu blamed Angola, while President Neto counter-claimed that Zaire harboured FNLA and Cabindan rebels waiting to invade his country. According to a journalist close to Savimbi (Bridgland 1986), Zbigniew Brzezinski, President Carter's national security adviser, on a visit to China in May 1978, discussed ways of countering Soviet activities in Africa, and persuaded his hosts to supply 600 tonnes of arms to UNITA. Savimbi received his guerrilla training in China. 'From Mao and the Communists', he once wrote; 'I learned how to fight and win a guerrilla war.' By then 500 UNITA recruits were completing their military training in Morocco.

Savimbi became the lynchpin in the joint American–South African programme to destabilize Angola. He visited Cape Town in March 1982 for secret talks, but with his base so close to the Namibian border, the two allies could get together whenever they wished. Soon, UNITA was claiming responsibility for numerous disruptive operations across a wide swathe of Angola. Western artisans were kidnapped and marched around and around for weeks on end, priests and peasants were murdered, the Benguela railway was occasionally blown up, coastal oil depots destroyed. Savimbi's stock-in-trade was to foster the belief that his ubiquitous troops were encroaching ceaselessly on government-held territory. Yet he never succeeded in holding a single town of any size in this vast country. His capital, Jamba, lay a short flight from the Caprivi Strip. In May 1985, FAPLA forces captured a white South African commando, Captain Wynand du Toit, a member of a nine-man reconnaissance mission to blow up the American oil installations in the

Cabinda enclave, as far away from Namibia as you can get in Angola. Du Toit carried UNITA propaganda leaflets to be left at the scene of the attack. He also admitted to participating in a 1982 commando raid on a bridge near Mocamedes, which UNITA had claimed as its success (Bridgland 1986, p. 442).

So the Cubans remained in Angola because the South Africans, whose invasion had precipitated the Cuban escalation in the first place, refused to get out of Namibia. And South Africa stayed in on the pretext of 'the communist threat' posed by the Cubans. In Luanda, the MPLA viewed a UNITA armed and cossetted by the SADF as a threat to their very existence. The stalemate suited South Africa. Very few whites were dying. Washington could say it wanted an early solution, but no American lives and very little money were at risk. It was the Namibians, Angolans, Cubans, overwhelmingly black, who did most of the dying, at least until 1988.

No more ministerial level meetings of the group were held after October 1983. Indeed, the French government withdrew from the Contact Group on the grounds that everything was in place for the plan to go ahead. The British and West Germans for their part followed the US line in private, while fudging in public. A succession of Foreign Office Africa ministers declared that 'Cuban withdrawal is not a formal pre-condition for a Namibian settlement.' (Cranley Onslow, 28.7.82, to AAM delegation.) But in the Commons in 1984 Mrs Thatcher said that Namibian independence would not occur 'until there is, in parallel, also the withdrawal of Cuban troops from Angola.' By not firmly distancing themselves from the United States, the British endorsed linkage. Whether the Americans would have persisted in placating South Africa without the wink-and-nod support of its trans-Atlantic ally will never be known.

The Reagan administration spent the years of 'linkage' trying to grind the MPLA into a frame of mind suitable for sending the Cubans back home. The two-pronged attack of Crocker diplomacy and SADF scorched earth was reminiscent of the good-guy-bad-guy interrogation employed by South African security police. After Crocker impressarioed a South Africa–Angola meeting on Cape Verde, Pik Botha spoke of a 'preliminary package that included South African military withdrawal from Angola'. But at the subsequent meeting of the South African State Security Council, the foreign minister was apparently bitterly rebuked by General van der Westhuizen, who feared a deal on a SADF pull-out without a Cuban quid pro quo (SAIRR 1983, p. 619).

The period 1983 to 1987 were dark, frustrating years yet the combined might of the strongest military powers of two continents failed to break the will of the Namibian and Angolan peoples. Black Namibians, however, despaired of US policy and the US lost much of the moral authority that decades of its anti-colonial policies had achieved. In October 1984, the Council of Churches general secretary, Dr. Abisai Shejavali, lamented that:

> Our people thought that the West was serious when they came up with this Contact Group and said they were going to negotiate with South Africa. We thought they were honest . . . we now see them wavering and they don't want to let this resolution be implemented. The American government, as the leader of the group, is really losing credibility with our people. [NCC interview 14.10.84.]

Bishop Dumeni described Reagan's re-election in 1985 as 'the re-election of our suffering'. (NCC, 18.6.86.)

Angola did, however, bend under the sustained battering, though without ever accepting the concept of linkage. Its *Plataforma* of November 1984 proposed a phased Cuban withdrawal from southern, but not northern, Angola in exchange for South Africa implementing 435. Crocker dangled diplomatic recognition (only Taiwan, South Africa and the USA did not recognize the MPLA). The proposals were stymied by continued SADF operations in Angola and US support for UNITA. Again, in 1984 Luanda initialled an agreement which would have South Africa withdrawing from Angola in exchange for PLAN guerrillas being reined in by the MPLA. An unhappy period ensued, with Pretoria stalling its withdrawal and unconfirmed reports of FAPLA arresting, even shooting, SWAPO guerrillas. Crocker, for his part, proclaimed high hopes that this agreement would lead to Namibian independence in 1985. He did admit, however, that 'predictions get you into trouble in this business.' (*Star*, 25.2.85.) South Africa completed a troop withdrawal in April 1985, but instead of signing a ceasefire, it switched to the other track and set up an 'interim government'.

In Angola, the government had agreed in principle on the reciprocity of withdrawals, but not on as rapid a timetable as the US or South Africa sought. To encourage Dos Santos, Reagan sent $15m. of CIA covert aid (though it was publicly announced) to Savimbi, largely in the form of Stinger anti-aircraft missiles. The Kamina airfield in Zaire was upgraded for the on-transport of the weapons. There is good reason to believe that, even before this new aid, the CIA had armed Savimbi through donations from wealthy American right-wingers. The perceived effect of the arming of UNITA, surrogate of the apartheid government, hardly improved the US image in the developing world, while the comparatively small amount of arms hardware on offer could not have swung the balance in South Africa's and Savimbi's favour. Indeed, it gave the Soviet Union and Cuba the opportunity to upgrade support to MPLA, ultimately leading to the humiliation of South Africa. By now

South Africa's townships were in revolt and the American public, fed nightly scenes of state brutality in their living rooms, demanded action. As a direct outcome, the Congress voted sanctions against South Africa (including Namibia) and the American corporate community began a helter-skelter disinvestment from apartheid. Despite the sanctions, Namibia faded into the background as an issue.

The Puppets Can't Dance

Content in the knowledge of Western support, or at least of no hint of reproach, over its activities in Angola, South Africa turned to the more enduring problem of finding a credible alternative to SWAPO, and a leader to place at the head of it. Anyone would have sufficed, even one without charisma, though he had to be black to stand the least chance of acceptability. A Savimbi would have done. But there was not even an Abel Muzorewa, the bishop called in to front Rhodesia's 'thousand years' of white rule.

Since the Turnhalle conference in 1975, Pretoria had experimented with several variations of local rule, interlaced with direct control through an administrator-general; each time it failed. The political party which grew out of the Turnhalle, the Democratic Turnhalle Alliance, became the leading player in the National Assembly, which in turn became a constituent assembly, with a cabinet with limited powers. By 1982, the DTA-led cabinet was falling apart at core and seam. White conservatives, inspired by the outlandish *Herstigte Nasionale Party*, resisted the inroads on apartheid, while Peter Kalangula, the DTA president, complained that the ethnic make-up of the alliance discouraged Ovambo support. He resigned to form his exclusively Ovambo Christian Democratic Action for Social Justice Party (CDA), claiming the support of all but seven of the 58 members of his tribal legislature.

By then a ('modest' for blacks, 'thin-edge-of-the-wedge' for whites) start had been made on repealing racist law and practice. Mixed marriages, taxis, many hotels, public buildings, cinemas, official resorts, were 'opened'. So were residential areas, but the few blacks who could afford to buy a house in Klein Windhoek still had to transport their children to a black school miles away as, except for a handful of private institutions, classes remained rigidly segregated. Railway carriages and hospitals were also segregated. By 1983, Namibia was probably the most over-administered country on earth, with a constituent assembly, bantustan legislatures and several tiers of local authority structures. This fiscal bottomless pit offered effortless opportunities for corruption. The secretary for finance, Johan Jones, in a 1983 document, talked of the Namibian bantustans as 'parasites feeding on the fruits of the land without any control or supervision . . . which is leading to the rapid collapse of the entire economy.' (*Cape Times*, 7.1.85.) When the assembly broke up in 1983 it was over an arcane dispute about the abolition of the Day of the Vow, an emotive relic recalling the Voortrekker victory over the Zulus in 1838. Under right-wing pressure, the abolition bill was returned to the assembly by the AG. The white chairman, Dirk Mudge, and his ministers' council resigned (SAIRR 1983, p. 602).

The AG once again assumed the role of colonial governor. But it was important that South Africa be seen as moving the territory towards independence, and a new grouping was formed, the Multi-Party Conference (MPC). In June 1985, President Botha converted the MPC into a Transitional Government of National Unity. This interim government (IG) was rejected by the churches and many political parties, including SWAPO. On 16 June, the day before its installation, Police Major-General Dolf Gouws warned the churches against political activities. In defiance, with police and Koevoet patrolling, the churches held meetings across the territory, concluding with the prayer, 'Will you allow, oh Lord, our children to live under the destructive burden of colonialism into the coming century?' (NCC, 17.6.85.)

Namibians were lured to the official ceremony on the white side of town with offers of free transport and food. Koevoet troops were brought in to Windhoek to assist the Special Task Force, their southern counter-insurgency counterparts. A counter-rally of 4,000 people was held at a sports field in Katutura. It was peaceful, but outspokenly critical of 'a government that has no support from the majority of the suffering Namibian people.' Afterwards, 1,500 marchers streamed into the streets of the township singing and chanting '435 Now'. Casspirs ahead and behind blocked the procession, and fired tear gas. An American volunteer teacher, Gary Nelson, saw 'the Koevoet getting out of the trucks, throwing batons at cars and beating the people. A woman was lying on the ground, covering her head with four Koevoet beating her.' Protestors heard the constables pleading with their white officer, 'Please baas, give us the permission to kill them.' 'Not now,' they were told, 'there will be a chance later.' Across the town invited guests and journalists watched white doves of peace soar into the sky.

Shocked by the brutality of the day, Vice-Bishop Zephania Kameeta declared; 'The devils are really among us now.'

The interim government was seen by many as a precursor of a Rhodesia-type UDI. Though it had six political parties in its make-up, the sole identifiable common factor was an extreme antipathy towards SWAPO. White nationalists, of the same ilk as P. W. Botha's party in the Republic, were the largest component. The whites, and the equally ethnic-minded Rehoboth Basters, were the only groups elected by the people they represented. The government was hoping that the inclusion of men with some, albeit tarnished, resistance credentials would make the IG acceptable in black Africa. But cabinet ministers Andreas Shipanga, Moses Katjiuongua, a former Maoist who returned from exile in Scandinavia, and Jariretundu Kozonguizi, were viewed with contempt. Shipango's creation, SWAPO-D (for democratic), had a barely visible following in Ovamboland, while SWANU (MPC) comprised only a rump of Namibia's oldest political party, many of whose followers now supported SWAPO. Thus, the MPC was unable to dent the racist bodywork of Namibia. To acquire credibility, it needed to abolish AG 8, the South African edict which formed the legal basis for the division of the land into a dozen unequal ethnic packets. Thus, a white minister, Eben van Zijl, rejecting protests about a hospital being built by the white second-tier administration in Swakopmund, explained that white patients needed 'the right milieu' — code language for 'we want to be ill among our own people.' If the treatment failed, they had the satisfaction of burial in a segregated cemetery. The black minister of national health and welfare, Katjiuongua, complained that 'apartheid, tribal and racial discrimination and inequality of opportunity are not dead in this country.' (NCC, 25.6.86.) But he and other ethnic ministers and a fast-growing pool of officials were aboard a gravy train they could not afford to get off.

The Herero administration was one of the more venal, and had to be bailed out with a R10 million central government loan to fulfil its health and education obligations. One of its critics, Chief Munjuku Nguvauva of the (Herero) Mbanderu Council, said the money would be 'consumed by corruption and inefficiency.' (*Windhoek Observer*, 9.4.88.) The succession of scandals over overspent ethnic budgets and ministers' land speculation led to the Thirion Commission of Enquiry into corruption, but a system which countenanced eleven education departments for a country of one and a half million people was by its nature wide open to peculation. Nor were the ministers able to halt the enormous mineral drain by foreign companies, something attempted, however ponderously, by the United Nations.

By inheriting responsibility for the police and the South West Africa Territorial Force (SWATF), the MPC became answerable for Koevoet's behaviour, though it was plainly controlled by South Africa. Still, black ministers relished the task. Four of them toured the north in May 1986 praising the security forces for their role in 'defending the country against aggression'. (*Observer News Service*, 20.6.86.) At the same time the IG failed to abolish the Terrorism Act, though long repealed in South Africa, nor other detention-without-trial laws. Cabinet members Katjiuongua and Kozonguizi swore affidavits opposing access to

161

political detainees by relatives and lawyers. Detentions, prison deaths, disappearances persisted. Church processions were banned. The Anglican bishop, James Kauluma, was shot at while trying to protect schoolchildren.

Whatever the ministers tried rebounded against them. A University of Pretoria Military Information Bureau assessment noted SWAPO's success in using the transitional government to generate an 'emotional wave'. (1987, p. 10.) When South Africa freed several Pretoria trialists in 1984, the IG gave the impression that it had been in response to its request. The gesture backfired. Shipanga visited his erstwhile comrade Andimba Ya Toivo in Windhoek prison prior to his release, but the SWAPO veteran sent him packing. Others were soon reinvigorating the trade unions or working for SWAPO or the churches. But it was the tragedy of another ex-Robben Islander, Immanuel Shifidi, who unwittingly did more than anyone to expose the IG's subservience to Pretoria.

After his 18 years in prison, Shifidi, a quiet, self-effacing man, was found a job with the Council of Churches. One day in November 1986, he attended a SWAPO rally in Windhoek to mark the UN Year of Peace. It was orderly until a group of men in plain clothes charged the outdoor rally brandishing *knobkerries* (heavy sticks), pangas (machetes), bows and arrows and guns. Dozens were injured, some stabbed, but the only fatality was Shifidi, knifed in the chest. The Security Police were waiting outside, and they fired tear gas and rubber bullets, pursuing the terrified crowd through the streets. One man was followed into a Lutheran church and sjambokked in the chancel. The authorities hoped to give the impression of black-on-black violence. But a bus driver who had ferried the attackers the several hundred miles from Ovamboland explained all. The men belonged to 101 Bn, the Ovambo military unit known for its violent treatment of Angolans and Namibians. The inquest magistrate found that the meeting was peaceful until the *agents provocateurs* arrived. Almost a year later, four white officers, including a Colonel Johannes Vorster, and two black men, were charged with Shifidi's murder and public violence. The prosecution had 50 police and soldiers as witnesses to the conspiracy. On the day of the trial, however, as members of Shifidi's family waited outside the court, President Botha quashed the proceedings. He invoked a clause in the Defence Act empowering him to issue a certificate halting a trial of members of the security forces where they had acted 'in good faith while combating terrorism in an operational area.' When lawyers for the Shifidi family appealed, a full bench of the Windhoek Supreme Court invalidated Botha's certificate. The president in turn lodged an appeal. By the time it is heard, the white officers may well have left Namibia for good.

It was not the first Defence Act intervention. In November 1985, a

48-year-old father of five, Franz Uapota, had been attacked as though by 'a pack of wild dogs' (in the words of his widow) by four white soldiers outside a shop in Ovamboland. He was kicked and butted with rifles, but did not fight back as, blindfolded, he was dragged by the neck into the bush to die. His injuries included a crushed skull, broken neck, partial strangulation, nine broken ribs, a ruptured spleen, multiple bruises, abrasions and burns on his arms, thorax, abdomen and back. It took a charge of murder laid by Uapota's widow, helped by a church lawyer, to bring the four white soldiers to court. A preliminary hearing was held in December. On 27 July 1986, Botha told the interim government to issue a certificate under the Defence Act to halt the proceedings. The Windhoek Bar Council described the state president's refusal to give reasons for stopping the trial as an 'insult to the dependents of the deceased, the judiciary, the courts, the attorney-general, the legal fraternity and the citizens of this country.' (NCC, 4.8.86.)

Earlier, in 1984, the Cassinga raid surfaced in court when it was learnt that over 100 survivors had been held for six years at a prison outside the southern town of Mariental. They were, by any definition, prisoners of war. When Namibian bishops went to court to have them released, the South African justice minister, Kobie Coetzee, issued a certificate stopping the proceedings which were, he said, 'not in the national interest'. They were later released following pressure by the International Red Cross and Windhoek lawyers.

An international public relations effort was mounted over a 'Bill of Fundamental Rights' included by P. W. Botha in the proclamation establishing the interim government. It was fine-sounding measure which occasionally served to hoist ministers on their own petard when citizens invoked it. The bishops used it unsuccessfully in an effort to show that the curfew infringed freedom of movement and worship, but a German-born Namibian successfully challenged a law providing for the deportation of non-Namibians. In these and other cases the government opposed the application of the freedoms ostensibly guaranteed by its own law. Then, in October 1986, the Supreme Court struck down a major provision of the Terrorism Act which forced an accused to prove their innocence. The section, said Judge Harold Levy, conflicted with the right to a fair trial as enshrined in the Bill of Rights. The decision came as a prelude to a trial in which eight Namibians were accused of 187 counts under the Terrorism Act. As a result, 50 acts of terror allegedly committed after the Bill had come into effect were withdrawn. Acts of terror committed before the enactment of the Bill of Rights, however, remained actionable. The case was an example of the Supreme Court taking a less executive-minded view of the law than would its South African counterparts. Andreas Heita and Salomo Paulus, PLAN guerrillas, and four SWAPO supporters, were sentenced to a total of 58 years in prison, which did not take into account their two years in pre-trial custody. They were not convicted for murder. The case was dominated by evidence that a Koevoet officer, Captain Frantz Ballach, had marched into the hospital where the badly-wounded Heita was being treated, tore a drip from his arm and flogged him mercilessly. The judge recommended that Ballach and other police officers be prosecuted. They were not.

In an effort to bolster their image among an increasingly sceptical populace, four of the six MPC parties drew up a draft constitution which made no mention of 'group', in other words, 'white' rights. Its contents were not made public, but it prompted the two big brothers, Pik Botha and General Magnus Malan, to fly to Windhoek to inform the MPC parties that the draft was unacceptable. Shipanga and Katjiuongua were forced to climb down as the IG announced the decision to go along with Pretoria was unanimous. In March 1988, ministers finally received a copy of a proposed constitution drawn up by retired Judge Victor Hiemstra. It was rejected by the whites and Basters, and by the South African government. These events hardly helped the IG out of its isolation. Nowhere in the world was it recognized, though it had friends. In April 1988 a visiting delegation of British Conservative MPs, including Mrs Teresa Gorman, were able to describe the IG as 'the custodian and champion of democracy and free enterprise'. (*Namibian* 15.4.88.)

The stalemate in the war in Angola corresponded with a profound radicalization of Namibian society. Church, trade union and student activism almost exactly paralleled that in the Republic. The IG responded by intensifying its war against the Namibian churches, which it rightly believed to be on the side of liberation. The IG forcibly took over a Catholic hospital in Swakopmund and slashed subsidies to the church's schools, making it difficult to feed children in the lowest economic stratum. The churchmen did not hesitate to speak their minds, in the pulpit and out, at home and abroad. In Brussels, Bishop Dumeni accused the United States of participating in 'the theft of our freedom', adding that 'we will never retreat in our demand for freedom, there is no reverse gear in this vehicle.' Calling for economic sanctions, he explained that 'even though people may suffer, it is better to suffer illness for one day and then get cured, rather than to be an invalid for the rest of your life.' (NCC, 6.5.86.) The Roman Catholic Bishop of Natal, Denis Hurley, was awarded damages of R25,000 for malicious prosecution when the state withdrew Police Act charges relating to his allegations about Koevoet and Security Police atrocities.

The case of Ida Jimmy illustrates how the authorities were unable to accept people's Christian beliefs if they were SWAPO activists. While serving a seven-year prison term for non-violent 'terror' activities. Jimmy gained a Bible studies diploma. So impressive was her performance that the Bible college recommended that she teach other prisoners. The prison matron objected, but Ms. Jimmy was helped by a God-fearing wardress who smuggled Bibles into the prison. She held clandestine Bible discussions with five 'non-politicals', after which the dangerous volumes were hidden in a rubbish bin. 'This was one of the good experiences,' she said on leaving prison in 1986, 'because while South Africa say SWAPO do not know God, they were at the same time trying to stop us studying the Bible.' (NCC, 1.5.86.)

This closeness between the churches and the political parties was formalized in the *Ai-Gams Declaration*, an alliance of all the major churches (not the Afrikaner Dutch Reformed Church nor the small white Lutheran grouping), SWAPO, SWANU, the Damara Council and other southern political parties, and student and women's organizations. (*Ai-gams*, or more properly, */Ai//Gams*, using the click sound of the Nama language, means 'hot springs', original designation of the Windhoek area.) This CCN initiative inaugurated a new, heightened phase of the struggle, aimed at 'mobilizing and conscientizing the masses so as to actively resist the status quo.' In a series of countrywide meetings *Ai-gams* speakers called for the implementation of 435, while castigating the unholy alliance of South Africa and the United States. IG ministers could only threaten to pass a law banning *Ai-gams* meetings.

These meetings were made easier to hold by a show of independent-mindedness on the part of the Namibian Supreme Court, which ruled that SWAPO did not have as its aim the overthrow of the state — a judgement which might have surprised some of its followers. The Notification and Prohibition of Meetings Act, the 1981 measure designed to smother SWAPO activities, according to Judge Levy, 'made serious inroads into the liberty of the subject.' (*Namibian*, 4.7.86.) The movement's first legal rally in years, in Katutura, attracted 13,000. Now the voice of Namibia could be heard direct. Asked by Revd. Hendrik Witbooi, a SWAPO vice-president, if they favoured sanctions, they thundered back, 'Sanctions now!' Enthusiastic meetings around the country emphasized that the court judgement had been a milestone in SWAPO's fortunes.

Now the unions, dormant for some years, came back to life. Ovambo workers had been the early bedrock of the OPO and SWAPO, and had won limited reforms of the contract labour system in the 1971 strike. In 1978, internal SWAPO launched a general workers' union, the National Union of Namibian Workers (NUNW). However, bogus Terrorism Act arrests decimated the leadership and it was not till the release of the Robben Island prison veterans that Namibia's workers became a real force. This time they made sure that unions were industry-based, rather than the general union of previous years. John Pandeni founded a food and agricultural union (NAFAU) in September 1986. In its Luderitz stronghold, employees in a chemical plant went on strike over a worker dismissed for refusing to wear a faulty safety mask. The dispute triggered action over wages and dismissals at Atlas Organic Fertilizers, a small guano-collecting firm, a symbolic link with an earlier commercial activity in the colony.

The launch of the Mineworkers Union of Namibia (MUN) was clearly the most significant in terms of the national economy. Again, an ex-islander, Ben Uulenga, was the guiding spirit at the launch attended by 100 delegates from most of the country's mines. The Consolidated Diamond Mine's 50th anniversary celebrations were boycotted by some 3,000 black workers. The MUN subsequently signed an agreement with the company providing for the election of shop stewards and prohibiting the victimization of its officials. This success was followed by recognition at Rossing. Tsumeb, the third giant, was a tougher nut. By July 1987 it was one-third owned by the American company, Newmont, with a minor BP Minerals interest, but with control in the hands of Goldfields, South African subsidiary of the British company Consolidated Gold Fields. The union was anxious to improve the lot of members working under conditions of primeval exploitation. It struck, seeking better wages, a 45-hour week, pensions, paid annual leave, an end to segregated and single-sex 'bachelor' quarters, housing for their wives and children. Their action had an overtly political dimension with a call for the abolition of white supremacy and a demand that the company, which was run by white South African officials, condemn the war. Despite widespread workers' support for the action, the general manager refused to negotiate on the grounds that 'we do not recognize the union as it has not yet proven its membership.' (*New York Times*, 3.8.87.) Some 3,100 men were sacked, on the technical point that the strike had not followed government rule book procedures.

With the metal and allied workers, teachers and public servants all unionized by 1987/8, only the worst-off sectors of the work force, the farm and domestic workers, had still to come under the wing of the National Union of Namibian Workers. By 1988, its estimated 70,000 members made the NUNW the fastest-growing union federation in the world. It had developed strong links with unions in Scandinavia and Britain, notably the mineworkers. The unions showed their muscle and commitment in June 1988 in solidarity with the 40,000 boycotting schoolchildren. Workers arrived home one evening to find their children had been teargassed, beaten or arrested. Now they joined their children in demanding that defence force bases be removed from the vicinity of schools. There being no official response, workers took impressive action. At Rossing, the strike was almost 100 per cent successful. Some firms refused to reinstate the absentees, and this in turn became a rallying point for union expansion.

The IG and Pretoria were stunned by the integrated nature of resistance, where workers as parents supported children as unarmed freedom fighters (see Chapter 4). The IG attempted to tame NANSO's 3,000 plus students with the Protection of Fundamental Rights Act, which carried maximum fines of R20,000 and 10 years imprisonment. Student leaders were jailed for, among other things, influencing fellow workers to strike or students to boycott classes.

If workers, students and the church were part of the liberation movement led by SWAPO, other groups as well called for the implementation of 435. Most notable was Namibia Peace Plan 435, a pressure group of lawyers, businessmen and academics led by the prominent advocate, the Afrikaans-speaking Brian O'Linn. They were not SWAPO supporters, but neither did they want the dead hand of the occupation to continue. SWAPO held consultations in Stockholm with leaders of commerce, the law and acadème and followed with a larger meeting in Lusaka. In 1984, Anton Lubowski, a Windhoek barrister, became the first white to 'come out' publicly for SWAPO, although a white South African, Peter Manning, had in 1977 been detained for SWAPO-related activities. In a sign of spreading resistance, several white graduates and students had by the mid-1980s left the country to avoid army service. One of them, Hanno Rumpf, worked in the SWAPO office in Bonn, while Wilfred Brock taught at UNIN in Lusaka. Both came from established German–Namibian families. Others, for security reasons, kept their allegiance a secret for the time being.

From 1985, the war was made even more inaccessible to reporters by a requirement that police permits were needed to visit the 'operational area'. But with the launch in August of that year of the *Namibian*, the country became better informed about the north. The paper's lawyers cited the freedom of speech clause in the Bill of Fundamental Rights when challenging the R40,000 deposit it was forced to pay as a guarantee of 'good behaviour', while other papers favourable to the regime were overlooked. They won their point. Unashamedly on the side of SWAPO, the *Namibian* was not shy to rap the movement over the knuckles if necessary. It was said to have a readership of 100,000, and its appearance on Fridays itself tended to radicalize public opinion. Perhaps the army, police and government turned to it to find out what Namibians were thinking. The editor, Gwen Lister, leading reporter Chris Shipanga and photographer John Liebenberg were its stars, but it was a team effort. When, on 10 October 1988, a mystery bomber destroyed offices and equipment, the staff could still get the paper out for the Thursday night deadline. Within six weeks, a state-of-the-art computer system, courtesy of Western governments, had been installed. The firebombing, said to be the work of the neo-Nazi *Wit Wolwe* (White Wolves), was part of a campaign of harassment which included the detention of Lister for five days, police death threats to Liebenberg, and interference with the brakes and tyres of staff cars.

Other forces aligned themselves with SWAPO. Chief Munjuku Nguvauva, a long-time supporter, persuaded his Mbanderu Council to join the movement in 1988, against opposition from SWANU Progressives. It was a significant blow to the establishment Hereros. The administrator-general had earlier shown his distaste for the chief's politics by refusing to discuss his grazing and watering rights until he denounced SWAPO and agreed to accept the suzerainty of another chief.

But if SWAPO was recruiting at home, abroad it was going through another exile crisis. On a Sunday in February 1986, SWAPO's information secretary, Hidipo Hamutenya and the foreign relations secretary, Theo-Ben Gurirab, briefed journalists and NGO representatives in London. It was a brave initiative for a movement in the midst of a desperate war, though rumours were already circulating in Windhoek. They disclosed that a network of at least 100 South African spies had been uncovered in SWAPO offices in Zambia and Angola. Four were members of the central committee, the policy-making body. A few of those involved were dead. The most surprising name was that of Tauno Hatuikulipi, said to have committed suicide in a Lubango prison following accusations of treachery. He had risen rapidly in the PLAN hierarchy after fleeing his post of director of the Windhoek Christian Centre, a forerunner of the CCN. Colleagues recalled him as intelligent and industrious.

By the time the network had been detected in December 1983, both the political and military wings were said to be penetrated. Most of those identified claimed to have been forced into their work by threats or blackmail. Many were apparently the more urban and educated Nama-speaking southerners whose administrative skills would be valuable in exile. A 'video confession' was shown in which one man admitted to being recruited while in a detention cell in Namibia. He told of threats to his family if he did not work for South Africa. He was trained as a spy while in detention, he said, released, then redetained by the police to provide extra credibility, before using a SWAPO escape route to join PLAN (NCC, 17.2.86).

The detainees were said to have been tried by a SWAPO military court in a camp near Lubango. Gurirab said those in custody 'are not our enemies, most of them have been misled and we will not victimize them.' But others were 'real traitors' and could not be rehabilitated. 'SWAPO is not a charity organization, but is engaged in the liberation of our country. These men have provided information to our enemy that was used for killing our people.' There was no further clarification. SWAPO, he said, had been and would remain committed to basic human rights. The news was grist to the anti-SWAPO mill. The International Society for Human Rights launched a 'Release the SWAPO 100' campaign to project its pro-Pretoria viewpoint. Others spoke of ethnic rifts, or of a generation gap between the old SWAPO guard and the young blades.

When, in July 1989, 153 SWAPO detainees were returned to Namibia, they spoke of dehumanizing detention, starvation and being tortured to give video-taped confessions. Women said they had been raped by their guards. Some claimed that detainees who refused to confess to being spies had been beaten to death. One name mentioned, Victor Nkandi, caused particular distress for he had suffered imprisonment and the extremes of torture at the hands of the South African security police. When the allegations were made public in Namibia, Gurirab declared that 'as a SWAPO leader I will never defend the humiliation and suffering of torture.' If the allegations were true, he said, 'I apologize to the victims and their parents and pledge to you now that the SWAPO leadership will take the necessary steps to bring those involved to book.' (*Times of Namibia*, 10.6.89.)

Either way, the case of the SWAPO detainees could be a focus for disharmony in the new state. But few would question South Africa's ability to destabilize. It would have been strange had they not attempted to plant human 'bugs' on their enemy. Commanding huge resources, a network of contacts throughout black Africa, and experienced in setting black against black, it was an easy card to play. Yet SWAPO, its headquarters abroad, dependent on the charity of neighbours, fighting the continent's best organized and most wilful power, was still expected to behave like a paragon.

The exile crisis notwithstanding, diplomatic support for SWAPO was growing in the mid- to late 1980s. In 1988, the organization opened offices in Moscow and India, the latter granting it the status of an embassy. Nujoma, Ya Toivo, Gurirab, Information Secretary Hidipo Hamutenya and other senior officials travelled the world offering the message of a free Namibia. It was not a life for the weak-kneed or those with indifferent digestions. In 30 years of exile, Nujoma himself had flown several million miles. He lived out of a suitcase, home was a plane or a hotel room, in between meeting a foreign minister or a Namibian exile, speaking at a rally, a press conference, cocking an ear at a diplomatic cocktail party, briefing the local SWAPO office, all the while having to be supremely conscious of his personal security. The exile of a Garibaldi or a Lenin were sedentary by comparison.

Mrs Helir Kondombolo Nujoma also suffered for her political connections. In December 1986, Koevoet called at the Okahao kraal of the president's aged mother to swear at her and ask her about her son. 101 Bn also came, flaunting hand grenades and guns and cursing her for being 'the mother of SWAPO'. (NCC, 30.1.98.)

As SWAPO's popularity grew, so too did PLAN's military activities. SWATF reported that:

> armed contacts with PLAN rose from 176 in 1986 to 118 in the first three months of 1987. These figures tally closely with those released by PLAN, whose figures also include sabotage action against South African 'security' and strategic installations. PLAN reported 130 'combat actions' in the first quarter of 1987, including 50 sabotage actions and twenty attacks on SADF bases. Given the somewhat disadvantageous geographical conditions for guerrilla warfare in Namibia, and the vast numerical imbalance in troops and equipment between the SADF and PLAN, this continued level of armed struggle by the nationalist movement is impressive. [Wood 1987, p. 5.]

By the late 1980s, the war was taking its toll. White farmers in the strategic far north were quitting for reasons related both to guerrillas and drought. Many had received cheap loans under the 1979 Law on the Promotion of Population Density aimed at countering the land drain. In mid-1989, the white politician, Jannie de Wet, had to issue a warning against leaving their farms before the 10-year contractual limitation period had expired.

Visiting American correspondent Joseph Lelyveld noted that the guerrillas 'never had to be a match for the South African military machine. . . . In the kind of anti-colonial struggle they have been waging . . . survival and victory are virtually synonymous. And SWAPO have survived.' (*New York Times*, 11.8.82.) In late 1987, as the war of liberation began its final bloody lap, the International Institute for Strategic Studies in London declared that 'SWAPO had suffered severe casualties and, although incursions continue to be attempted, they have little effect.' It was the sort of judgement made about Algeria in 1960 and Vietnam in 1967.

Cuito Cuanavale to New York

'A waste of time' was how Chester Crocker described the round of US–Angolan 'peace' talks in July 1987. Angola, he complained, had 'nothing new to say.' (*Worldnet*, 22.7.87.) The Angolans had lots to say, but what really exasperated Crocker was Angola's ability to soak up punishment and yet stick by its friends. The Angolans were behaving much like Ronald Reagan said the little guys should when standing up to the bullies. Angolan intransigence might also have been related to the latest SADF invasion, Operation Modular, launched in the same month and aimed at capturing the strategic town of Cuito Cuanavale in order to set UNITA up as the alternative government in south-east Angola.

However, Angolan fortunes had been slowly reviving from the days in 1983 when Savimbi boasted of an impending capture of Luanda, and the capital endured two lengthy power cuts. The irregular MPLA guerrilla force was now more of a disciplined national army, though it was in effect fighting a second war of liberation. In late 1985, FAPLA forces based in the southern, or fifth military, region in Lubanga had attempted to capture the airstrip at Mavinga, a strategic village leading on 150 kilometres southwards to Savimbi's capital, Jamba. After initial gains, the SAAF rescued Savimbi by destroying the Angolan armoured column. With the stakes rising, the Soviet Union poured in a billion dollars of armaments, including their lethal MiG 23 fighters, piloted by Angolans and Cubans, and far superior to South Africa's ageing Mirages. These proved decisive in 1986, when South Africa and UNITA tried and failed to capture Cuito Cuanavale in a campaign in which 32 Bn alone was said to have lost 100 men.

Modular soon went wrong. Soviet prestige was at stake. Along with further arms shipments, came Russian generals and technicians. The Angolans counter-attacked, cutting UNITA off from their supply lines, but they failed again to capture Mavinga. Having blunted the Angolan counter, 'the South Africans were tempted into an ill-fated effort to score a knock-out blow against the MPLA at Cuito Cuanavale.' (Freeman 1989, p. 134.) The Angolans stood firm. When the SADF ordered in fresh Namibian troops from 101 and 102 Bns, hundreds mutinied, claiming they were being used as the white man's cannon fodder. Once white national service mechanized units were sent in, casualty figures could no longer be hidden. By November, 3,000 of their troops were bogged down on the Lomba River.

Now, after years of spreading the lie that there were two separate wars, South Africa against SWAPO and UNITA against the MPLA, the SADF chief, General Jannie Geldenhuys, was forced to admit that they were fighting alongside UNITA. In aggrieved tones he noted that 'elements of the SADF and SWATF were compelled to take limited action against surrogate forces. . . . Russians and Cubans, using tanks and sophisticated ground-to-air missiles, fighter aircraft, including MiG 23s, and attack helicopters entered the battle.' (*The Independent*, 12.11.87.) When Geldenhuys explained that his forces had rushed to the aid of UNITA to save them from annihilation by the Angolan army, he was flatly contradicted by a 'very surprised' Savimbi, who claimed a great victory over those same soldiers. (NCC, 14.12.87.) The *Windhoek Observer* commenting on the contradictory statements said, 'Only Luanda seems capable of issuing balanced press statements.' (*Action on*

Namibia, Spring 88.)

The phantom war had at last become real for white South Africa. The *Star* (12.3.87) carried a letter from a parent:

> While I trust that my son has been raised as a true and patriotic South African and is committed to his two-year stint, I am extremely dismayed and perturbed that he and his fellow troops have apparently been thrust into an area of conflict not of their choosing and after only a few short months of basic training.

With the stalemate, the battalions off Cuito faced disaster. Readers of the *Star* were told two days before Christmas 1987 how their army:

> faced the greatest dilemma since cross-border operations began. If they could not advance, neither could they withdraw. A pull-back to the Namibian border would (rightly or wrongly, given the extent of human and material loss) have been seen as a retreat. This would have demoralized UNITA, spurred FAPLA on, and incurred the wrath of the South African public which enjoys being on the winning side.

There was very little doubt, the piece continued, that if South Africa left Angola, the Luanda forces would sweep down the dusty roads of southern Angola, through Mavinga and possibly down to Jamba. South Africans suddenly realized that they were turning Angola into a regional superpower.

General Geldenhuys tried to cheer up troops returning from the front line. They had 'experienced more than many soldiers in the first and second world wars,' he told them. 'You fought hard, you fought well and you won.' (*Paratus* January 88.) But with the loss of the SAAF's dominance of the skies, the tide had turned. The MiG 23s, flown by confident Angolans alongside Cuban pilots, restricted the air cover South African and UNITA troops had come to expect. In the early months of 1988 the SAAF was said to have lost more than 40 Mirage and Impala jet fighters which they could not replace. There was talk of Angola becoming South Africa's Vietnam.

South Africa knew Cuito well. It had grown from a Portuguese hunting lodge to an attractive village then to an encampment in the colonial war against the MPLA. South Africans had helped build the airfield, using it as part of the military link with northern Namibia and Katima Mulillo. Bogged down, the SADF began shelling Cuito in January 1988, and on March 23 launched an armoured assault, hoping to capture the airstrip that would provide Savimbi with *lebensraum* and a seat at the negotiating table. The 82nd brigade of P. W. Botha's Presidential Regiment was among the elite units employed in the desperate throw. For the first time in a dozen years, the Cubans moved in to take on South Africa face-fo-face. General Arnaldo Ochoa

Sanchez, deputy foreign minister, directed operations from Menongue. Cubans manned the radar and provided rear logistic support. The artillery bombardment was to last for months, but the G-6 shells, sometimes 200 a day, did minimal damage to the well dug-in troops. The civilian population had been moved out. It was Africa's largest battle since El Alamein.

Several times the Western media, briefed by the SADF, reported the fall of Cuito. But Fidel Castro, in Crocker's words, 'raised the ante and sent 15,000 fresh troops.' (*Optima*, June 1989, p. 52.) Equipped with armour and anti-aircraft weaponry, they made a diversionary counter-attack towards the Namibian border through Cunene province west of Cuito (which was in Cuando Cubango province). 'Until then,' wrote Freeman, 'this area had been the unimpeded hunting preserve of South African forces against SWAPO. It was also the site of dams on which northern Namibia depends for its water supply.' (1989, p. 134.) Caught by surprise, SADF units withdrew, leaving their 4,000 colleagues outflanked, bogged down by heavy rains, without the means to escape by helicopter from the proximity of Cuito. There were reports of 'tipsy troopies' running into minefields and doctors doing amputations in the field. A visitor to No. 1 Military Hospital in Pretoria talked of scenes redolent of Florence Nightingale's Scutari.

By May, the Cubans had advanced to within 40 kilometres of the 'cut line'. White South Africa's nightmare had become reality. A SADF intelligence officer, Major Desmond Burman, reported 12,000 Cubans in southern Angola, with three mixed SWAPO–Cuban battalions, one with tanks, in southern Cunene. The offensive towards the border was expected at the latest by the end of July. Burman disclosed that, since the beginning of the year, MiG 23s had crossed four times into Namibia, apparently unchallenged, though without carrying out ground strikes (BBC 'Focus on Africa', 16.6.88).

But the Cubans held back. They, like the Angolans, had had enough of fighting. They had come to see Angola as a quagmire, a vast cemetery for their sons. They could afford to be magnanimous. They saw themselves as having won the war and now they wanted to achieve the objective for which they had come to Africa in the first place — to make an MPLA Angola secure. President Botha and his generals needed little persuading. Facing the electorally-ruinous prospect of hundreds of young white soldiers dying in Angola, they were desperate for talks.

The first meeting in the final diplomatic marathon took place in London in May 1988, with Crocker bringing the South Africans, Angolans and Cubans together, and the Soviet Union as a background observer available for consultation. So each faction had a minder breathing down its neck. Pretoria's delegation comprised Neil van Heerden, worldly-wise director-general of foreign affairs, the defence chief, Geldenhuys, and the national intelligence services director, Neil Barnard (a Namibian by birth and schooling). One comparative peacenik against two bitter-enders, SWAPO was not formally represented at the deliberations, though Gurirab was kept informed of developments by the Angolans and Cubans. From the start, Crocker had tried to downgrade SWAPO to the level of the DTA, though before his arrival it had been an equal negotiating party with Pretoria. The exclusion of the major voice of the Namibian people would contribute to the tragic guerrilla incursion in April 1989.

The initial talks made slow progress. However, when 12 white soldiers were killed by a single Cuban missile on the border at Ruacana in July 1988, South Africa's fragility was exposed and the knot began to unravel. *Die Kerkbode*, journal of the NGK, the main Dutch Reformed Church and spiritual home of two-thirds of Afrikanerdom, suggested that the apparent permanence of the army in Angola could be questioned on Christian ethical grounds. South Africa, it complained, 'could be drawn deeper into a battle on foreign soil with increasing loss of life.' (*Guardian*, 8.7.88.) Decoded, the message read 'Enough is enough'. In August, South Africa hastily agreed to a withdrawal from Angola by the end of the month. The foreign press was flown in to witness the troops retreat back to Kavango. Their 'heroes welcome' barely concealed the fact that they had got out by the skin of their teeth. Not everyone in Botha's government was happy. Defence Minister Malan muttered about the 'red flag' (for SWAPO) over Windhoek being irreconcilable with the efforts South Africa was making for Namibia. The struggle, he said, 'is worth the difficulty and the expense.' (AWEPAA, 3.4.89.) In Malan's mind, the apparent human cost had been slight. He told parliament on 18 May: 'We lost 31' (i.e., whites), adding that, 'with reference to the SWA Territorial Force they lost 12' (i.e., blacks). The enemy, on the other hand, had lost between 7,000 and 10,000. Incredulous South Africans noted that, despite the enormous disparity, 'we' still lost the war.

Murmurings of further American sanctions combined with South Africa's poor economic performance tipped the balance. At the second Brazzaville meeting, Pretoria agreed to a phased Cuban withdrawal that would end well after Namibia's independence day. 'Prior withdrawal', the gospel for seven years, had gone by the board. The peace agreement was signed at the United Nations in New York on 22 December 1988. The Namibian independence process, UN Security Council Resolution 435, was set to start on 1 April 1989, leading to elections to a constituent assembly seven months later, and formal statehood early in 1990, though no date was specified. In addition to this trilateral accord, was a bilateral Cuban–Angolan agreement regulating the troop withdrawal, starting with 3,000 by 1 April 1989 and ending with the last of the 50,000 by 1 July 1991. The undoubted Western media hero of the agreement was not Angola, certainly not SWAPO, which did not even feature as a signatory, but Chester Crocker. Adulation knew no bounds: 'Stiff upper-lip when all hell breaks loose' (*Argus*, 24.12.88), and 'Crocker's patience leads him to Africa's Holy Grail' (*The Independent*, 17.11.89). How much of a diplomatic triumph it was for Crocker and the US was open to question. After all, in the days before linkage, Carter's team had argued that once South Africa left Namibia, the Cubans would have no reason to stay on in Angola.

A striking illustration of how linkage had failed was the increase in the numbers of Cubans in Angola. In January 1976, after the first South African invasion, they numbered 12,000. The figure climbed dramatically after South Africa's Operation Protea in 1981, and was 30,000 by 1985. In mid-1987, the *International Herald Tribune* (12.6.87) talked of 35,000 Cubans. Pretoria's Cuito offensive boosted them to 50,000. So linkage, far from driving Cubans out, had the opposite effect. All the while, South Africa was granted *carte blanche* to devastate Angola and Namibia, with deaths in the tens of thousands, and material damage in the billions of dollars.

Why South Africa Had to Go

Before the battle for Cuito Cuanavale, South Africa had no serious intention of leaving Namibia. The government had never really accepted Resolution 435 and was determined to put off the evil day when '*Suidwes*' would 'go black'. But once the SADF had invested its prestige in capturing the airfield of a remote Angolan town, and failed, the chemistry of the sub-continent changed. Like it or not, the non-victors had to abide by the rules of the game. In the peace accords, Pretoria was awarded a single face-saver, the closure of the seven African National Congress camps in Angola. None of the major aims — pre-conditional or even parallel Cuban withdrawal, a role for UNITA in the government in Luanda, or better still, the MPLA's overthrow — was realized.

The capacity of sanctions to force changes in Pretoria's policies has become a matter of acrimonious debate. Often it is skewed by those who suggest that because 'it hasn't worked', it is not worth continuing. But sanctions hold out no instant solution. As Rhodesia had shown, they bite gradually, hitting at investment and trade especially when there is a world or domestic recession. The real argument should turn on the role of sanctions as one pressure point among several. In the case of Namibia, and, indirectly, South Africa, sanctions, and the threat of more of them, were effective. No better example can be found than the failure to replace the obsolete French fighter planes. The arms boycott stranded the airforce and its expert pilots in a time capsule. A free-for-all aerial escalation might not have altered the long-term outcome, but South Africa would have won more time. Sanctions have also worked to stop Rossing's customers, among them British and Japanese utility companies, renewing their contracts. Anti-apartheid lobbyists have engineered embarrassing scenes at RTZ and other annual general meetings in London, as well as in Japan, Holland and the USA. As a result, the mine has been reduced to 80 per cent capacity.

White South African politicians and businessmen deride US corporate disinvestment and, as a result, the US may have lost some of its ability to lever reforms. But the psychological impact has been profound. It is also likely that South African business, for three centuries dependent on the importation of capital and technological know-how from Europe and the US, may contract 'investment scurvy'. The debate often overlooks a more damaging consequence to South Africa's trade. The 1986 congressional sanctions, though limited, have had the effect of reducing the Republic's exports from US$2.5 billion in 1986 to US$1.4 billion a year later. *Krugerrands*, affected by EEC measures as well, accounted for 91 per cent of the world trade in gold coins in 1978. Nine years later the share was 3 per cent. Members of Congress and European Community governments wanting to tighten the sanctions screw were in the minority in 1988. A refusal to budge on Namibia would have invited further action.

The drying-up of international bank loans dates from President Botha's 1985 'Rubicon speech' in which, finger-waving, he told the world to mind its own business. It did, and for four years no state loans worth mentioning were forthcoming. In late 1988, South Africa was servicing a total foreign debt of US$22 billion, with more than US$3 billion due for repayment in 1990–91. The post-Rubicon halved rand compounded the problem. Four months after the New York accords, Citicorp rolled over loans totalling US$670 million due for repayment in 1990. A small pat on the back for Pretoria, though Dr. Gerhard de Kock, governor of the Reserve Bank, admitted that it remained impossible to raise long-term loans abroad (*Financial Times*, 20.4.89). The Trust Bank of South Africa estimated that by 1990 South Africa's losses of foreign reserves since 1984 due to sanctions would amount to some SAR30 billion (about UK£7 billion) — roughly half the government's revenue in the 1989 budget. The average South African might, as a result, be 30% worse off (*The Independent*, 5.4.89). During confirmation hearings for Crocker's successor, Herman Cohen, the chairman of the Senate foreign relations committee, Claiborne Pell, said that:

There are those who believe that the result of sanctions is to a great extent responsible for the successful negotiations in Namibia; that but for the credit problems that South Africa faces . . . it is questionable whether South Africa would have come to the conference table and negotiated as they have. [*AWFile* 9.5.89.]

Even without sanctions the war and the occupation were a heavy burden. In 1984 the war was said to be costing R1.5 million a day. The exponential increase in arms use on the last foray into Angola, with 40,000 shells fired on to Cuito Cuanavale alone, would have taken them well over budget. The 1987/8 national defence budget, at R7.4 billion, was three and a half times the level of the first year of the decade.

Then, out of the blue, the bear toned down its roar. So sudden was the impact of the Gorbachev era that it must have seemed to those caught up in it as though America and Russia were now playing on the same side of the chess board. Crocker was to say that the Angola–Namibia settlement 'transformed a major irritant in East–West relations into a remarkable example of US–Soviet co-operation in the settlement of regional disputes.' (*Topic*, June 89.) The withdrawal of Soviet troops from Afghanistan was a pointer to a reduction in involvement further afield. War weariness and disastrous economic performance at home added up to a conciliatory attitude abroad. At the same time, the Kremlin stood by its friends, as shown by the immense injection of material and technical assistance in the final push in Angola. Pretoria must have been bewildered by this thaw in relations with the 'evil empire'. What was to become of 'total onslaught' when Russian journalists toured the Republic and Soviet and South African scholars met in London to trade their world views? 'Total response' would now have to carry a clause warning of Russians bearing gifts.

Doubts expressed by influential Afrikaners about the war were shared by a growing band of conscientious objectors. Mostly their reasons were religious, though others, who were not against soldiering as such, refused to fight an unjust war against black fellow-countrymen. In Namibia, the military refrained from calling up northern blacks for fear of widespread disaffection. Two Herero-speaking pro-SWAPO youths had appealed to the courts to stop their conscription, but the final outcome had not been settled by the time of the cease-fire. In the Republic, thousands of young men were estimated to have left the country, either before their call-up or after their national service, to avoid the annual camps. Those who stayed to face the music risked six years in prison. What must have been disconcerting to the government was the number of Afrikaners refusing to fight. One of them, Etienne Marais, had been an army captain in Angola. He recalled walking into kraals where 'small children ran away in fear.' Occupation, he said, 'is a very neutral word; it encompasses none of the menace and sense of hostility that exists when an army of people— mostly indoctrinated into a racist ideology— arrogantly invade a community to forcibly uphold a political order, which happens to oppress the very people they are supposed to be "protecting"'. (*Sash* March 89.) Views like these, when held by Afrikaner officers, could play havoc with discipline when things went wrong on the battlefield.

In the first and the last resort, however, what 'persuaded' the South Africans to agree to leave Namibia were the Namibian people themselves. They did not all support SWAPO, but they despised South Africa and held the empty shell of the interim government in contempt. But no amount of UN resolutions, peace marches down Kaiser Street, sermons from the pulpit, or requests from Western capitals would have moved South Africa one millimetre southwards. Something more was needed. In Poland, Solidarity could achieve its aims through non-violent action, helped by the West lobbying for its cause. Namibia had much in common with Poland— a Christian people, decidedly against their government— but, as we have seen, it could not rely on the West. So it was forced into an armed struggle. While deriding the efforts of PLAN, it is clear that South Africa's initial military problem was an inability to counteract the guerrillas. As a result, the war was pushed into Angola, which led to confrontations with FAPLA, in turn, inviting increased Cuban and Soviet assistance, and ineluctably to Cuito Cuanavale, there to commit the elementary mistake of turning counter-revolutionary warfare into a conventional confrontation far from home.

Freedom Road?

In finally accepting the implementation of 435, had South Africa accepted an unfettered SWAPO victory?

At 8.30 a.m. on the morning of 7 September 1988, the SWA National Security Council met at the Bastion, Windhoek, to discuss 'the practical implications of 435'. Little was known of this shadowy organization until the minutes of the meeting, the eleventh in 1988, were leaked to the press. Its members were the leaders of the colonial establishment, with Dirk Mudge as chairman, black and white politicians, civil servants and security chiefs. Not present on that day, though sending apologies, was A. G. Visser who, as chief electoral officer of Namibia, would preside over the coming 'free and fair elections'. The minutes record that the council had discussed the security considerations of implementing 435. General Lloyd, secretary of the South African State Security Council and former chief of SWATF, was present. Now, S. F. Gous, secretary of the Central Personnel Institute, asked the members to 'establish what could be done to beat SWAPO in an election.' To this end, said Gous, cabinet and heads of government departments 'must work together as a team to give urgent attention to an overall strategy.'

The black politicians agreed. Katjiuongua, complaining that 'so many opportunities had slipped through their fingers in three years of interim government rule,' spoke of eliminating 'the perception that only SWAPO can do something for this country. . . . Everyone around this table should get together as soon as possible to discuss these matters in depth.' (*Namibian*, 7.6.89.) The military view, expressed by Brigadier G. J. C. van Niekerk, was that South Africa wanted a friendly government in Namibia. All the negotiations on an international level were worthless if SWAPO won an election, he said. Many discussions would have to be held to establish what would happen and 'only when certain plans for the elections had been tabled by SWA could funds be sought.' Having grudgingly accepted the fact of independence, South Africa was preparing a damage limitation exercise, or, more precisely, plotting to frustrate a SWAPO victory.

The 435 plan was riddled with flaws, omissions and obscurities, and then compounded by concessions to Pretoria following private negotiations which never received the Security Council's ratification. The years of delay in implementing the plan provided Pretoria with additional opportunities for its undermining, while the election of Ronald Reagan meant that South Africa, and not the long-suffering people of Namibia, was treated as the aggrieved party in the negotiations.

Most serious was the lack of effective authority and options available to the UN special representative to enforce 435. Even if, in the event of violation, he assumed a tough stance, the UN's only real power was for the Security Council to withhold approval by halting the process. However, in the past the West had invariably acted to prevent punitive action being taken against South Africa. One indication of the lack of bite in the plan was the clause guaranteeing 'full freedom of speech, assembly, movement and press' in the campaign period. Yet after 1 April the state radio and television countinued to pour out anti-SWAPO vitriol as if the fighting had never ceased, in stark contrast to the Rhodesian independence elections when the liberation movements were allowed to put their case on the state-run media. These, of course, were flaws only if one or both sides were intent on upsetting the applecart.

But right from the outset it has been clear that South Africa would not play fair. In February 1989, Louis Pienaar announced that the 20,000 members of SWATF would remain on the payroll, even after being decommissioned. Many then found jobs as drivers and bodyguards, and even as full-time organizers, for the DTA. A more sinister flaw in the peace arrangements, however, was the deployment of Koevoet. Pretoria's original characterization of it as a 'police unit' was deliberate, for under 435 the police did not have to be disarmed and demobilized. They would be 'disbanded', Pik Botha announced after signing the December peace accords, 'as a gesture of goodwill'. There was a general sigh of relief. But the goodwill was of short duration, for all 3,000 of them were immediately integrated into the SWA police, which thereby doubled in size to 6,000. Koevoet's task was to enforce law and order during the campaign. One moment they were hunting guerrillas like dogs, the next they were authorized to monitor their self-same prey's good behaviour.

In mid-March, South Africa's intentions became clearer. Two former Koevoet constables swore affidavits describing how, on the day in January when the disbandment was announced, they were patrolling in Ovamboland. They were told by radio that they should no longer wear their Koevoet badges. That was 'the only thing that changed in our lives.' They were not required to sign any forms, their commanding officer was the same man, for a while they still wore the light-green uniform of Koevoet. But they had 'to tell people we were now members of SWAPOL, the South West Africa Police.' One of the men, Petrus Davids, said a white officer in Rundu, Captain Engelbrecht, warned that 'it does not mean we are still not going to make war.' He cited the example of the venomous snake which 'loses its skin, but still remains a mamba.' The commanding officer, the recently promoted General Dreyer, told a group of constables being reassigned to police units to go on providing information about SWAPO activities.

The two constables refused to continue in the police and their affidavits prompted official instructions to serving members of the army and police to 'refrain from unlawfully harassing and interfering with' SWAPO and student activists (NCC, 17.3.89). Within weeks, this agreement was to prove an empty shell.

To accomplish his peace-keeping task, Martti Ahtisaari expected to oversee a UN Transitional Assistance Group (UNTAG) military unit of 7,500 troops, as outlined in the 1978 plan. But the five permanent Security Council members were in a cost-conscious mood and insisted on swingeing reductions to 4,650 troops and 500 police. The secretary-general, the frontline states, the OAU, SWAPO and the Namibian churches argued that the understrength force would be insufficient to contend with the increased size of South Africa's security forces. South Africa was, of course, pleased — the fewer blue berets, the better. The permanent members, including China and the Soviet Union, argued that, with a monitoring force on the Angolan side of the border under the Tripartite Agreement, the peace-keepers could be reduced. They ignored the fact that UNITA had prevented the monitors from moving in along the Kavango and Caprivi border, and the fact that SWATF and Koevoet did not exist when the plan was drawn up. With all the wrangling, authorization for the UNTAG force was not voted until 16 February 1989, leaving too little time for full deployment before the peace process began on 1 April.

The most glaring omission in the final documents of 435 related to the disposition of SWAPO guerrillas inside Namibia at the time of the ceasefire. Early drafts, agreed by South Africa, made it clear that those inside Namibia would report to UNTAG, which would then confine them to a base. That there were SWAPO troops inside the country was known to all. On a visit to the north in March 1989, journalist Tony Weaver was told by a senior police officer that large numbers of guerrillas were in the country, doing what the officer termed 'political work'. The formal ceasefire to the war in Namibia was 'pronounced signed' by the Secretary-General, Perez de Cuellar, on 30 March. It was accomplished by post, as South Africa refused to sit down with SWAPO in the same room to exchange the formal documents. The ceasefire would take effect at 4 a.m. the next day, a Saturday.

That morning, contingents of armed SWAPO soldiers appeared openly in Ovamboland, seeking out UNTAG troops to whom they would give themselves up. It was not long before South Africa broke the ceasefire, as 30 battles were fought over a 200-mile front. Weaver said that the level of fighting indicated that the South Africans 'knew where the guerrillas were and more or less laid a trap for them.' (*Africa News*, 1.5.89.) In Windhoek, Ahtisaari was besieged by Pik Botha claiming that SWAPO had infiltrated armed terrorists into the country in violation of the accords. The episode was complicated by a lightning visit by the British prime minister, Margaret Thatcher, on a tour of Africa. She attended the A-G's meeting with Ahtisaari and, from utterances when back in Britain, apparently lent her voice to the criticism of SWAPO. Basing his decision solely on this one-sided version of events, Ahtisaari authorized the release of six South African battalions, including 101, to assist the Koevoet units in hunting down SWAPO. The UN thereby gave South Africa a licence to kill the soldiers of the liberation movement.

Had SWAPO been a party to the negotiations the tragedy might well have been avoided. There were grounds for differing interpretations of the August 1988 Geneva Protocol, which sought to deploy PLAN above the 16th parallel (150 kilometres north of the border) until the South African withdrawal from Namibia was completed. The argument went back to the earliest days of the negotiations, when South Africa refused to accept that there could be PLAN bases in the Namibian north. As the Protocol did not specifically amend 435, it could be interpreted as referring to guerrillas inside Namibia when the ceasefire formally started, awaiting the arrival of the UNTAG monitors.

Here was a tragic irony of men returning to their motherland, with nothing but peace in their hearts, only to be waylaid by surrogates of the very government they had just defeated. Thus the eyewitness account by a farmer, Jekonia Ngenokesho, on the fatal morning.

> I was walking with my brother when I heard a whistle. There were two men in a tree. They asked me for water. I recognized these men as SWAPO fighters. They were keeping guard. I saw a group of people I identified as SWAPO fighters. They told me they were not there to fight but were regrouping in order to hand themselves to UNTAG and were asking me if I had seen any UN people in the area. And if they couldn't find such people, they would be going back up north (to the border). While my brother was getting water, we heard Casspirs and they told us to run, the South Africans were coming. The South Africans started shooting first, and I was shot in the leg. The next thing I found myself in Oshakati hospital [NCC, 3.4.89].

As was their habit, Koevoet and 101 took few prisoners. The human rights lawyer, David Smuts, accused them of a shoot-to-kill policy. Many of the dead were shot in the face, despatched 'at close range with small calibre weapons'. (*Sunday Telegraph*, 9.4.89.) The bodies were buried hurriedly but after proceedings by church lawyers some were disinterred for post-mortem examination. Despite a request to attend, UNTAG missed the opportunity to be present at the autopsies, and the pathologist's report was not expected to be publicized before the elections. But everyone knew what had happened. Koevoet, declaring that 'the hunting season is open again', seemed surprised that prisoners should be treated any other way. The 300 or more young men massacred were seen as martyrs. It would have been small consolation to SWAPO that the episode was said to have improved SWAPO's electoral support (author's interview with Tötemeyer, May 1989). SWAPO's allies, in particular President Dos Santos, made no secret at what they considered SWAPO's rash action. SWAPO's enemies had a field day. The Voice of America, reflecting the US government's view, broadcast a piece entitled 'SWAPO violence in Namibia'. (*AWFile*, 6.4.89.)

The United Nations plan was suspended until South Africa was satisfied that the guerrillas were outside the territory, north of the 16th parallel. By 19 May 1989, South Africa's forces were again confined to base and a 'de facto cessation of hostilities' was proclaimed by the administrator-general and the special representative. The war was now officially over.

After They Have Gone

Namibia faces problems which leaders of many newly independent African countries will understand. The difference is that elsewhere the birth pangs have usually been treated with sympathy by the outgoing colonial power ready to accept that an era was about to end. Once the flag is raised over the new-born Namibia, a new set of problems will come into focus. The security of living in peace with one's neighbours, of being allowed to enjoy the fruits of the bountiful land, of coming to terms with the enormous social deprivation, can by no means be taken for granted. South Africa's hold on the new state will provide a range of options from puppeteer to strangler.

Whatever government comes to power, Namibia seems destined for the foreseeable future to remain South Africa's fifth province in financial terms. This structural dependency was described in a report by the Association of Chambers of Commerce (Assocom), which sought to place a silver lining on the black cloud of independence. South Africa, it noted, financed the central government budget of Namibia by some R700 million in transfers during 1987/8, compared to internally generated tax revenue of about R780 million. South Africa owned the railways, the international airline, the main port, it supplied the territory's coal and oil, bought the ranchers' beef, and fish, tin, zinc and salt, it had a finger in almost every major mining, fishing and farming pie, while technical and middle management skills were mostly in expatriate hands. South Africa, it was said, knew every light switch in the place. Assocom's report saw Namibia as an economic springboard to black Africa and the world beyond, a conduit for the export of surplus capital and manufactured goods. Through this back door would enter imported goods prohibited by sanctions.

Yet Namibian blacks hoping to share in the bonanza of one of the continent's best-endowed mining countries might have to wait a while. They have no access to private capital with which to invest in their own natural resources. The abrupt termination of the military largesse will wreak havoc, the more so in the north, where many businesses, not excluding the *cucas*, face bankruptcy. Since 1980 South Africa claims to have borrowed more than R750 million from foreign institutions to pay for the occupation. Much is in the form of bonds, managed and underwritten by South African financial bodies. In international law, such debts are not to be inherited by Namibians, but it remains to be seen whether they will be made to pay for an occupation they have long resisted.

There will be, too, the question of the pastures seized from the Hereros and Namas by the Germans and, despite the 'Sacred Trust', not restored to them by South Africa. Today, the white five per cent of the population own 60 per cent of the land in the fertile south and centre, while those who lost it live in poverty in arid homelands. The future of the 5,000 white farmers, their holdings averaging 18,000 acres, is as much an emotional as an ideological matter. Almost half of all white farms are said to belong to foreign absentee landowners.

Perhaps the most serious of the obstacles to peace and prosperity will be Walvis Bay. After the German defeat in 1915, the governor-general, Lord Buxton, wrote that:

> it is easy to appreciate the feeling of envy and bitterness that the Germans must have felt [at not having Walvis Bay] all these years, at having to put up with the open roadstead at Swakopmund, and create their town and carry on their development from there, when, almost within a stone's throw, a fine harbour existed of which practically no use was made. [Cabinet papers 37/127, 29/3/15.]

That will remain the position at independence. From 1922 the enclave of 1,124 sq. kms was administered as an integral part of 'South West', until, in 1977, as independence loomed, South Africa restored it to direct control. Its white voters were now assigned to a Cape Town parliamentary constituency, its courts placed under the jurisdiction of the Cape division.

Just as crucially, South Africa is attempting, against the will of the UN, to retain the 12 guano islands, stretching for hundreds of miles along the coast north and south of Luderitz. Guano is not so thick on the rocks these days, but diamond recovery vessels work the gravels along their shores. When the new government extends its international waters to the maximum 200 miles, South Africa, as the occupier of Walvis Bay and the islands, will claim some of the fishing revenues. No wonder P. W. Botha has said that the use of the port would be negotiated with a friendly Namibian government.

The priority of the new incumbents of the *Tintenpalast* (state house) will be to right the historic wrongs. Too much innovation, however, and they face 'correction' from the South African Air Force or from a fifth column of SWATF or Koevoet. Too little, and this nation of fewer than one and a half million, having heroically rid their land of one of the most hateful forms of racial domination ever devised, will feel a terrible let-down. For now, the century of struggle behind them, Namibians must become masters of their own destiny.

Bibliography

1. **Newspapers, Periodicals and serials**
    Action on Namibia, Namibia Support Committee, London.
    Africa Analysis, London.
    Africa News, Durham, North Carolina.
    Anti-Apartheid News, Anti-Apartheid Movement (AAM), London.
    Argus, Cape Town (formerly *Cape Argus*).
    Armed Forces, Johannesburg.
    AW File (formerly *Worldnet*), US Embassy, Paris.
    Cape Times, Cape Town.
    CCN Information, Newsletter of the Council of Churches in Namibia, Windhoek.
    CCN (press releases), Council of Churches in Namibia, Windhoek.
    Citizen, Johannesburg.
    Combatant, People's Liberation Army of Namibia (PLAN), Lubanga, Angola.
    Dateline Namibia, Africa Fund and the Namibia Christian Communications Trust, New York.
    Defence and Armament, Paris.
    Financial Times, London.
    Flight International, Sutton, Surrey.
    Focus on Political Repression in Southern Africa, International Defence and Aid Fund (IDAF), London.
    Guardian, London.
    Independent, London.
    International Herald Tribune, Paris.
    Jane's Defence Weekly, London.
    Namibian, Windhoek.
    NCC (press releases), Namibia Communications Centre, London.
    New Statesman, London.
    New York Times, New York.
    Observer and *Observer News Service*, London.
    On Record, news magazine of the Information Service, Windhoek.
    Optima, Johannesburg.
    Paratus, South African Defence Force (SADF), Pretoria.

Bibliography

Pretoria News, Pretoria.
Rand Daily Mail, Johannesburg.
Resister, Committee of South African War Resisters (COSAWR), London and Amsterdam.
Scope, Johannesburg.
Servamus, South Africa Police (SAP), Pretoria.
Shipping Research Bureau, monthly bulletin, Amsterdam.
Soldier of Fortune, Boulder, Colorado.
South African Digest, Bureau of Information, Pretoria.
Star, Johannesburg.
The Times, London.
Times of Namibia, Windhoek.
Sash, Black Sash, Johannesburg.
Sunday Telegraph, London.
Weekly Mail, Johannesburg.
West Africa, London.
Windhoek Advertiser, Windhoek.
Windhoek Observer, Windhoek.
Worldnet (now *AW File*) US Embassy, Paris.
World Campaign against Military and Nuclear Collaboration with South Africa (press releases), Oslo.

2. **Official Documents/Archival Records**
    Colonial Office Files Public Records Office, London.
    Hansard, House of Assembly, Cape Town.
    Hansard, House of Commons, London.

3. **Books and Articles**
Anti-Apartheid Movement (1987) *Britain and the Arms Embargo*. London: AAM.
Bar Council of South West Africa (1984) 'Memorandum of . . . the society of advocates in regard to the Commission of Inquiry into Security Legislation', *Lawyers for Human Rights Bulletin*. No. 4, pp. 55–90.
Benson, Mary (1989) *A Far Cry: The Making of a South African*. London: Viking.
Breytenbach, Jan (1986) *Forged in Battle*. Cape Town: Saayman and Weber.
Bridgland, Fred (1986) *Jonas Savimbi: A Key to Africa*. Edinburgh: Mainstream Publishing.
Carlson, Joel (1973) *No Neutral Ground*. London: Davis-Poynter.
Cawthra, Gavin (1986) *Brutal Force: The Apartheid War Machine*. London: IDAF.
Cooper, Allan (1985) 'From Colony to Dominion to Republic: South African nationalism and its consequences for Namibian independence', paper presented to the Pacific Coast British Studies Conference.
Crocker, Chester (1980) 'South Africa: Strategy for Change', *Foreign Affairs*, 59, Winter, pp. 323–51.
Crocker, Chester and Lewis, William H. (1979) 'Missing Opportunities in Africa' *Foreign Policy*, Summer, pp. 142–161.
De Villiers, Dirk and Johanna (1984) *PW*. Cape Town: Tafelburg.

Drechsler, Horst (1980) *Let us Die Fighting: The Struggle of the Herero and Nama against German Imperialism (1884–1915)*. London: Zed Press.

Dugard, John (ed.). (1973) *The South West Africa/Namibia Dispute: Documents and scholarly writings on the controversy between South Africa and the United Nations*. Berkeley/London: University of California Press.

Du Pisani, André (1986) *SWA/Namibia: The Politics of Continuity*. Johannesburg: Jonathan Ball.

Ellis, Justin (1979) *Elections in Namibia?* London: British Council of Churches/Catholic Institute for International Relations.

First, Ruth (1963) *South West Africa*. Harmondsworth: Penguin.

Freeman, Charles (1989) 'The Angola Namibia Accords', *Foreign Affairs*, Summer, pp. 126–41.

Gordon, Robert (1984) 'The San in Transition: What Future for the Ju/Wasi of Nyae-Nyae?' *Cultural Survival Quarterly*.

Gordon, Robert (1988) 'Anthropology in the Service of Apartheid', *Southern Africa Report*, 4,3, pp. 22–5.

Grundy, Kenneth (1988) *The Militarization of South African Politics*. Oxford: Oxford University Press.

Hooper, Jim (1988) *Koevoet*. Johannesburg: Southern.

International Commission of Jurists (1968) *Report on the Trial of SWAPO Members*. Geneva: ICJ.

International Defence and Aid Fund for Southern Africa (IDAF) (1989) *Namibia: The Facts*. London: IDAF.

Katjavivi, Peter (1988) *A History of Resistance in Namibia*. London: James Currey.

Moorsom, Richard (1982) *Transforming a Wasted Land*. London: Catholic Institute for International Relations.

Moorsom, Richard (1986) *Fishing: Exploiting the Sea*. London: Catholic Institute for International Relations.

Morgan, Kenneth (1984) *Labour in Power*. Oxford: Clarendon Press.

Murray, Christina (1983). 'The Status of the ANC and SWAPO and International Humanitarian Law', 100 *SA Law Journal*, p. 402.

Nambala, Shekutaamba (1987) 'How the Church Came to Namibia', *Lutheran Quarterly*, 1,4, pp. 513–69.

Ndadi, Vinnia (1989) *Breaking Contract: The Story of Vinnia Ndadi*. London: IDAF.

Reid Daly, Ron (1982) *Selous Scouts, Top Secret War*. Alberton, Transvaal: Galago.

Rotberg, Robert (ed.) (1983) *Namibia: Political and Economic Prospects*. Cape Town: David Philip.

Scott, Michael (1958) *A Time to Speak*. London: Faber and Faber.

Smith, Susanna (1987) *Namibia: A Violation of Trust*. Oxford: Oxfam.

Soggot, David (1986) *Namibia: The Violent Heritage*. London: Rex Collings.

South African Institute of Race Relations (SAIRR) (1986) *A Survey of Race Relations in South Africa*. Johannesburg: SAIRR. Also 1967, 1972, 1973, 1977, 1983, 1988.

Steenkamp, W. (1983) *Borderstrike!* Durban: Butterworths.

SWAPO (1981) *To be Born a Nation: The Liberation Struggle for Namibia*. London: Zed Press.

Bibliography

Swilling, Mark and Phillips, Mark (1989) 'The Powers of the Thunderbird: The Nature and Limits of the Emergency State', unpub. Seminar Papers, Institute of Commonwealth Studies, London, pp. 1–23.

Tötemeyer, Gerhard (1978) *Namibia, Old and New: traditional and modern leaders in Ovamboland*. London: Hurst.

Tötemeyer, Gerhard, Vezera Kandetu and Wolfgang Werner (eds) (1987) *Namibia in Perspective*. Windhoek: Council of Churches in Namibia.

UNICEF (1989) *Children on the Front Line: The impact of apartheid, destabilisation and warfare on children in Southern and South Africa*. Paris and New York: UNICEF.

Vance, Cyrus (1983). *Hard Choices: Critical Years in American Foreign Policy*. New York: Simon and Schuster.

Vigne, Randolph (1987) 'SWAPO of Namibia: a movement in exile', *Third World Quarterly*, 9, 1, pp. 85–107.

Williams, A. F. (1945) *Botha, Smuts and South Africa*. London: Hodder and Stoughton.

Wood, Brian (1987) 'Namibian Independence and British Policy: breaking the diplomatic deadlock', paper presented to the Oxfam Conference on Namibia, London.

Wood, Brian (ed.) (1988) *Namibia 1884–1984: Readings on Namibia's history and society*. London: Namibia Support Committee.

World University Service (1987) *Namibia: Education in Conflict*. London: WUS (UK).

Ya Otto, John (1981) *Battlefront Namibia: An Autobiography*. London: Heinemann.

Glossary

A-G	Administrator-General
ANC	African National Congress of South Africa
ASSOCOM	Association of Chambers of Commerce
AWB	Afrikaner Weerstandsbeweging (Afrikaans Resistance Movement)
AWEPAA	Association of Western European Parliamentary Associations
BBC	British Broadcasting Corporation
BNFL	British Nuclear Fuels Limited
BOSS	Bureau of State Security
CANU	Caprivi African National Union
CDA	Christian Democratic Action for Social Justice Party
CDM	Consolidated Diamond Mines
CIA	Central Intelligence Agency
CCN	Council of Churches in Namibia
COIN	Counter-Insurgency Unit
CONSAS	Constellation of Southern African States
DEMCOP	Democratic Cooperative Party
DTA	Democratic Turnhalle Alliance
DMZ	Demilitarized Zone
FAPLA	People's Armed Forces for the Liberation of Angola
FNLA	National Front for the Liberation of Angola
Frelimo	Front for the Liberation of Mozambique
ICJ	International Commission of Jurists
IDAF	International Defence and Aid Fund
IG	Interim Government
ISCOR	Iron and Steel Corporation
LWF	Lutheran World Federation
MARNET	Military Area Radio Network
MPLA	Popular Movement for the Liberation of Angola
MUN	Mineworkers Union of Namibia
MPC	Multi-Party Conference
NAFAU	National Food and Agricultural Workers Union
NANSO	Namibian National Students Organization

189

NATO	North Atlantic Treaty Organization
NCC	Namibian Communications Centre
NUDO	National Unity Democratic Organization
NUNW	National Union of Namibian Workers
OAU	Organization of African Unity
OPC	Ovambo Peoples Congress
OPO	Ovambo Peoples Organization
PAC	Pan-Africanist Congress
PIDE	International Police for the Defence of the State (Portugal)
PLO	Palestine Liberation Organization
POQO (pure)	Underground political movement linked to PAC
PRO/CO	Public Records Office/Colonial Office Files
RTZ	Rio Tinto Zinc
SAA	South African Airways
SAAF	South African Air Force
SADF	South African Defence Force
SAIRR	South African Institute of Race Relations
SANLAM	South African National Life Assurance Company
SSC	State Security Council
SWABC	South West Africa Broadcasting Corporation
SWANLA	South West Africa Native Labour Association
SWANU	South West Africa National Union
SWANU (MPC)	South West Africa National Union (Multi-Party Conference)
SWAPO	South West Africa People's Organization
SWAPO-D	South West Africa People's Organization-Democrat
SWATF	South West Africa Territorial Force
SWAKARA	South West Africa Karakul Association
SYL	SWAPO Youth League
UDI	Unilateral Declaration of Independence
UNICEF	United Nations Children's Emergency Fund
UNITA	National Union for the Total Independence of Angola
UNTAG	United Nations Transitional Assistance Group
UNIN	United Nations Institute for Namibia
WHAM	Winning Hearts and Minds
ZANU	Zimbabwe African National Union
ZAPU	Zimbabwe African Peoples Union

Index